Volleyball Skills & Drills

American Volleyball Coaches Association

Kinda S. Lenberg
Editor

Human Kinetics

Library of Congress Cataloging-in-Publication Data

Volleyball skills & drills / American Volleyball Coaches Association; Kinda Lenberg, editor.
p. cm.
ISBN 0-7360-5862-1 (soft cover : alk. paper) 1. Volleyball--Training. I. Title: Volleyball skills & drills. II. Lenberg, Kinda. III. American Volleyball Coaches Association.
GV1015.5.T73V656 2006
796.325--dc22

2005017608

ISBN-10: 0-7360-5862-1
ISBN-13: 978-0-7360-5862-9

The Web addresses cited in this text were current as of September 2005 unless otherwise noted.

Acquisitions Editor: Jana Hunter; **Developmental Editor:** Kase Johnstun; **Assistant Editor:** Cory Weber; **Copyeditor:** John Wentworth; **Proofreader:** Sarah Wiseman; **Graphic Designer:** Robert Reuther; **Graphic Artist:** Tara Welsch; **Photo Manager:** Dan Wendt; **Cover Designer:** Keith Blomberg; **Photographer (cover):** Associated Press; **Photographer (interior):** Tom Kimmell, unless otherwise noted; **Art Manager:** Kareema McLendon; **Illustrator:** K&M Services; **Printer:** Versa Press

We thank Joan Powell and Coronado High School in Colorado Springs, Colorado, for assistance in providing the location for the photo shoot for this book.

Human Kinetics books are available at special discounts for bulk purchase. Special editions or book excerpts can also be created to specification. For details, contact the Special Sales Manager at Human Kinetics.

Printed in the United States of America 10 9 8 7 6 5 4 3

Human Kinetics
Web site: www.HumanKinetics.com

United States: Human Kinetics, P.O. Box 5076, Champaign, IL 61825-5076
800-747-4457
e-mail: humank@hkusa.com

Canada: Human Kinetics, 475 Devonshire Road, Unit 100, Windsor, ON N8Y 2L5
800-465-7301 (in Canada only)
e-mail: orders@hkcanada.com

Europe: Human Kinetics, 107 Bradford Road, Stanningley
Leeds LS28 6AT, United Kingdom
+44 (0) 113 255 5665
e-mail: hk@hkeurope.com

Australia: Human Kinetics, 57A Price Avenue, Lower Mitcham, South Australia 5062
08 8372 0999
e-mail: liaw@hkaustralia.com

New Zealand: Human Kinetics, Division of Sports Distributors NZ Ltd.
P.O. Box 300 226 Albany, North Shore City, Auckland
0064 9 448 1207
e-mail: info@humankinetics.co.nz

Contents

Introduction

It is a privilege for me to introduce *Volleyball Skills & Drills,* an outstanding book that will become an invaluable resource for you. *Volleyball Skills & Drills* is a compendium of skill and drill instructions from the very best coaches in the game today and is presented to you by the American Volleyball Coaches Association (AVCA). The six major skills of volleyball—serving, receiving, setting, attacking, blocking, and digging, as well as the tactics of team defense, team offense, and transition—will be presented and discussed in a way so that you can apply them to any level of play. Every chapter will provide detailed instruction, including many progressions and variations, and will be supported by drills specifically arranged to help your athletes progress through the varying levels of difficulty within the skills and tactics.

Volleyball was first played more than 100 years ago as a non-strenuous lunchtime activity and has now become a fast-paced, action-oriented sport played worldwide. The 1964 Olympic Games in Tokyo were the first to feature men's and women's indoor volleyball, and this great spectator sport has been an Olympic fixture ever since. Volleyball boomed in the United States with the passage of Title IX, when it became one of the premier women's sports. With the advent of rally scoring, the game has become much more understandable for the average fan. The intricacies of volleyball skills, techniques, and tactics—while steeped in tradition—are constantly evolving. *Volleyball Skills & Drills* contains all the new and updated techniques and tactics and will become a fixture in your volleyball library. This book will be a great resource for your coaching and teaching of this great sport.

Volleyball is unlike any other sport when it comes to teamwork. A team cannot attack if a proper set has not been executed. Of course, the proper set cannot materialize unless a solid pass has been implemented. With the advent of rally scoring, whereby every error is a point for the opponents, teamwork becomes more crucial. Truly, each player's actions and skill level on the court affect the five other members of the team—for every rally.

In addition to the concept of teamwork in the truest sense of the word, volleyball is a unique team sport because of the following features:

- **Separation of Teams.** The physical barriers of both a net and centerline separate the teams. Except for the dynamic hitting and blocking above the net in the attack zone, there is no defending, jostling for position or hands in your face as one performs his or her contact with the ball.
- **Small and Congested Playing Area.** The volleyball half-court area of approximately 900 square feet (81 square meters) is the smallest team sport playing area. Since there are six players in this half court, they must learn to perform in a limited area. Intricate movement patterns must be executed very quickly, must be efficient and must involve a minimum amount of movement.
- **Rotation.** According to the rules, the six players must rotate on the court in a clockwise fashion following each service change. The original intent of this rule was to create an environment in which there was a generalization of skills.

Today, there is more specialization for two reasons: (1) multiple substitutions at the collegiate and high school levels and (2) the addition of the libero—a player who can play back row for all six rotations. However, rotating still puts players in different positions and presents different situations where players must both perform different movements and utilize different skills. In addition, rotation results in new positions and perspectives for the entire team, presenting many different relationships and spatial orientations among teammates. Finally, rotation creates a new personnel orientation for the opponents as they attempt to identify the hitters, setters, libero, and so forth, on the other side of the net.

- **Concept of Rebounding.** Volleyball rules stipulate that the ball should never visibly come to rest. However, at the international and collegiate levels, there has been much more latitude given to the first contact. Even with this liberalization of rules each contact is, in effect, a rebound. The spatial positioning of the ball, as well as the sequence of the contact, determines which individual technique or skill will be employed in rebounding the ball. Rebounding is alien to our American sports culture, since almost all of our sports skills have a "catch and throw" orientation. Rebounding implies non-possessiveness, so in volleyball every player is in contact with the ball for a fraction of a second. For this reason, in most cases it is very important to assume a stable and balanced position prior to contact.
- **Cause and Effect.** Other than the skill of serving, each volleyball skill is entirely dependent on the previous skill executed. Each contact is built upon the previous contact. Each player involved in the rally is part of the chain reaction. A cause-and-effect principle underlies every contact.
- **Unit Versus Individual.** Volleyball is one of the best examples of teamwork in sport. As a result of the small and congested playing area, the concept of rebounding and the cause-and-effect principle, it is very difficult for one player to dominate a match completely. Each player must think of his or her role to *better the play* or *make his or her teammate successful.*
- **Fast Pace.** Because of the small playing area, one is constantly transitioning from offense to defense in a split second. Both the serve and spike can travel at speeds of 50 to 70 miles per hour, and a player may have only a few hundredths of a second to react to the ball.

As for skill development, ball control has always been a cornerstone for my teams at every level that I have coached. Very simply, the teams that have the best ball control and mastery of the six volleyball skills (serving, serve receiving, setting, attacking, blocking, digging) will be a contender at their respective levels. With the advent of rally scoring, the premium at the lower levels should be, more than ever, an emphasis on ball control! Every error results in a point. At the higher levels—top collegiate and international—attacking (particularly in transition), blocking, and serving factor heavily into determining the winner. As a beginning coach, I often followed the principle that at the lower levels serve-receiving will determine the level you play at and serving will determine who wins at that level. This holds for almost all levels except for top international volleyball, where successful attacking is often the most important ingredient to success.

Once the coach and the players understand the unique features of this sport, the key to having a successful team is to teach and drill the correct six skills as well as the correct offense, defense, and transition tactics. To produce or become an accomplished volleyball player, it has always been my philosophy and belief that you must teach and learn these fundamentals with sound biomechanical principles and proper pedagogic methodologies every day in your practice environments. In addition, design your drills so that outcomes are easily measurable and observable. Also, make your practice environment as gamelike as possible. I have often repeated to my players and staff—*practice does not make perfect; perfect practice makes perfect.* By striving for perfection, even though you may not always accomplish it, you will be surprised how often you may catch some *excellence* as a byproduct. Your team will not be the best that it can be if you simply go through the motions while teaching (and learning) skills and tactics, if you use concepts that you are not sure about, or if you run drills without knowing their intent or purpose. *Volleyball Skills & Drills* will provide the proper guidance for you to be able to accomplish all of your teaching and coaching goals.

In order to attack successfully, all good teams must have above average left-side hitters. In recent history, all the top international and collegiate teams have outstanding attackers on the left side. This player is required to hit a high ball and to be able to direct it to several areas of the opponent's court. This player will also be required to block, pass, serve, and set. In order to have a balanced attack, a team must also have good attackers from the right side, from the middle, and from the back row. The setter, if in the 5-1 system, will be the quarterback of your team; if in a 6-2 system, he or she will be one of two players responsible for delivering the second ball to the attacker. The key to an effective block will be your middle blockers—they set the tone for stopping the opponent's attack in all zones of the net. These players must have very good "reading skills" to be able to get to the right zone of the net and must also develop quick arm swings if they are the focal point of the quick attack in the middle of the court—both in serve receive and in transition.

The middle blocker will be complemented by the left-front and right-front blockers. These "end pieces" will set the block as predetermined by your tactics (blocking line, blocking angle, and so on).

This is an era of specialization with the libero and with an additional 12 to 15 substitutions per game. Now you are able to have a libero who will be able both to serve receive and dig balls throughout an entire game or match. However, it will still be important to teach defensive positioning for right front (RF), left front (LF), left back (LB), right back (RB), and middle back (MB) positions so that you may be able to position your players both technically and tactically.

MENTAL AND PHYSICAL CONDITIONING

According to Iradge Ahrabi-Fard, PhD, former head women's volleyball coach at the University of Northern Iowa (now retired),

> *The development of a volleyball player depends on the athlete's potential, level of commitment and working habits, as well as the quality and quantity of training. The entire developmental process of a volleyball player is the result of several complex, individually tailored conditioning programs, including physical, technical, psychological, cognitive and competition conditioning.*

Coaching—and becoming the true volleyball athlete—takes discipline in and commitment to all five aspects of conditioning. Truly, the information available on physical and mental conditioning alone could each fill the pages of two additional books. More than anything else, coaches and athletes should engage in proper physical conditioning to improve performance, prolong endurance during intense training sessions and competitions, and to prevent—and rehabilitate—injury.

From a psychological conditioning aspect, the most important responsibility of the coach is to motivate the athletes and influence their behavior via attainable goal setting. In addition, the coach is charged with the duty of influencing the athletes and encouraging them to develop a committed attitude toward both training and competing.

***Volleyball Skills and Drills* is divided into 10 chapters:**

Serving—Coach Tom Peterson of men's NCAA 2004 national champion BYU will present the stance, the toss, contact and follow-through. Several different serves (float and jump) will be discussed, as well as the strategy of serving. Tom makes a case for missing fewer serves and presents a strategy and drills to do so.

Receiving—Venerable coach Marilyn Nolen (former head women's volleyball coach at Saint Louis University, now retired) will present body stance, positioning, movement to the ball, and contact with the ball. Tactically, several systems of passing will be shown.

Setting—Coach Sean Byron of the men's team at Rutgers-Newark will elaborate on body stance and positioning, footwork and movement, hands and arms, and contact. Sean describes four basic phases of setting: (1) get to target, (2) be ready to move from the target, (3) beat the ball to spot, and (4) stop and set. Drills are presented for each phase.

Attacking—Coach Jim McLaughlin, head women's volleyball coach at the University of Washington, will discuss body positioning, footwork, the approach, plant, jump, timing, arm swing, contact, follow-through, and landing. Tactically, different types of attacks will be discussed.

Blocking—Coach Don Hardin, who is at the helm of the women's volleyball program at the University of Illinois, will present body positioning, footwork, balance and body control, jump, arms, hands, and landing. Tactically, different types of blocks that involve one, two, or multiple sets of blockers will be presented.

Digging—Coach Joan Powell of Coronado High School in Colorado Springs will discuss body positioning, leg position, footwork, platform, contact, timing, base and ready position, sprawl, the extension or shoulder roll, barrel roll, overhand pass, and beach dig. Joan presents 12 drills emphasizing all of the individual defensive techniques.

Playing Offense—University of North Carolina head women's volleyball coach Joe Sagula will present concepts such as attacker-setter timing, multiple-attacker movements, covering the attacker, executing down balls and free balls, reading defenses, and communication.

Playing Defense—Julie Backstrom and Mike Schall of Penn State, along with Coach Russ Rose, will discuss how to defend hard-driven spikes, tips and dinks, back-row attacks, free balls, down balls, playing defense behind a split block, reading offenses, and communication. Also discussed in detail are proper attitude, the big picture, sequence of events, physical characteristics of the defensive player, various defenses (perimeter, middle-up, rotational), and out-of-system plays.

Transitioning—Macalaster College head coach Stephanie Schleuder will present concepts such as movement from serve receive to offensive positions, moving from serving to base defensive positions, individual transition movements, and communication. Stephanie does an excellent job of presenting the visual cue for all the different movement sequences. The transition skills are broken down into individual skills and team-related skills. Drills are provided for all types of transition situations and sequences.

Practicing—Paul Arrington, venerable high school and club volleyball coach in Hawaii, will present how to plan and design a practice—but from a unique perspective. In this chapter, three determinants for quality practices will be discussed in detail—preparation, execution, and evaluation—along with the importance of having fun while learning the main emphasis.

When I was a beginning coach, there were very few print resources available. There were only a handful of books and none were as thorough as *Volleyball Skills & Drills*. Please take some time to go through each of the chapters carefully. Also, remember to use the American Volleyball Coaches Association (www.avca.org) as a resource.

Volleyball Skills & Drills will provide you with many valuable teaching and coaching tools. It will enhance your coaching abilities. Your volleyball coaching will be an exciting and wondrous journey; enjoy every minute of it!

Taras Liskevych
Head coach of women's volleyball, Oregon State University

Key to Diagrams

- - - - - - - - - -	Ball movement
————————	Player movement
A	Attacker
[ball cart symbol]	Ball cart
B	Blocker
C	Coach
D	Digger
H	Hitter
LB	Left-back player
LF	Left-front player
L	Libero
MH	Middle hitter
MB	Middle-back player
MF	Middle-front player
NP	Non-passer
OH	Outside hitter
P	Passer
X	Player
RB	Right-back player
RFH	Right-front hitter
RF	Right-front player
RS	Right-side player
Sv	Server
S	Setter
T	Target

1

Serving

Tom Peterson

Courtesy of Cal State Fullerton

Volleyball coaches and players have long recognized that serving and passing are the two most important skills in volleyball. Dr. Gil Fellingham, professor of statistics at Brigham Young University and consultant for the men's volleyball team, has conducted research on the BYU team, as well as on international teams. Dr. Fellingham recently shared some of his conclusions drawn from statistical research in relation to the importance of serving in volleyball. He found that a kill in volleyball is perhaps the most beneficial play in terms of a team winning a game, while the most detrimental play is missing a serve. However, he also found that serving "easy serves" (serves that allow an opponent to pass the ball directly to the target, allowing the setter to set all possible options) had an even more negative impact on winning a game than missing serves, simply because in a typical match, easy serves occur more frequently than missed ones. In short, Fellingham discovered that missed serves and easy serves are the two greatest detriments to winning a volleyball match, especially at a high level of competition.

Considering that missed and easy serves are the two most detrimental misplays when trying to win volleyball matches and that the more kills a team has, the more likely it is to win a game, one can conclude that during high-caliber competition, players must serve tough (hard and strategically accurate) to reduce the opponent's ability to make kills, and they must make these tough serves without missing a significant number of them. This, of course, presents quite a challenge for servers—and considerable frustration for coaches. However, as you would expect, navigating the fine line between tough serves and missed serves is made easier by devoting due time and attention to working on the serve, both in and out of practice.

Decreasing the number of missed serves is vital to success. This is best accomplished, first, by setting individual and team goals for percentages of serves made. Second, players must get in as many serving repetitions as possible, especially under gamelike situations. During these reps, they should always focus on the *quality* of serves, not only on getting them in.

Coaches should include feedback on serve quality during practice, again focusing on both accuracy and speed. Because serving is one of the few skills that can be practiced without having to rely on teammates, there's no excuse for players not getting their repetitions in. The more reps players do on their own time, the better prepared they will be for games. All they need to get going is access to a cart of volleyballs and a court. Of course, getting in reps with the addition of focused strategy, motivation, goals, and feedback is even more effective. Passers will obviously get better if they're practicing receiving all those extra serves.

MOTOR LEARNING FOR SERVING

You'll find many players do better when they understand the basic motor learning principles behind the skills they are practicing. A good book for information on motor learning as applied to volleyball is *The Science of Coaching Volleyball,* edited by Carl McGown, PhD.

When learning motor skills for serving, players shouldn't try to take in too much information at once. It works best to break skills down into keys or cues to help process the information. This helps them commit the information to memory and recall what needs to be done during the execution of the skill in practice or competition. Following are some motor learning concepts that work well when teaching and learning particular skills, including the serve:

- Eliminate extra movement. Extra movement, such as an unnecessarily high toss during a serve, makes a skill more complicated to learn and master. Experienced players sometimes display extra movement as part of their personal style. When less-experienced players try to imitate the skilled player, they include these unnecessary extra movements, which can prevent them from focusing on executing the basics of the skill properly, often leading to a delay in development.
- Demonstrate proper technique. Players will understand a skill and execute it more effectively when they see the skill's proper technique demonstrated. Demonstrate each phase of the serve, including the correct stance, toss, contact, and follow-through.
- Use repetition and provide feedback. A demonstration of a good serve, followed by directed, gamelike repetitions and accompanied by the coach's feedback will help players learn much better than simply talking about a good serve.
- Make practice gamelike. Spend the majority of practice time in gamelike drills without breaking down each skill separately for long periods of time. When possible, initiate all gamelike drills with a serve instead of a toss from the coach.

In addition to learning and implementing motor learning principles, it would be helpful for the teacher to have acquired proficiency in executing a particular skill himself or herself before teaching that skill to others.

BASIC MECHANICS OF SERVING

A serve may be executed anywhere directly behind the endline. Indeed, it might be most effective to serve from various places along the length of the endline. During the course of a match, passers tend to get into a groove with their passes. Serving from different areas can help prevent an opposing passer from getting too comfortable. Being forced to adjust to serves coming from different places along the endline can also disrupt the flow of the passers in relation to each other.

For our purposes here, we'll limit our discussion of the serve to the basic float serve and the basic jump serve. Other serves are either variations or combinations of the jump and float or are uncommon enough to be beyond the scope of this chapter. Techniques discussed here are for a right-handed player and will need to be reversed for a left-handed player.

Figure 1.1 Position to rotate body through torque.

The Float Serve

The float serve (figures 1.1-1.5) is used to keep opponents on their toes. In most cases, the receiver does not keep an eye on the ball for its entire flight over the net. As a result, a float serve, which changes direction (slides left or right, up or down because it's hit without spin), can be most effective when opponents seem to be getting lazy.

Footwork. To execute a float serve, the server stands with upper body facing the direction to which the ball will be served with the feet positioned to allow the upper body to rotate easily through a throwing motion. This motion of throwing or "torque" is performed more easily if the feet are placed with the left foot forward and the body and feet pointing toward the right. Notice in figure 1.1 how the weight of the body is distributed and how the ball is held in the nonhitting hand with that arm slightly extended.

Draw the hitting arm back. Drawing the arm up and back takes longer than the toss, so begin to draw back before tossing the ball (figure 1.2).

Small step and toss. In the float serve, the toss or lift is out in front of the body and only high enough so contact with the ball can occur without waiting for it to drop significantly (figure 1.3). The small step is with the left foot; at the same time, some body weight transfers toward the left foot and in the direction of where the ball is being served. If beginning players need more power when serving, they can gain extra momentum by starting in back of the endline far enough to take a step with the right foot first. Then they step onto the left foot and complete the serve as described. Most beginners will quickly gain the coordination and strength to serve without requiring this extra movement.

Hit the middle of the ball with the palm of the hand. When the server contacts the ball with the hand during a float serve, the ball should be hit very firmly (unless the serve is intentionally short) with the palm of the hand, not with a clenched fist (figure 1.4). There's no need for excessive follow-through except to decelerate the

Figure 1.2 Drawing arm back.

Figure 1.3 Small step and toss.

Figure 1.4 Hit ball with palm of the hand.

arm and hand after hitting the ball. If the ball is hit in the center, it will not have spin as it travels over the net. This allows the ball to "float" and move in reaction to the air currents acting upon it. It's this movement that can make a well-executed float serve so difficult to pass.

Drag the back foot. Many beginning players make the mistake of taking a big step with the left foot and then a big step with the right foot. When this occurs, the player usually ends up facing far to the left while trying to hit to the right, which makes it difficult to step into the direction of the serve. To assist players in developing the habit of taking a step only with the left foot, it's helpful to drag the back foot as the ball is being hit (figure 1.5). This is similar to a tennis player dragging the back foot during the serve.

Figure 1.5 Drag the back foot.

Coaching Points for the Proper Execution of Basic Float Serves

- Footwork (left foot in front, feet turned to the right, upper body facing direction of the serve).
- Draw back (elbow up and back).
- Small step and toss (step with the left foot as the ball is tossed).
- Hit the center of the ball with the palm of the hand.
- Drag back foot.

The Jump Serve

The jump serve (figures 1.6-1.9) is now prevalent at higher levels of competition. For the jump serve to be effective, it must be accurately placed and hit very hard. When executed properly, this serve forces the passer to move and to pass the ball outside of his or her body line. A poorly executed jump serve can be rather easy for a good passer to handle. A jump serve has spin on it, which prevents air currents from acting upon its flight (unless the currents are strong). Thus, it's necessary for the jump serve to come with a great deal of speed, decreasing the passer's reaction time. Accuracy and speed are essential elements of successful jump serving.

The jump serve should not be viewed as a player's best serve—or even as an effective serve—unless he or she can hit it with a high level of accuracy, velocity, or both. The jump serve is effective if the server can direct the ball enough to cause the passer to move out of a stable passing position or if the server can hit the ball with such velocity that it causes the passer's ball control to be erratic.

To be effective, the jump serve must usually get to a passer (serve receiver) very quickly, almost to the point of surprising him or her. A player or coach must decide if the jump server has the skills to make this happen. If the jump server misses too many serves and is too erratic in simply getting the ball into the court, then even a very hard jump serve is not effective overall.

The jump serve is usually more aggressive than the float serve. When a team needs to make up ground on another team quickly, a more aggressive serve is generally advantageous. If a player's jump serve is not effective, the most aggressive serve might be a float serve hit harder than normal.

It's best to start a jump serve far enough behind the endline to allow the server room for a "spikelike" approach. It's legal to jump or "take off" from behind the endline, serve, and then land in front of the endline. Players should try to get to the point where an efficient broad jump and vertical jump are used to an advantage rather than complicating the skill and hindering performance.

Although some jump servers like to hold and toss the ball with both hands or with the nonhitting hand, it's usually best to hold and toss the ball with the hitting hand. The toss must be high enough and out in front of the server so that he or she can contact the ball at the peak of the jump. To do this, the server must initiate the approach with a small step and toss.

Figure 1.6 Jump serve small step and toss.

Small step and toss. Take a small step with the right foot (for a right-hander) and toss the ball as you put weight on that foot (figure 1.6). Essentially, this leaves three steps of a four-step approach to "spike" the serve. In essence, the jump serve is tossing the ball to oneself to spike. (For details on the proper spike approach, refer to chapter 4.)

Medium height toss. In the jump serve, the toss is out in front and at a medium height so the three remaining steps of the approach don't have to be slowed down, sped up, shortened, or lengthened too much. Another way of stating this is to toss the ball only high enough to hit a second-tempo set (a fairly low set in which the first step of a four-step spike approach has already been taken before the ball is set). Occasionally, players toss the ball very high and then take a four-step (or more) approach after the toss. You see this most often in international play. However, as mentioned previously in this chapter, eliminating extra movement simplifies the skill and makes it easier to learn (figure 1.7).

Spike. When executing the jump serve, contact with the ball is like an attacker spiking the ball. As shown in figure 1.8, the ball should be contacted with the palm of the hand when the hitting arm is extended and slightly out in front. By snapping the wrist on contact with the ball, you put topspin on the ball. The higher the contact and the faster the armswing, the more topspin is generated. A ball with topspin travels harder and faster to the floor and is thus more difficult to pass to target.

Figure 1.7 Medium height toss.

Figure 1.8 Spike.

Coaching Points for the Proper Execution of Jump Serves

- Accuracy and speed are essential.
- Use a spikelike approach.
- Hold and toss the ball with the hitting hand.
- Toss the ball high and out in front.
- Use a small step and a medium toss.
- Contact the ball with the palm of the hand.
- Snap the wrist.

Although serves other than the float serve and jump serve aren't discussed in detail in this chapter, it's worth noting that the jump float serve has now become quite common. The jump float serve is executed with a lower toss than the jump serve, with the palm of the hand contacting the center of the ball to avoid creating spin. As shown in figure 1.9, the hitting arm does not "torque" as much during the jump serve. It combines the upper body execution of a float serve with the lower body execution of a jump serve approach.

Figure 1.9 Torque of jump serve.

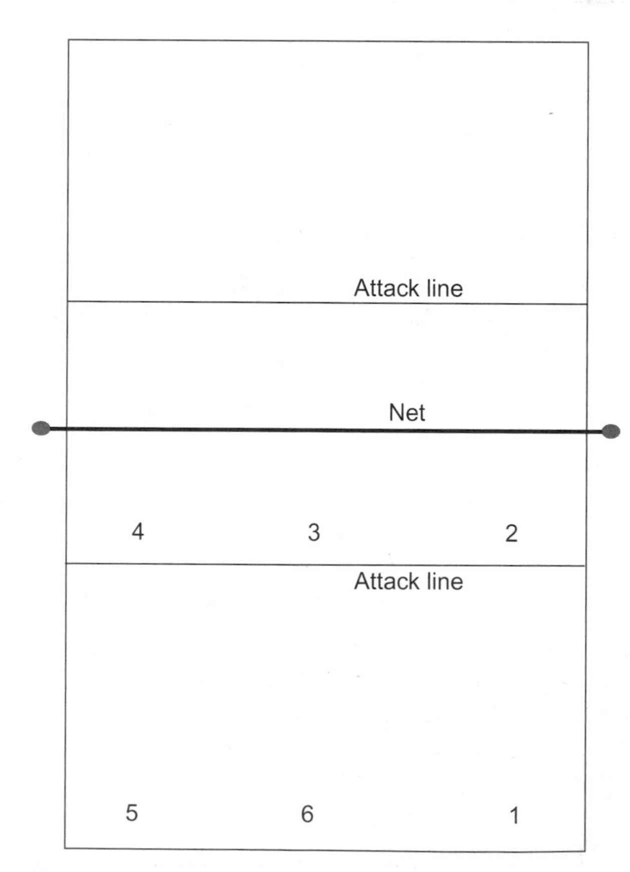

Figure 1.10 Six areas of the court.

A jump float might be preferred to a jump serve if a server or a team is having trouble getting a hard jump serve in consistently. The jump float is generally more accurate than the regular jump. One of our team goals is not to miss more than four serves each game. If we're missing many more serves than that, we might float more. This also goes for any individual who's missing too many serves. If a team is able to hit "hard jumpers" into the court consistently (four misses or fewer per game), then the hard jump serve is preferred.

A player or coach will have to decide whether a standing float or a jump float serve is the most effective for a particular server and for a given serving situation. Most servers naturally become better using one type of serve or another. The jump float is hit at a higher contact point (and sometimes closer to the net) than a standing float is hit. But because the jump float is more dynamic in nature, it's also often more difficult to execute.

SERVING STRATEGY

What serve to use and when to use it are not easy decisions. One bit of advice is to make sure you're prepared to make an accurate and effective delivery, no matter what serve you choose. Also, strategy and research can help make these decisions easier. Following are some tips for developing or improving strategies employed during games.

1. Know your opponent. It's helpful to know ahead of time the weaknesses and strengths of each passer on the opposing team. Know who the weakest passer is in each rotation. It might be that one passer doesn't move well in a certain direction. Or a particular passer might not do as well if the ball has to be passed in a certain spot in relation to his or her midline. Perhaps one type of serve is more effective against a certain passer. Knowing who the front-row players are is also important. Making a front-row passer move further away from the intended line of his or her spike approach might make that hitter less efficient. Serving short, deep, or to the side might take a step away from that hitter's approach. A team can gain many advantages in serving by being familiar with the opponent.

2. Get some advice. Most coaches and players use a system in which the court is divided into six areas with corresponding numbers (figure 1.10). Many teams have a member of the coaching staff who spends time becoming familiar with the strengths and weaknesses of the passers on an opposing team. This coach can then use

hand signals to indicate to his or her servers the most strategically beneficial area to serve against that opponent in any particular rotation. The coach usually holds up a hand and flashes to the server a number of fingers that indicates which area to serve (a fist could mean area 6; a crooked finger could mean a jump serve). Such hand signals can be of great help to servers, especially those without a lot of experience with serve selection and placement. However, it's still preferable for servers to use their own creativity and instinct to determine the proper serve in a particular situation rather than continually looking over to the bench for guidance.

3. Recognize the times when it's critical to get the serve in. Volleyball is a game of momentum. The better a team can retain momentum, the greater the chance to win. One way to stop momentum dead in its tracks is by missing a serve. Although missed serves do occur, in some situations they have a much greater negative impact. Players will want to be extra sure to get the serve in the following situations: the first serve of the game, at game or match point, following a timeout, when the previous server missed his or her serve, after a substitution, after a spectacular rally, after a run of points by either team, and near the end of a game or match.

Well-prepared servers are practiced, know their own strengths and weaknesses, and are familiar with the strengths and weaknesses of the opponent. Well-prepared servers can quickly determine the best serving strategy to employ in any situation.

Coaching Points for Serving Strategy

- While serving hard or "tough" serves is critical, serving a high percentage of serves inbounds is also very important.
- To serve well, a player should develop and execute the skill using sound mechanics.
- Strategy is a critical component of serving.
- Using motor learning principles to govern the development and implementation of drills makes for much more effective practices, which in turn results in well-prepared servers.
- Done well, serving can gain any team a huge advantage over an opponent by taking the opponent "out of system" (the inability to set all options) as much as possible.

SERVING DRILLS

Marv Dunphy, head men's volleyball coach at Pepperdine University and head coach of the 1988 gold-medal winning USA men's national team, was once asked what he thought were the best passing drills. He replied, "serve–pass–set–hit." He was then asked what he thought were the best setting drills. He replied, "serve–pass–set–hit." Clearly, Dunphy believes that good serving drills are also good for passing, setting, and hitting. Designing and using drills that incorporate all or as many volleyball skills as possible takes creativity and flexibility. Coaches who design their practices around such drills will develop players who have an easier time transitioning from competing in practice to competing in actual games.

In almost all drills, following general principles of behavior modification—establishing a goal for the desired behavior and a consequence for the outcome—is recommended. The consequence can be positive (reward) or negative (penalty). Behavior modification is basic to coaching and critical for skill development.

The drills included in this chapter are just a small sampling of the many possible drills for serving. Use your creativity to modify the drills to fit the needs of your team. The best drills have the following elements in common: they are goal-directed, they provide for maximum repetitions, they are gamelike, they put players in a position of performing under pressure, and they allow for feedback from the coaching staff.

Partners

Purpose: To practice serving to target

Setup: One player stands on one side of the court and one on the other.

Execution: Partners take turns serving at each other.

Coaching Points: If players are beginners, they may stand far inside the baseline to serve the ball. As they develop more skills, the partners back up until they can serve from behind the baseline. There may be several sets of partners on each court. A progression from serving directly to a partner could be to serve to areas of the court where the partner is standing.

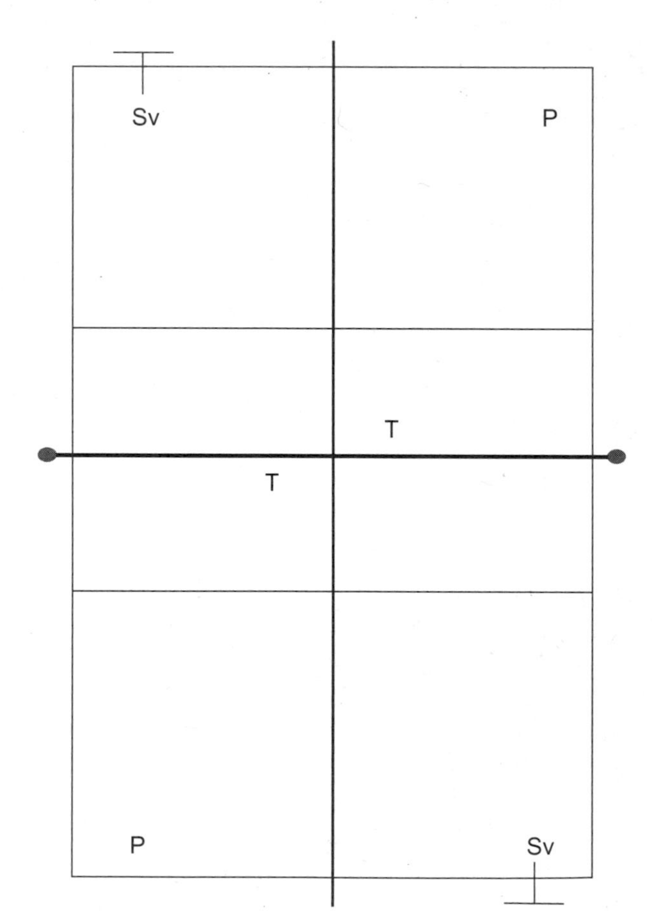

Figure 1.11 Groups-of-Three.

Groups of Three

Purpose: To practice serving with a "live" passer

Setup: One player stands on one side of the court, and two stand on the other side of the court. Groups of three make it convenient to practice the skill of serving.

Execution: A server on one side of the court serves to the passer on the other side of the court while a target catches the ball and feeds the server. The group of three rotates after a set time or set number of reps. Beginning servers may stand within the court and then step back as skills develop (figure 1.11).

Coaching Points: Drills using three players can range from very basic skill-level drills to those that require a high level of proficiency.

Three in a Row

Purpose: To employ a more advanced serving drill for a group of three players

Setup: Place a server on one side of a modified court, with a passer on the other. A judge (another player) is on the passer's side to begin. The boundary for this game is half of the court divided lengthwise.

Execution: The server competes in a game to three against the passer. The passer's target is the judge. A small point is given to the server if the passer can't pass a "good" pass, as determined by the judge. The passer receives a small point for a good pass or for a serve that goes out of bounds. A big point is awarded to either the server or the passer after either has won three small points in a row. The target then switches with the winner of the big point, and a new game begins. If any of the three players gets stuck having to perform the same skill more than two games in a row, then all three players rotate to a different position. Big points are then tallied after a set time (15 to 20 minutes) to see who has the most. About halfway through the drill, the passer may switch to passing on the other half of the court. The server will continue to serve to that passer from the same serving position. First-, second-, and third-place finishes are then determined (a tie-breaking system might be needed). With larger groups, a number of tournament "systems" may be implemented in which first-place finishers compete against other first-place finishers, and so on.

Coaching Points: This drill is excellent for practicing both serving and passing with ball control.

Butterfly

Purpose: To provide repetition practice in up to four skills

Setup: Place three players on the court, one as the server on one side of the net and the other two as a passer and a target on the opposite side.

Execution: A server serves to the passer. The server then takes the passer's position, and the passer becomes the target. The previous target becomes the server (figure 1.12).

Coaching Points: This is a good drill for warm-up or as part of regular practice.

Variations: To incorporate setting into the drill, the target could set the ball to a player standing near the antenna. To add spiking to the drill, the setter could set a hitter. This basic drill is used frequently in practice, camps, and clinics. Other variations include servers jogging to the other side of the court and passers staying for a set time; in this variation, the targets are nonplayers who throw the ball to the servers as the servers jog to the other side.

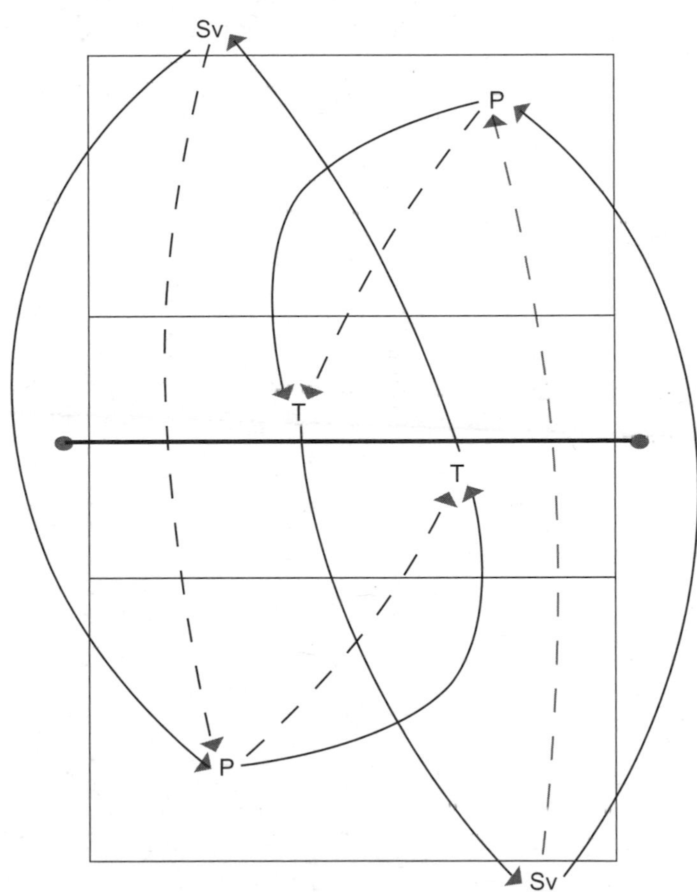

Figure 1.12 Butterfly.

***Stat*-ing Servers**

Purpose: To encourage proper passing to a target, focusing on getting the ball to a certain location and using proper skill technique; it also allows coaches to identify the team's best servers

Setup: To "stat" servers, select two to three passers for each side of the court. Have servers and a target on each side of the court.

Execution: Servers serve at the passers, and statistics are kept using a 4, 3, 2, 1, 0 scale. The serve is rated in relation to how well or poorly a receiver can pass it. A score of 4 is given for an ace or for a shank by the passer where no other teammate can control it. A score of 3 is given to the server for a poor pass in which the other team can only "get the ball up" or in which the setter doesn't have more than one setting option. A score of 2 is given for a serve in which the passer passes the ball and the setter can set the ball only to the outside hitter on either side. (This means the pass was poor enough that the setter couldn't set a quick-hitter or could not set all three options.) A score of 1 is given when the pass allows all three options open to the setter. A score of 0 is given if the server makes a service error (hitting out of bounds or faulting). Rating servers can be done on paper, a white board, or a computer.

After a set time, servers or passers switch to different positions on the court (they can even switch sides). After another set time (or after each server or passer has had a set number of attempts), results are tallied. Using a white board to record scores allows everyone to see them (figure 1.13).

Coaching Points: Statistics can motivate performance and are useful in determining the best servers and passers, as well as problem areas that need to be worked on in certain serving and passing rotations. The formula for determining a serving percent-

	4	3	2	1	0	
John	I	II	III	~~IIII~~ II	II	23/15 = 1.53
Sam	II	III	~~IIII~~	~~IIII~~ I	IIII	33/20 = 1.65
Jim		II	~~IIII~~	~~IIII~~ II	III	23/17 = 1.35
Tom	IIII	III	~~IIII~~	~~IIII~~	I	40/18 = 2.22

Figure 1.13 Sample chart for *stat*-ing servers.

age is as follows. Total points scored by the server are divided by that server's total number of attempts (TP/TA = SP). Scores can be kept on both individual servers and on the entire team. This gives each player a serving percentage based on a scale of 0 through 4. The statistics for servers are the opposite of the statistics for passers. If the server serves a 1, the passer must have passed a 3. If the server serves a 2, the passer passed a 2. If the server serves a 3, the passer passed a 1. If the server serves a 4, the passer scored a 0.

A good serving percentage or rating depends on the level of play. For a collegiate men's team, a good server averages approximately 1.8 or better. After some experience with this rating system, it's easy for a coach at any level of play to determine a realistic serving percentage for his or her team to shoot for. A rating system like this is more revealing than knowing the percentage of serves in the court. You can design drills based on the information gathered from the statistics. *Stat*-ing servers and passers also provides valuable information for individual and team strategy.

Servers Versus Passers

Purpose: To promote a friendly game of competition between servers and passers while providing gamelike reps

Setup: Place one server and two passers on each side of the court.

Execution: A typical servers-versus-passers drill consists of the main passers from the team (it's helpful to have at least two passers on each side of the court). Other players are serving and are divided so half of the servers are on one side of the court behind the baseline, and the other half are on the other side of the court behind the baseline. Two players serve as targets and are at the net where the passers want to pass the ball. The targets can be coaches or, better, setters on the team who want to get their "location reps" by setting the passed ball to a target.

An individual server on one side serves to the passers on the other side, trying to make the serve difficult enough that the passer doesn't pass a "good" pass to the target. Either the coach or the target at the net decides if the pass was good or bad. Then a server from the opposite end of the first server serves, trying to make it difficult for the passers he or she is serving to. The servers continue to alternate sides serving while a running score of good or bad serves is kept. Whichever team scores a set number of points first wins.

Coaching Points: There is one scoring method in particular that can be changed to fit different levels of play. In order for servers to score a big point, they must make passers pass two poor passes in a row. Conversely, for passers to score, they must pass four good passes in a row (more or less, depending on the playing level). The competition could go to so many big points or for a certain time period. At a high level of play, passers will pass more good passes than bad passes, so a common scoring system could require passers to pass three good passes in a row to receive a point. In contrast, the servers will need to make the passers pass only two bad passes in a row to receive a point. At a lower level of play, the scoring might be two versus two little points (passers and servers both need to pass or serve two good ones each in order to rotate).

Serving at Targets

Purpose: To motivate servers to improve accuracy

Setup: The target could be a marked area of the court, a ball cart, a chair, or a plastic cone.

Execution: Servers line up along the endline and serve directly to the designated target.

Coaching Points: The ability to execute a serve with accuracy is perhaps the most important element in serving. It goes without saying that the coach makes for a motivational hitting target. Getting a reward (e.g., a piece of candy) for hitting a target can also provide motivation.

Variation: The best serves force receivers to move, so serving at the area near the target rather than directly at the target itself might make for a better drill. You might lay two or three towels on the court in places at which passers could easily get to the ball. The servers could then try to land their serves between the towels without hitting them.

Work-Ups

Purpose: To encourage players to serve to a target

Setup: More than one court may be used. Passers may also be involved.

Execution: To complete this drill successfully, the server must execute a set number of serves from and to designated areas on the court. This drill can be set up as a competition between players or as an individual exercise that must be completed within a certain time.

Coaching Points: This drill uses the term "work-up" loosely. You can create your own work-up drills to target specific weak areas on your team.

Serving Pressure

Purpose: To encourage players to serve to a target in high-pressure situations

Setup: At the end of practice, one coach stands along the endline and another coach stands along the sideline, thus marking off a section of the court as a target area for serving. One or two players are chosen as servers; the rest of the team lines up on a sideline.

Execution: The server serves to a designated target. If the serve lands within the target area, no penalty is suffered. If the server misses, his or her teammates run lines (figure 1.14).

Coaching Points: When athletes realize they're not going to be criticized for their mistakes, they no longer fear making them. Make sure that the penalty, whatever it is, is not fear induced. (See Chapter 10, Practicing, for an excellent description of fear-induced penalties.)

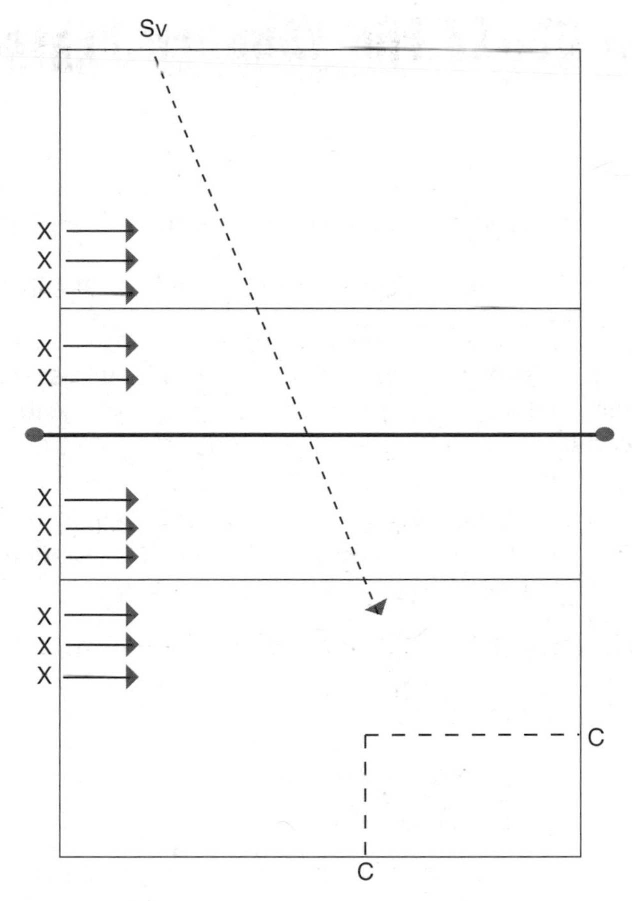

Figure 1.14 Serving Pressure.

Serve and Serve-Receive Ladder

Purpose: To encourage poor servers to improve their serving and serve-receive ability as statistically determined by the coach

Setup: One player is on one side of the court and two players are on the other side.

Execution: To start the ladder at the beginning of the season, arrange players in descending order from weakest at the top to strongest at the bottom. Challenges can then be made each week (perhaps with a limit of two per week). The two players involved in the challenge get together and ask someone to be their target. Each player serves 50 times at the other player (25 down the line and 25 cross court). The target keeps score of the number of good serves or passes. The player with the most good serves or passes wins the challenge.

Coaching Points: This ladder is similar to a tennis ladder. As coach, you get to decide who will get to challenge whom each round. I like to have at least the potential primary passers on the team be part of a serve-receive ladder. These challenges can take place either during practice or outside of practice.

FUN SERVING DRILLS FOR YOUNGER PLAYERS

PIG

Purpose: To encourage young players to serve over the net and to a target

Setup: Two players set up along the same endline. Each serves the ball to the opposite court.

Execution: This game is similar to the game of HORSE in basketball. One player announces where or what kind of serve he or she is going to attempt. If he or she makes the serve as described, the other player has to make the same serve. If the first player makes the serve and the second player misses, the second player earns a letter P. If the first player misses the serve, the second player becomes the leader and gets to choose what serve he or she will attempt. The player who gets all three letters of the word PIG first loses the game.

Coaching Points: Make sure the target is varied for different players at different levels. For instance, with young players, have them hit within a few feet of the target or make the court smaller or the target larger.

Asteroids

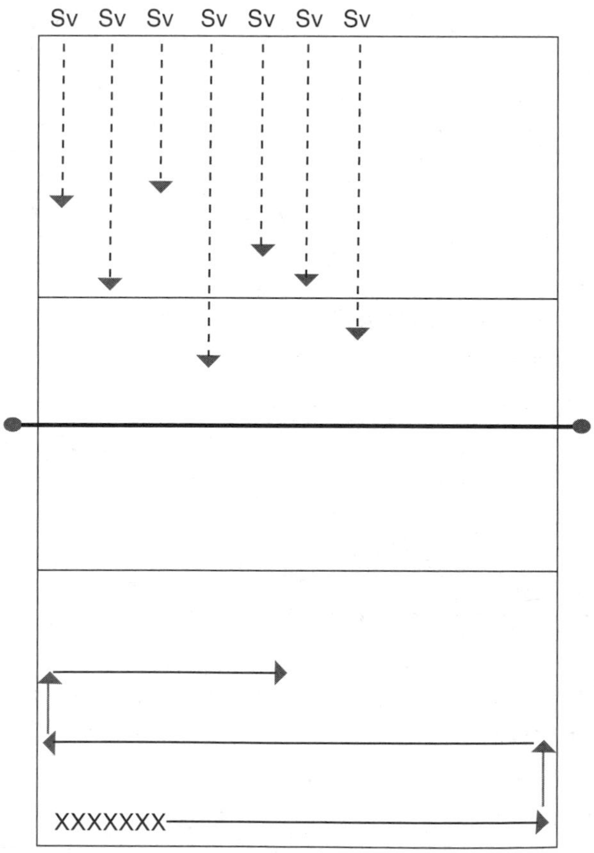

Purpose: To promote server accuracy and team camaraderie

Setup: Players divide into two even groups; each group goes to its own side of the court. One group is chosen to serve first, and the other group is the "asteroids." The asteroids group lines up along its baseline with backs toward the servers on the other side of the court.

Execution: The asteroids interlock arms and then shuffle-step sideways in a straight line from one sideline to the other. When the asteroid group reaches the other sideline, the entire group of asteroids takes one big step backward and toward the net. Then the asteroids shuffle to the other sideline and take another big step backward toward the net. This process continues until the asteroid group actually touches the net. While this is going on, the serving group tries to hit the asteroids by serving volleyballs (figure 1.15). When an asteroid is hit, he or she leaves the group, and the rest of the asteroids interlock arms once again and keep going. Once the asteroids get to the net or they are all hit, the two groups switch. Whichever group has the most remaining asteroids when they reach the net wins the game.

Coaching Points: Keep an eye out for "cheating" asteroids.

Sv Sv Sv Sv Sv Sv Sv

XXXXXXX

Figure 1.15 Asteroids.

Six

Purpose: To promote controlled serving to target

Setup: Players divide into two teams. Each team lines up at its respective endline, ready to serve, with the exception of one player from each team. This player goes to the opposite court and sits in area 1. (The court has been divided into the typical six designated areas.)

Execution: Both teams start serving, one player at a time, trying to serve to their teammates sitting on the opposite court. If the teammate on the other side can catch the serve while sitting down, the player who served the ball sits in area 2, and the previous sitter goes to the endline to serve. This continues as both teams race to see which team can complete catching the serve in all six areas of the court.

Coaching Points: A bit of friendly competition is inherent in this drill, and it has several elements of a great drill: it is goal-directed, provides for maximum repetitions, is as gamelike as possible, puts the player in a position of performing under pressure, and allows for feedback from the coaching staff.

CONCLUSION

Like all other skills in volleyball, serving has evolved over the years from simply a way to put the ball into play to a true offensive—and even defensive—weapon. The serve is the only skill in volleyball that affords players complete control of its execution. Unlike any other skill in the game, only the server can determine if the serve will be successful.

2

Receiving Serves

Marilyn Nolen

Courtesy of FIVB

According to Mike Hebert, PhD, head women's volleyball coach at the University of Minnesota, "A quick offensive tempo begins as a concept on the coach's clipboard. It can become a reality only if the team can pass accurately, a setter can be trained to run the offense, and a full complement of quality hitters can be trained to attack within the system."

Pay particular attention to the first 12 words of the second sentence: It can become a reality only if the team can pass accurately. Undeniably, serve receive is the single most important component in the overall offensive scheme of a volleyball team, no matter the level or gender. If a team cannot receive the opposing team's serve and transition into an effective attack, the coach and team members might as well pack it up and go home. With the widespread use of rally scoring, a breakdown in receiving the serve is truly the precursor to defeat.

What does it take to teach and to become a great serve-receiving team? According to Carl McGown, PhD, former head men's volleyball coach at Brigham Young University, "Because of the magnitude of its importance, at least half of practice every day should be involved with serve and serve receive."

Half of practice is a considerable amount of time to spend on one skill in a multiskilled sport. But do not underestimate its importance. Training excellent serve receivers as individuals to meld together as an efficient serve receiving team is critical to any team's success.

TRAITS OF EFFECTIVE PASSERS

To clarify, the "serve receiver" and the "passer" are one and the same. Because the serve receiver's primary task is to pass the ball to another player, he or she is frequently called a passer instead of a serve receiver. For volleyball coaches, the two terms are synonymous.

First and foremost, an effective serve receiver (passer) must have the proper visual skills to be able to track the ball from the exact moment it leaves the opposing server's hands to the time it reaches his or her arms. A good serve receiver must have excellent distance vision—the ability to see clearly at a distance of 16 feet or more; very good depth perception (stereopsis)—the ability to judge distance from self to others and objects; visual pursuit—the ability of the eyes to follow smoothly, easily, and accurately when tracking an object, such as a volleyball coming off a server's hand; and visual concentration—the ability to concentrate on an object while dealing with other visual stimulation occurring within range of sight.

In addition to keen visual skills, a truly effective serve receiver has the ability to concentrate. Sean McCann, PhD, director of Sport Psychology Services at the United States Olympic Training Center (USOTC) in Colorado Springs, determined a number of mental skills crucial to sport success in terms of offense. These skills include confidence, competitive focus, mental preparation, quality of training, and use of imagery. Especially for the serve receiver in volleyball, confidence, competitive focus, and mental preparation stand out as the most desirable traits. Mental preparation, or the ability to think in the present, is paramount. A good passer must be able to move on from past mistakes and not worry about future performances. In addition, he or she should be able to focus on the process of improving without thinking about the overall outcome or results. Confidence translates into the ability to trust one's own skills, thus invoking the ability to perform automatically, without hesitation or second thoughts.

Finally, a good serve receiver must have the physical ability to get the job done. A player's ability to move efficiently to the ball determines his or her serve-receive success rate. When receiving a serve, passers should attempt to get to the ball in three steps or fewer. They should also be able to move to the point at which they can actually intercept the ball before it gets there. In other words, the effective passer should be waiting for the ball to arrive. A major fault that poor serve receivers display is waiting until the ball actually reaches them before taking that first step. From a purely physical standpoint, a coach must ensure that his or her players have adequate flexibility, especially in the ankles, so they can pivot and turn as quickly as possible.

Unfortunately, when it comes to teaching and learning effective serve receive, form and success don't necessarily go hand in hand. In other words, the player with the nicest technique might not be the one who's able to get the ball to target on successive attempts. Similarly, a player might be able to pass the ball in certain situations but might not be a strong passer overall. For instance, a player might be very good at receiving a short serve or receiving when he or she is in the right back or middle position. However, if that same player is passing from the right front, where there are refractory angles, it becomes more difficult for him or her to get the ball to the setter. The principal hindrance to effective serve receive is the inability to perform under pressure. Sure, an athlete might be able to pass nails during practice, but what happens when his or her team is down 18-17 and it appears the opposing server likes to serve to his or her particular spot?

Just as with setters and middle blockers, serve-receive specialization is required. Not all players on a team, no matter the level, can be equally effective, so the ability to train two or three players to be efficient passers is paramount. Passers, like very tall blockers, play regardless of their other skills. It is therefore important to identify and train those passers who will be able to get the ball to the setter and initiate the offense.

PASSING PROCESS

The passing process begins with adequate preparation. First, ensure you have a wide base (feet spread slightly wider than shoulder width), with the ability to push off side to side and with one foot slightly ahead (figure 2.1). The knees should be slightly bent so that they are forward of the toes, which should be slightly in, not out. Body weight should be on the balls of the feet (figure 2.2). The back and shoulders should form a 45-degree angle to the floor (figure 2.3).

In addition to proper stance, perhaps the most important factor in effective serve receive is establishing the correct platform. At this point in the passing process, arms should be extended in front of the body and parallel to the upper leg (figure 2.4). The hands are not clasped prior to movement, and palms are up. The upper body remains relaxed in preparation to receive the serve.

Figure 2.1 Wide base.

Figure 2.2 Weight on the balls of the feet.

Figure 2.3 Back and shoulders form 45-degree angle to the floor.

Figure 2.4 Correct platform.

At this point, the ability to anticipate the serve and its trajectory comes in handy. The receiver must watch the server to predict what sort of serve he or she is going to release. For example, a toss in front of the server's body usually indicates a flat serve. A toss behind the server's body most often signals a spin serve. Of course, for a jump serve, look for the approach and jump.

Execution

Start in a comfortable stance in a medium (not low or high) position (figure 2.5). The receiver should be able to see the ball on contact for early eye fixation (reading the serve). The first step is to the ball without a jump or any other wasted movement prior to the step. This first movement is often referred to as the "step and plant" (taking a step toward the direction of the served ball and then planting both feet in the spread position). Set both feet behind the ball and stay balanced. As the receiver moves to the ball, his or her head stays at the same level (figure 2.6). Once he or she gets both feet to the ball, the shoulders are perpendicular (square) to the oncoming ball. The shoulders and hips should face the ball, especially if the player is forced to move during the pass (figure 2.7). Arms remain behind the line

Figure 2.5 Medium position.

Figure 2.6 Step and plant.

Figure 2.7 Shoulders are square. Shoulders and hips face the ball.

of the ball to the target, and the player should make sure not to open or pivot. Hips stay below the ball.

Simultaneous to planting the feet and forming the platform, the hands should "lock in." Several different hand positions have been taught over the years. The choice is up to the passer (or his or her coach). The overlap grip is one of the most popular and works well for all levels. Basically, the overlap grip is formed when fingers are across fingers and thumbs are parallel (side by side). The heels of the hands are also together (figure 2.8). At this point, the receiver pushes the wrists down, which helps to lock the elbows. This, in turn, elevates the shoulders forward and keeps the platform strong.

The receiver keeps the arms within vision range; he or she should be able to see both arms and hands. Although the legs and the body move, the platform doesn't change. Make sure the head doesn't go up and down. From the waist up, the skill looks very easy.

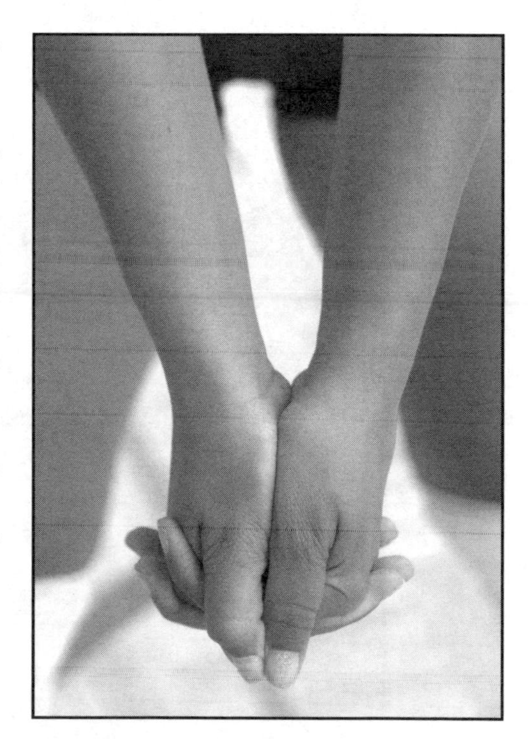

Figure 2.8 Heels of the hands are together.

Figure 2.9 Gentle shoulder shrug.

The receiver should play the ball in the top third of his or her vision, looking at the underside of the ball as it crosses the net and "watching" the ball into his or her arms. Focus on the line of the ball, since the target doesn't move. Once the ball comes in contact with the platform (the arms), the receiver gently lifts the platform into the ball. The arms should lift with a gentle shoulder shrug rather than a swinging motion (figure 2.9).

Location

According to McGown, "The majority of the world's great passers take the ball in the center of their bodies with feet slightly staggered. This allows them to get behind the ball quickly and efficiently."

Toshi Yoshida, 2004 U.S. Olympic Women's Volleyball Team head coach, agrees: "Passing linear refers to a player passing the ball between his or her knees. The play can have the most efficient power when contacting the ball between the knees."

However, volleyball is not a game of absolutes. Sometimes even the most efficient passer is not able to get directly in front of the ball and move through it, especially when the serve is a hard-driven jump serve and there are limited passers to cover a wide berth in the backcourt. Essentially, there are three ways to receive any served ball. Which one a passer chooses depends entirely on the situation.

Midline. When the receiver's body is directly behind the ball and the target is straight in front, the passer should pass the ball from the midline of the body. The feet should remain in a parallel position and might end with a step toward the target. This step occurs more often when passing from the back row as opposed to the front row, when momentum often takes some speed off the ball (absorption or cushioning of momentum).

Angle right. A ball received with the right-angle pass is the most commonly used. If the passer is directly behind the ball and the target is to the right, the passer takes the ball in front of the left hip, drops the right shoulder, and executes the pass with a lift-and-freeze motion. The right foot may be behind the lead foot (figure 2.10).

Figure 2.10 Angle right.

Angle left. If the passer is directly behind the ball with the target to the left, he or she takes the ball in front of the right hip. The left shoulder drops, and the pass is executed with a lift-and-freeze motion, as described for the right-angle pass. This time, the left foot may be the lead foot (figure 2.11).

Figure 2.11 Angle left.

Emergency Situations

Sometimes the ball can't be passed effectively via the three above-mentioned techniques. Perhaps the ball is served low or deep and above chest level. For a high serve, the passer must clear the shoulders of the path of the ball. The receiver tilts the shoulders and then angles the platform to the target (figure 2.12). For a low serve, the receiver might have to drop to one knee—or both, if necessary (figure 2.13, a-b). Sometimes the passer might

Figure 2.12 Receiver tilts shoulders and angles platform to target.

Figure 2.13a Receiver drops to one knee.

Figure 2.13b Receiver drops to both knees.

not be able to pass the ball from a stationary position. In this case, the passer must "shuffle through" the ball—that is, move through the ball while simultaneously executing the pass (figure 2.14).

Cushioning the Ball

Passers, especially at the younger levels, often find it difficult to receive (pass) a hard-driven serve. To receive a hard-driven serve, the passer should relax the shoulders on contact, allowing the arms to "give" with the ball instead of adding extra movement, possibly causing an errant pass.

Figure 2.14 Passer shuffles through.

Coaching Points for the Passing Process

- Know where the court lines are prior to the serve.
- End all conversation prior to the serve.
- Know where the intended target is prior to the serve.
- Focus on the ball before the server contacts it.
- If the ball is served on the left side, lead with the right arm and shoulder. Drop the inside shoulder so arms face the target. Do the reverse if the ball is served on the right side.

DEVELOPING A SUCCESSFUL SERVE RECEIVE

Once players learn the fundamentals of the serve receive, it's up to you, the coach, to determine the lineup on the court that makes for the best passes to the setter.

Kathy DeBoer, former head women's volleyball coach at the University of Kentucky, states,

> *Long ago we gave up on the idea that all our players are equally effective setters, middle blockers, left- or right-side hitters, or even servers. We specialize these positions at the elementary levels of play. Yet, in the area of serve receive, I see us peculiarly attached to the five-player pattern that tests only our opponent's ability to identify and serve our weak receivers.*
>
> *The reason for this must be that the skill of serve receive does not look difficult to us compared to other skills. A served ball travels 40 to 50 feet at a relatively low speed and is contacted by a stationary player with both feet on the floor. Further, if we put five of those players on a finite court, good passes should be guaranteed.*

Unfortunately, it doesn't always work that way. When it comes to the serve receive, coaches are always trying to find a combination of passers to optimize the team's chances for success. Depending on the level of play, there are four popular patterns of serve receive: five-, four-, three-, and two-person passing. (For details on these particular serve-receive patterns, see chapter 7.) Usually, at the lower levels, the more passers available to get to the ball, the better. In high school varsity and college, however, the three-person serve receive is more widely used. Fewer passers means less chance for miscommunication and misunderstanding about who's supposed to receive the serve.

Also, the best passers pass the ball.

Essentially, depending on the skill level of his or her team personnel, the coach must expose the team's best passers to the largest number of served balls while hiding the weaker passers. Good passers need more room for pursuit of the ball, and they should be encouraged to be aggressive in big areas. Conversely, the average passers (or the primary attackers, who need to focus on what the setter is running on offense), should have limited areas of responsibility during the serve receive. Basically, the goal of an effective serve receive is to get the setter to the intended target quickly and easily, while simultaneously getting the hitters into their optimal attack positions. An effective way to achieve this goal is to rate the passes of the receivers.

Rating Passers

James E. Coleman, PhD, venerable U.S. national team coach with more than half a century of experience as a player and an instructor, invented the most popular statistical system that rates the effectiveness of the team's serve receive on a five-point scale. For our purposes in this chapter, we'll use a modified scale in which the passer receives a 0, 1, 2, or 3, depending on the quality of the pass. The higher the number, the better the pass.

Points

0 = The passer is aced (no options are available to the setter).

1 = The setter can set the ball but has no choices, or another player must set the ball.

2 = The set is possible for two options.

3 = The passed ball reaches the target and all setting options are available.

The best kind of pass is low, about two feet above and off the net. Undeniably, the higher the pass, the more difficult it is to set the ball. In addition, passes that are too tight to the net decrease the setter's options.

There are some tried-and-true standards for comparison of passers in a team's serve-receive system. Basically, to be a successful team at the collegiate level, all primary passers must receive at a 2.0 level or higher. Conversely, if a player is below a 1.0, he or she is definitely a detriment to the team on serve receive and should be "hidden." Each coach must determine the appropriate levels for his or her team. For instance, you might not have any players who can pass at the 2.0 level; in this case, a 1.75-level passer is obviously preferable to one who scores a 1.25.

You can evaluate the passers on your team by doing a simple activity. Place one passer in a large area of the court (1/2 court) and have him or her face a variety of servers, from the best to mediocre. Use the rating scale just described (0–4) to determine the value of each pass. (As mentioned in chapter 1, servers can be evaluated at the same time with the same scoring system, but in reverse. However, servers will be more aggressive when there's no penalty for them. This keeps the pressure on the passer.) Determine the pass percentage on good serves, using 10 or more attempts. (For example, if a passer scored a 0, 3, 3, 1, 1, 1, 0, 2, 2, 1, he or she would receive a 1.2 rating.) Then do the same for 100 attempts.

Once the passers on the team have been evaluated, you can decide how many passers to use in the serve-receive pattern and who the passers will be. This is a difficult task that requires a clear understanding of overlap rules; the ability—and willingness—to use substitutions; and a little time spent drawing (and erasing) court diagrams.

The alignment (or overlapping) rule governs how you place your players in serve receive. The rule states at the moment of serve, players must be in their correct serving order and have at least part of one foot closer to their sideline, center, or endline than the adjacent player's two feet. (For more detailed information about the overlap rule and stacking, see chapter 7.) See figure 2.15 for examples of serve-receive options using three passers.

Placement of Passers

One of the most frequent mistakes coaches make is placing passers too deep in the court. To cover the court well, the base position should be about two-thirds of the way back from the net (halfway between the three-meter line and the endline). Of course, slight adjustments will need to be made depending on the server.

Whether in the front row or the back row, each of the six players on the court has a responsibility to begin serve-receive duties by focusing on the server. Even those players who are not passing and are transitioning to attack should focus all of their attention on the server and the ball coming across the net. Before the service toss, the front-row players should verbally identify the hitters and the setter on the opposing team and establish whether the setter is in the front or the back row. The receivers should call the ball as soon as it's served so that those players who won't be passing the ball can open up and give the passer room to move. Essentially, except for a ball served deep into the court, it's the responsibility of the player on the left to pass the ball when it's served between two players. At this point, because the intended receiver should be focusing on the pass, the other players should call the ball in or out.

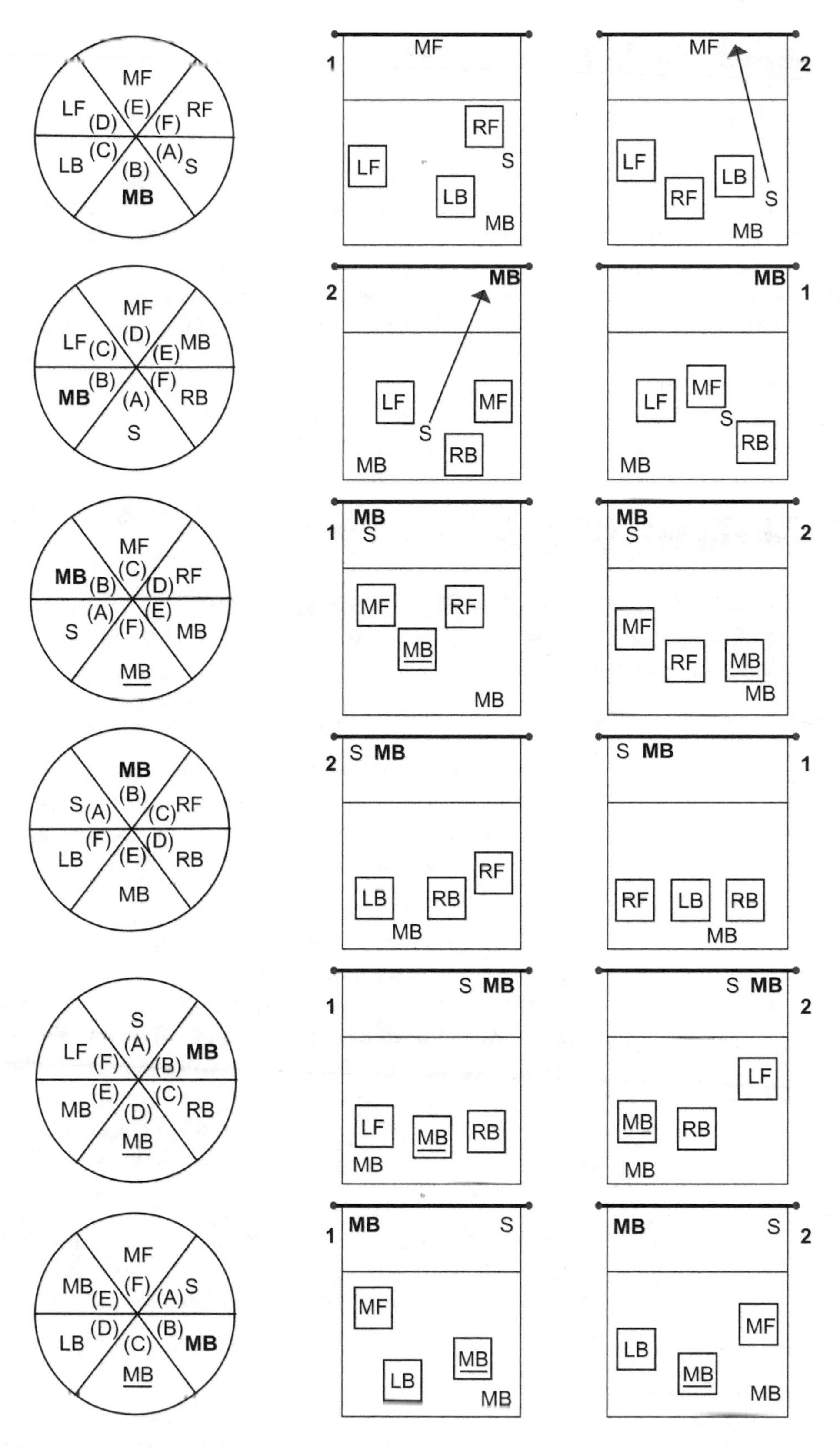

Figure 2.15 Serve-receive options using three passers. MB denotes the middle-back position, MB denotes the middle-back passer, and **MB** denotes the middle-back blocker.

COACHING POINTS

Approximately 60 percent of serves go to the middle-back position (position 6). Place your best passer there to increase your team's passing percentage automatically. Perhaps the most important key to ensuring that each player knows his or her responsibility when it comes to the serve receive is to practice with a definite lineup. A player needs to be familiar with the teammate who's passing next to him or her on a regular basis.

Have a passing captain or a setter prepared to make necessary adjustments, such as moving up or back, flooding to one side, covering the player being served or giving less area, switching to a front-row setter, or getting the best hitter in the easiest position to hit.

Take pass statistics in each rotation in practice initially and then again in matches so that weak rotations can be discovered and improved on.

SERVE-RECEIVE DRILLS

One-on-One Half-Court Serving and Receiving

(Courtesy of Kathy DeBoer)

Purpose: To help determine your players' abilities to pass

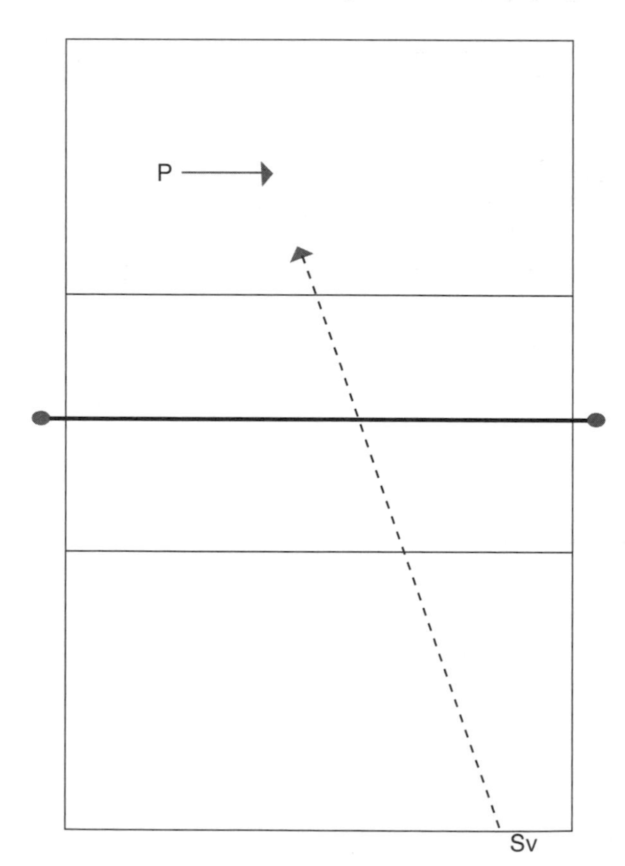

Figure 2.16 One-on-One Half-Court Serving and Receiving.

Setup: The server gets either the line half or the cross-court half of the court as an intended target area. A receiver is in the target area and attempts to make successful return passes (figure 2.16). Alternate servers line up on the endline.

Execution: The receiver is graded (or grades him- or herself) on all balls served in the designated half. Give receivers a set number of passes to complete and see how well they do with that much area to cover. (Passing scores will be lower than in game situations because the servers, in this case, are not penalized for overaggressive serving.) Make sure you rotate your servers and receivers in this drill because their varied serving abilities will affect the receivers' scores.

Coaching Points: Tell your players they are being evaluated. Certain athletes do better when score is kept, and others do worse. You should know this information before match situations.

Endurance Passing

Purpose: To encourage passing to the target while engaged in a long rally

Setup: Three to four passers circle two cones placed on each sideline.

Execution: Initiate the ball from the frontcourt or from across the net. The passers perform a set number of passes to the target area (figure 2.17).

Coaching Points: To increase the pressure of the drill, initiate the ball faster each time, giving the receiver less time to recover.

Variations

1. Instead of initiating the drill yourself, add a server on the opposite side of the net.
2. Add a live setter.

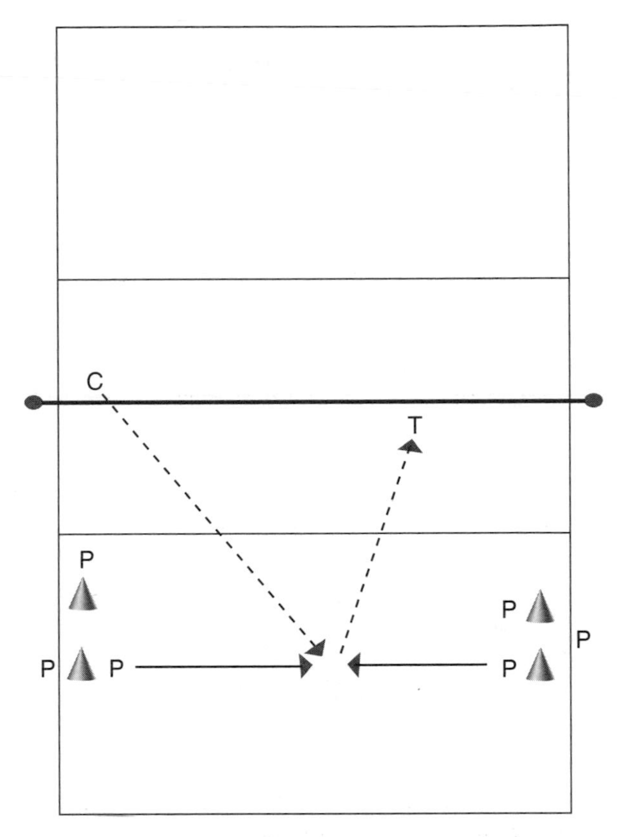

Figure 2.17 Endurance Passing.

Two Passers on Court

Purpose: To have players pass a set number of balls to a target

Setup: Two passers are on the court in proper serve-receive positions. A third player waits behind the endline to replace the passer who doesn't reach the target.

Execution: Initiate play via a serve from the opposing endline. If a passer doesn't get the ball to the intended target area, he or she is replaced by the player waiting behind the endline. The first passer to 10 points (10 proper passes to target) wins (figure 2.18).

Coaching Points: To become efficient passers, players must receive as many serves as possible. When evaluating serve reception, focus on each player's readiness to receive the serve.

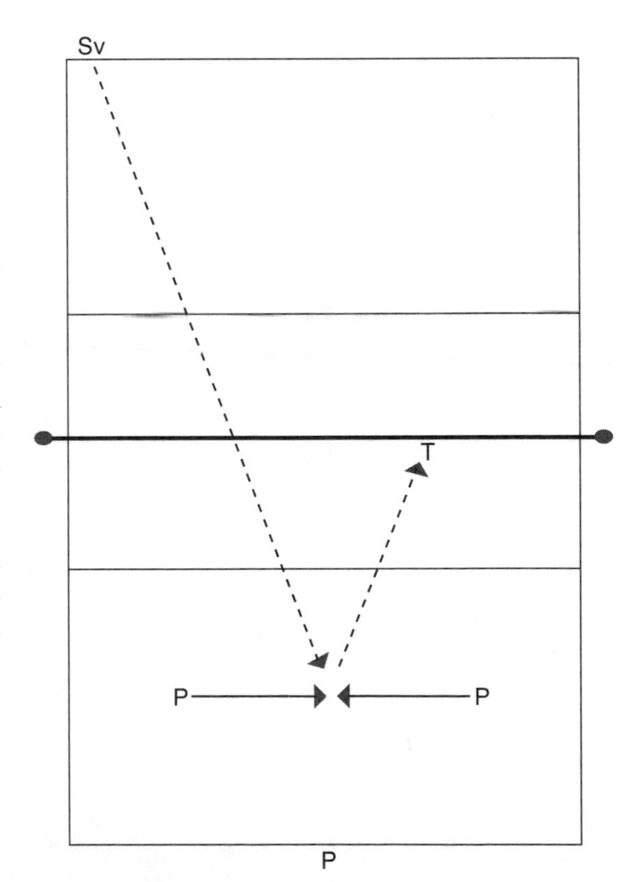

Figure 2.18 Two Passers on Court.

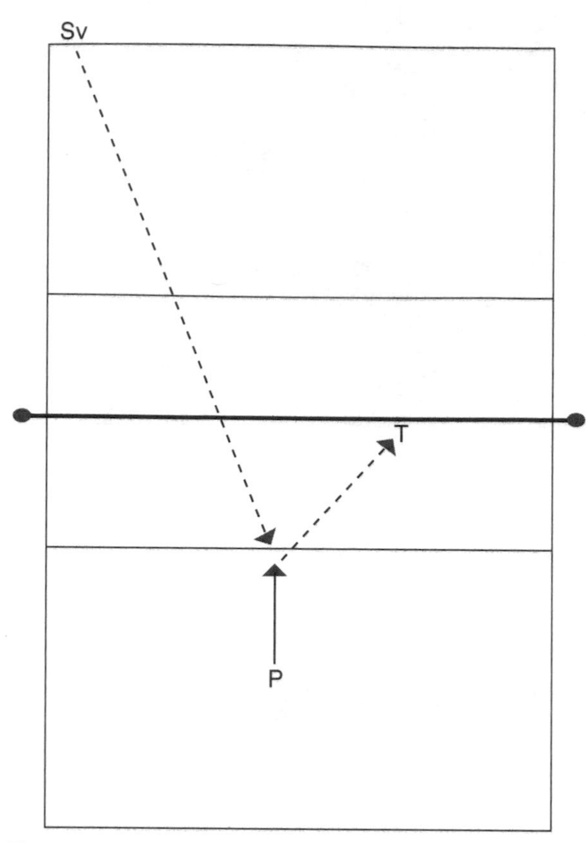

Figure 2.19 Three Players, Two Balls.

Three Players, Two Balls

Purpose: To have players pass to an intended target within a friendly competition

Setup: Place one server, one passer, and one target on the court. A coach or player can serve.

Execution: The ball is initiated via a serve; receivers pass a set number of times to an intended target (figure 2.19). Rotate the three positions or play a game of server versus passer, with the loser staying in place and the winner switching with the target.

Coaching Points: A receiver's success depends on his or her ability to read the server on the opposing team, move into position, and get set to receive the ball. Watch for your players' abilities to perform these skills.

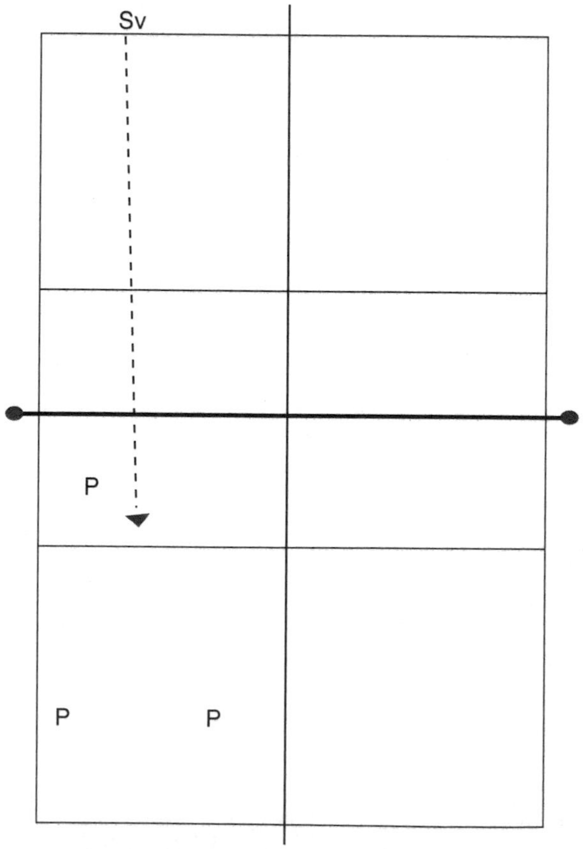

Figure 2.20 Three- to Five-Point Game.

Three- to Five-Point Game

Purpose: To practice within your team's normal serve-receive pattern

Setup: On half of the court, use half of your team's normal serve-receive configuration versus one server (figure 2.20).

Execution: Determine the point cap for the game (three or five points). The server initiates the ball to the receivers. The rally is played out. Record individual wins or serve 10 serves and take the percentage of wins and losses to determine the winner (e.g., 6 out of 10 = 60 percent).

Coaching Points: Encourage a friendly competition by rewarding the winning team.

Six Servers Versus Six Passers

Purpose: To provide repetitions of serving and serve receiving for all members of the team

Setup: One team of six servers positions against one team of passers (figure 2.21).

Execution: For the receiving team to score, the setter on the receiving team must be able to pass overhand legally. The servers score when the setter can't set the pass. The first team to score 10 points wins. Switch servers, passers, and the setter.

Coaching Points: The overhead pass or set can be used to receive any ball higher than shoulder level and that comes to the player with little force.

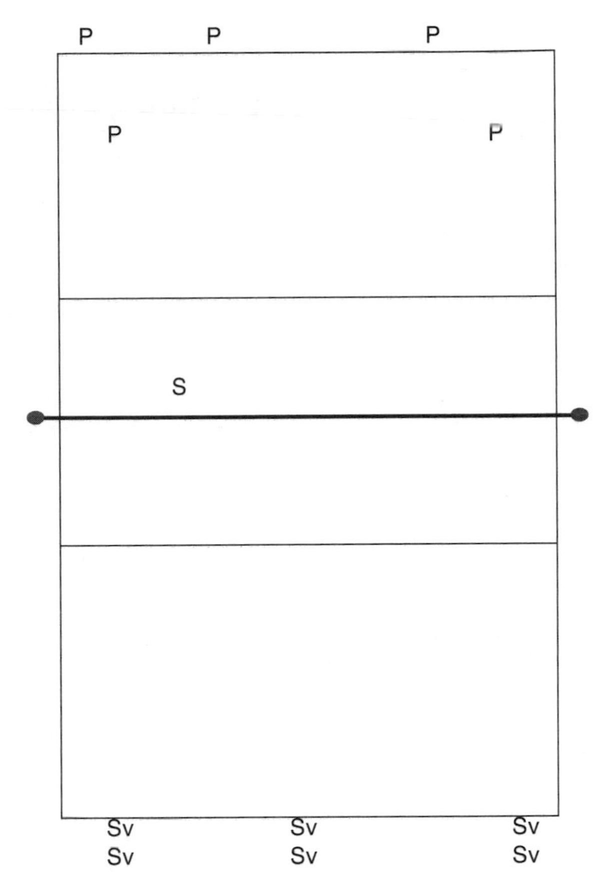

Figure 2.21 Six Servers Versus Six Passers.

Team Wash

Purpose: To promote passing to a target with the added pressure of wash drill scoring (a team must execute two or more elements in a row before receiving a point)

Setup: A normal serve-receive pattern (two, three, four, or five passers) sets up versus a server on the opposite side of the net (figure 2.22).

Execution: Each receiver must pass two good passes in a row to receive a point. To add pressure, the player missing the second pass is replaced and goes to the serve line.

Coaching Points: Competition usually elevates intensity and concentration in all team members, not just the receivers.

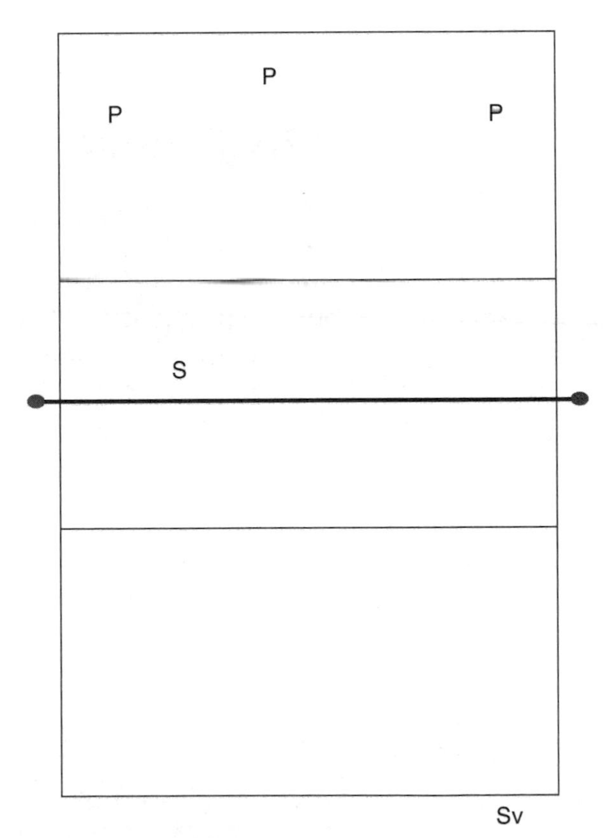

Figure 2.22 Team Wash.

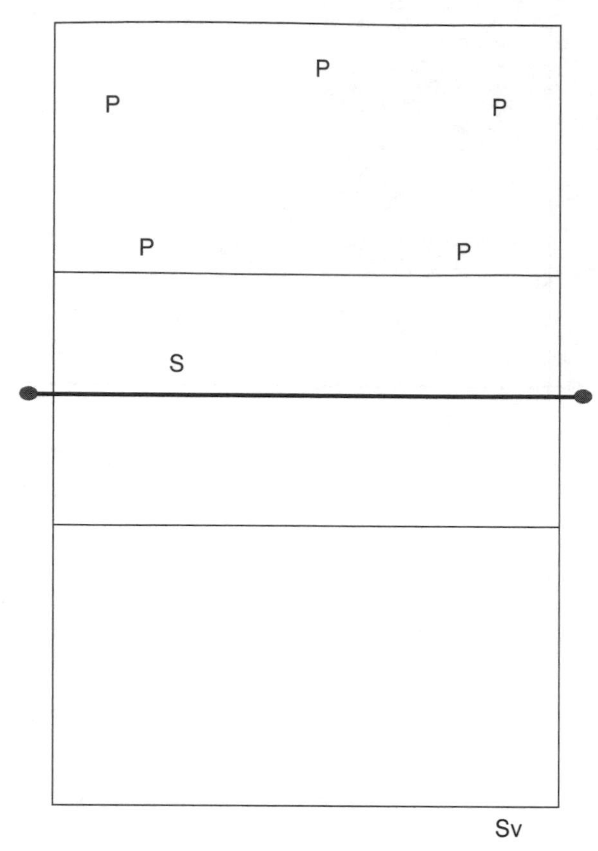

Figure 2.23 Rotate.

Rotate

Purpose: To give receivers several gamelike reps in each rotation

Setup: Place six players on one side of the court in a normal serve-receive pattern. Use one or several servers, depending on the number of players on the team (figure 2.23).

Execution: Play each rally to its conclusion. The team rotates on every third pass. When the team has completed an entire rotation, servers and passers switch.

Coaching Points: In practice, primary passers should receive serves as tough as—or even tougher than—those they'll see from opponents in upcoming matches.

Variation: The game can be served competitively to promote competition between servers and passers.

CONCLUSION

Because volleyball is a game in which each player's actions affect the other six on the court, the ability to receive the serve effectively is perhaps the most important skill in the game. The combination of the ability to read the serve and then perform the skill of passing flawlessly in a variety of situations is precisely what a coach should look for—and what a good passer should strive to do.

3

Setting

Sean Byron

Courtesy of FIVB

The skill of setting is crucial to every team's success. Your team's setter and all other players who deliver a controlled ball to be attacked by a teammate must be able to set effectively. The ability to attack and score points effectively corresponds to a player's ability to deliver a ball that is expected and located at the point the attacker wants it. Generating consistency in setting begins with creating many opportunities in practice for players to gain confidence using their hands. When players begin to learn and practice the skill of setting, the main objective for the coach should be developing their confidence in touching the ball with open hands. A second objective should be the quality of the contact. A third objective should be developing skills in deception and guile.

Too often, the only volleyball violations beginning players know are those involving the "double contact" or "lift." The strict adherence to these two rules for a beginner often leads him or her to resort to forearm passing all future setting opportunities, especially after a violation has been called. As a result, this yields fewer setting repetitions and an overall decrease in consistency in location and speed of each set. One of the worst things to see in beginners' volleyball is, after being called for a lift, how a player who has the opportunity to touch a ball with his or her hands chooses to duck away and use the forearms instead. A good rule for coaches in teaching setting is the more inexperienced the player, the more leeway should be given when it comes to hand contacts.

Another guideline to keep in mind when teaching setting is that floor setting is often good for the beginner who lacks shoulder and wrist strength. Floor setting is also easier than jump setting because of the external opposing force (the floor). Once the setter learns to jump set, he or she should jump set all the time. Usually players will release the ball from their hands quicker when jump setting, and some hitters (middles hitting quick sets) find it easier to hit from a setter who jump sets rather than sets from the floor.

To be sure, setting the ball requires more than confidence. Footwork, body position, and consistent movement technique are all important components of setting. We'll cover each of these components in depth in this chapter. Please read the skill acquisition section carefully before attempting to teach or learn the drills.

BODY POSITION

Body position refers to the setter's positioning just prior to, during, and following contact with the ball. The setter should be upright in stance with feet shoulder-width apart. Shoulders are over the toes with a slight flex at the waistline. The head is up. The feet are shoulder-width apart with a heel–toe relationship (figure 3.1). In other words, whether the player is floor setting or jump setting, the feet should be in the same relationship. Shoulders should be loose, relaxed, and forward (as opposed to upright).

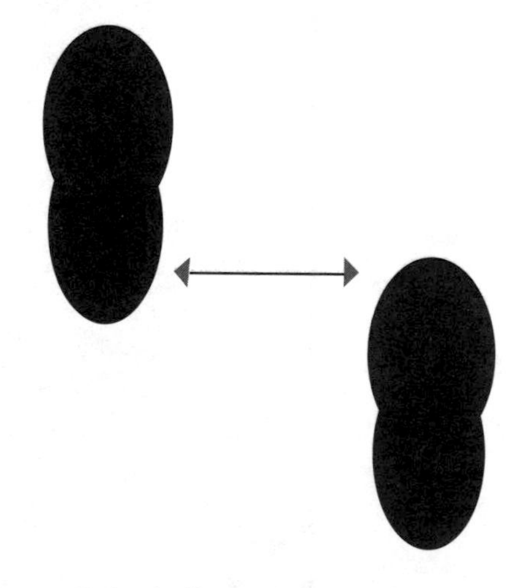

Figure 3.1 In floor setting or jump setting, players' shoulders are over the toes and relaxed, and the feet are in a heel–toe relationship.

FOOTWORK

Much has been written on setting footwork. Which step is correct? Which is incorrect? Stating simply, "Your left foot goes here" and "Your right foot goes there" is not practical in teaching today's setters. The setter position requires athleticism and the ability to adapt to a variant pass. Training and development should mirror the skill itself. Footwork can be broken down into four simple phases: get to a target, be ready to move from the target, beat the ball to the spot, and stop and set. Regardless of their skill level in other components involved in setting, players can enjoy early success by executing proper footwork. Let's look at each of the four phases in detail.

Phase 1: Get to a Target

Get to a target . . . any target (predetermined by the coach and team, of course) . . . but get there.

The setter releases from his or her court position at the moment of contact by the server. The ball traveling from server to passer and passer to target should allow the setter enough time to get from any court position to the target (figure 3.2). A common mistake for setters in this phase is to sprint to the attack line and then drift to the net. Remind your setters that the attack line (three-meter line) is not the finish line to his or her race.

The target can be the center of the net or just right of center or on the right sideline. Regardless of where the ball is after the first pass at contact (after a serve or attack not directed at the setter), the setter needs to sprint to the target as quickly as possible. Getting the right foot (the one closest to the net) to touch the centerline is also important for the next phase, Be Ready to Move from the Target. Often overlooked in training and game play, the initial phase of getting to a target will help setters tremendously because the act itself creates space between the setter

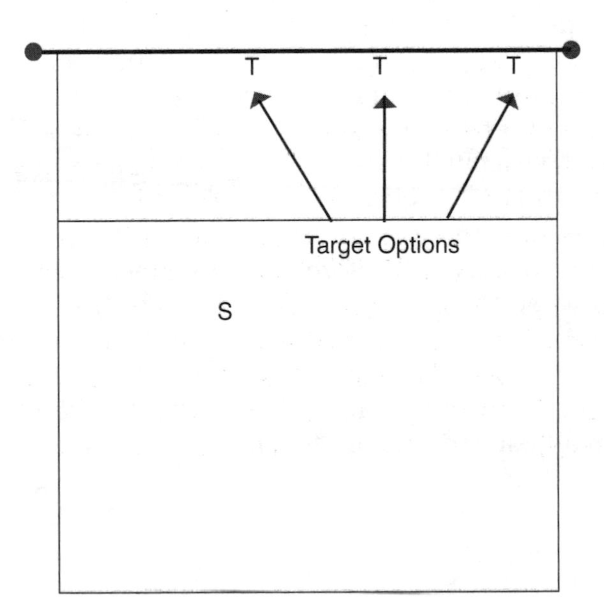

Figure 3.2 Setter goes from his or her court position to the target.

and the passer, allowing the setter more time to judge and adapt to the pass. It will also provide natural, dynamic balance after a few, short practice sessions. Dynamic balance is the ability to remain balanced while moving. A sprinter with a moving start will always beat a sprinter of equal speed who begins from a static starting position. Larger steps yield to smaller steps as the setter approaches the target (most athletes will do this naturally), and as steps become smaller, they should become quicker to allow the setter to slow down at a faster rate.

Phase 2: Be Ready to Move From the Target

Movement from the target should occur on every pass. The movement should become automatic and should occur whether a ball is passed 20 feet away from or directly to the target area. When dealing with the errant pass, the first thing the setter should do is step from the target area to the area where the pass is headed. For some players, this is not as easy as it sounds. Often, a player will take a "false step" to get into a dynamic balance position and waste valuable seconds distributing his or her weight to an appropriate moving position. If you watch videotape of setters in phase 1 through phase 2, you should be able to pause the tape and watch frame-by-frame continuity in movement (see the Two-Pass Reaction drill later in this chapter). A setter should adjust his or her feet even when the ball is passed directly to him or her because that dynamic balance scenario will, in fact, remain constant. Without these adjustment steps, players often try to adjust the hips or shoulders and become off balance in delivery. The setter's proficiency in phase 2 will develop in relation to his or her ability to judge passes, as well as his or her overall agility and movement skills.

Phase 3: Beat the Ball to the Spot

In phase 3, the goal is to anticipate where the ball is going to land and to get there before it does. Setters can get a head start on where the pass is going to go based somewhat on watching the passers prior to contact with the ball. If the passer has established a good passing platform prior to contacting the ball, and if he or she is still and calm, the setter can assume the pass will be of better quality than if the passer has made a bad read and is scrambling to get his or her forearms on the ball. The setter will have a much easier time adjusting if he or she can get a look at the passer before he or she passes the ball (figure 3.3).

Many advanced setters can arrive at the ball's intended location at the same time as the ball or a fraction of a second beforehand. An offense has no chance to deceive defensive blockers when the setter arrives too late to the ball location. If setters get to the intended ball location before the ball gets there, hitters can focus on the setter rather than on the ball. How many times have hitters said, "I just didn't think he [or she] could get there and get me the ball." Beating the ball to the spot also allows the setter to adjust and prepare for the act of setting the ball to a hitter.

Figure 3.3 Beating the ball to the spot.

Phase 4: Stop and Set

Stop and set is the final and most critical of the four phases of setting footwork; the fewer extraneous movements that the setter must adjust for, the easier the delivery will be. Setting a ball from the same body position requires the setter to execute phases 1 through 4 before ever touching the ball. Coaches use the term "float" to identify when the setter jumped from one spot, set the ball, and landed in another spot. Floating can be eliminated by stopping and setting (see Harlan Cohen's Footwork Series later in the chapter).

Coaching Checklist for Footwork Practice

- Get to a target.
- Be ready to move from the target.
- Beat the ball to the spot.
- Stop and set.

Figure 3.4 Setting movement technique.

MOVEMENT TECHNIQUE AND SET LOCATION

The setter needs to have his or her wrists "cocked" and fingers open to receive the ball. A good teaching cue for preparing to set is for a player to put his or her hands "in the shape of the ball" or pretend he or she is holding a cooler of water and then imagine dumping that cooler of water onto his or her own forehead. The entire finger pads (not just the tips) should be used at contact because the greater the surface area in contact with the ball, the greater the control. Elbows should be flexed and at chin level to allow high contact (figure 3.4). Beginning players often struggle with higher contact (above the forehead) because this requires more force to be generated by the wrists rather than by the shoulders and elbows. The wrists recoil at contact with the ball and extend toward the target. Strength in pushing the ball to the antennas can be generated with the increase in the speed of delivery. The elbows extend, and the hands "finish high" for the follow-through.

The setter's target is a multidimensional space, and once the ball is released, it needs to arrive within a specified time and take a relatively specified path to the hitter. The setter's target can be thought of as a large tube (imagine a cardboard wrapping-paper tube enlarged 10 times so that the diameter is big enough for a volleyball to fit through). Envision that tube hanging above a zone at a point on the court at which a hitter will be attacking. The setter needs to think of the ball going through that tube and passing across the zone for the hitter.

Let's begin with location. Each team should decide on an appropriate location for hitters to be successful and take time out of training to discuss with the setter(s) and coach where they want the set to be placed. The more specific the discussion, the easier the feedback can become later during the actual training. In terms of depth from the net, in the collegiate game most programs use a minimum of 4.5 ball widths from the net. Lay volleyballs down next to each other on the floor for a clear picture of how far off the net this is. Discuss the width from the sideline, as well as which shots the attackers are able to hit with each change in location. This conversation needs to happen for each of the play sets within the offense.

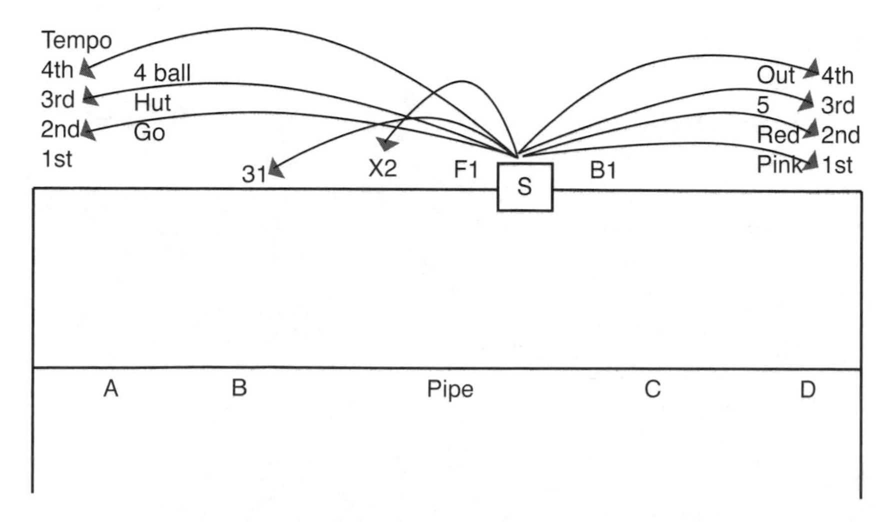

Figure 3.5 Set names and their general paths.

The specified path that the ball takes en route from the setter to the hitter is also crucial in determining the success—or what many coaches refer to as the "hitability"—of the set. The path the ball takes to the hitter is important because the hitter wants to spike the ball as it crosses a particular zone rather than at the point at which the ball completes its journey. Imagine a box raised above the net in a position away from the net (four ball widths) in which the set can pass through, allowing the attacker to spike it into the opponent's court. Hitters generally don't want the ball to pass through horizontally to the floor, nor do they want the ball to drop straight down into their lap. Figure 3.5 lists some set names and general paths the ball will take, as well as the locations on the court where the sets are made.

The pathways and tempos relate to what the set is called. For example, the 4 ball is the highest set for a hitter to contact on the left antenna. It's higher than a "go" and higher yet than a "hut." It often helps players understand tempo when pathways are used as visual tools to describe which path the ball should take. Obviously, balls that travel on lower, flatter planes arrive in the hitter's box sooner than balls that are set higher. The final evaluation of a set is how much time passes from the ball leaving the setter's hands to being contacted by the attacker. Using a stopwatch, a coach can give feedback to the setter for each set by simply reading the time it took for each set to reach its target. Give some specific goals on what time you're looking for for each play set. If the time goal is between 1.0 and 1.3 seconds, setters will quickly become accustomed either to speeding up or slowing down the set based on the number a coach calls out. Table 3.1 lists the approximate time it takes for the ball to go from the setter to the hitter for various types of sets.

Table 3.1
Approximate Times for Various Types of Sets

Set	Time from setter to contact with hitter
4 ball	1.5+ seconds
Hut	1.2–1.5 seconds
Go	1.0–1.2 seconds
Front 1	< 0.7 seconds
Red	.95–1.1 seconds

Coaching Points for Movement Technique and Location Selection

- Cock wrists and open fingers, with hands in the "shape of the ball."
- Use the entire finger pads.
- Flex elbows at chin level.
- Wrists recoil with ball contact and extend toward target.
- Elbows extend; hands finish high.
- Hitters are in appropriate locations.
- Hitters determine the specified path of the ball.
- Pathways and tempos relate to the set name.

TRAINING THE SETTER

Setter development requires repetitions in controlled settings and gamelike situations. Variety in repetitions is very important, and a plan for setter training (separate from team training) should be determined carefully before starting.

Coaches planning setter training should consider the following factors: the developmental stage of the setter, his or her ability and availability to train, and the team training schedule. It's important to train the setter specifically and outside of group practice with the team because the setter will touch the ball more than any other player on the team (table 3.2). When block planning the setter training for the entire season, it's a good idea to leave new skills for mid- to late season, which allows the setter to stay fresh and learn new things as the season progresses. This plan also provides opportunities for the setter to become good at certain components of setting rather than working on all parts of setting at once (table 3.3).

Developmental Stages of the Setter

Athletes learn motor skills in progressions from simple to more complex (e.g., crawling to walking to running); setting is a complex motor skill. Table 3.4 displays

Table 3.2
Planning Setter Training

Stage	Perfect pass reps	Bad pass reps	Strategy	Footwork	Dump/Attack
Beginner	High	Low	Low	Medium	None
Intermediate	Medium	Medium	Medium	High	Low
Advanced	Low	High	High	Included	Medium/High

Table 3.3
Sample Block Plan

Weeks	Beginner	Intermediate	Advanced
1–3	Perfect pass reps	Perfect pass reps Footwork	Bad pass reps
4–6	Footwork	Footwork	Bad pass reps Strategy
7–10	Perfect pass reps Bad pass reps	Strategy Bad pass reps Footwork	Attack Strategy
11–15	Bad pass reps	Perfect pass reps Bad pass reps Strategy	Perfect pass reps Bad pass reps Strategy

Table 3.4
Developmental Stages of the Setter

BEGINNER	HIGH SCHOOL/ INTERMEDIATE	COLLEGE/ADVANCED
Learning basic technique	**Mastering basic technique**	**Mastering various sets**
Ability to set high balls	Ability to set various sets	Understand offense, strategy
Understand location cues	Understand tempo	Think about game planning
Think about offense, strategy	Understand team psyche	

the stages of setter growth and the associated set of skills for each stage. The following three sections of text offer some corresponding training techniques for each stage's skill set. The techniques described will be helpful for planning each setter's training.

Beginning setters. The beginning setter is learning proper technique and has relative success at setting high balls to the antennas. The setter at this stage understands cues such as "too tight" and "inside the court" but has difficulty in consistently sending a ball to the exact location.

Training at this stage should focus on footwork separately from setting repetitions. Setting repetitions in a stationary position should be high in number. The setter should be allowed to make adjustments in technique before getting feedback on the location of the set.

It's a good idea for beginners to practice the skills specific to being successful at their given level. Many setters and teams can win by locating one type of set (e.g., hut, front 1). The beginning setter can gain confidence through team success and later develop a wider array of offensive options.

High school and intermediate setters. The intermediate setter has mastered the basic technique of setting and is experimenting with various types of play sets (quick sets, slides, combinations) as he or she begins to understand concepts of tempo and pace of sets. Cognitively, the setter should begin to think about offensive concepts and strategies. Examples of team strategies are a breakdown of the offense by rotation, by set effectiveness, and by player effectiveness. Some examples for setter strategy include reading blocker movement patterns, reading defensive team movements when the offense sets a specific set, and identifying what offensive structure opponents struggle with. In short, intermediate setters should be asking the questions, "What are they doing?"; "When do they do it?"; and "What do we do that works because they can't stop it?"

Training the intermediate setter should include movement and setting. Video of game play and discussions about decision-making promote cognitive development but obviously shouldn't replace the setter's time in the gym touching the ball. Setters in this stage need repetitions to be able to deliver the ball to a hitter from any position on the court on a consistent basis. Training for this requires the setter to use various movement patterns and should allow the setter to test his or her ability to set balls passed further and further away from the target.

Reading defenses is a complicated task and begins with watching the blockers. It involves noticing their ready position, understanding what moves they have made earlier in games, and identifying how successful they are at each move. An example might be the middle blocker who jumps every time with the quick-hitter on a perfect pass. He or she hasn't even tried to get to the antenna to block an outside hitter. Most setters and coaches would say, in this case, keep setting outside on the perfect pass. The advanced setter will evaluate the opposing blockers' effectiveness in the middle. Although he or she jumps every time with our quick hitter, our quick hitter is scoring better than the outside. This is a brief example of reading defenses.

College and advanced setters. The advanced setter can consistently locate and place hittable balls from anywhere on the court. Knowledge of team offensive strategy has been attained. The advanced setter should have no trouble responding to such questions as, "Why did you set that person? That set? That play?" with answers that match the goals of the offense. The advanced setter should be involved in aspects of game planning, such as what plays the offense can run against a particular blocking system or individual blockers. The advanced setter understands the team psyche and how to interact with individual hitters to generate the most from each player. Every player has a different viewpoint on competition and is motivated in different ways. The setter will have more interaction (both verbal and nonverbal) with on-court players than a coach will and, at the advanced stage, needs to be able to identify players who aren't performing up to standards. Training at the advanced stage should focus on group repetitions. Seeing an offense come at the setter, glancing at blockers' movements, and making decisions based on situational occurrences are the most important training elements. Practicing under gamelike conditions continues to be important for building confidence.

Advanced setters need to know their own hitters' strengths and weaknesses. Some players hit faster sets better, whereas others hit slower sets better. With the assistance of a coach, the setter can determine what speed and type of set fits into the team's offense.

Developmental stages are not specific to each skill set presented because each player will develop at his or her own rate. When training a player, match his or her current skill level with appropriate training techniques.

The Ability and Availability to Train

The ability to train as a setter depends in part on being able to focus on a task for a given amount of time and in part on the resources available. The setter's ability to focus is difficult to assess; however, some common sense can be employed. It's useless, for instance, to tell a seven-year-old that she's "staying in the gym until she gets 1,000 balls set to a target." Incrementally setting groups of 50 to 100 balls at a time allows the coach to give feedback, enables the setter to rest, and gives both the setter and coach a chance to maintain focus on the task at hand.

The resources available—the quality of volleyballs, ball tossers, shaggers, and coaches giving appropriate feedback—also influence a setter's ability to train. Feedback from coaches is crucial for the beginner and should be simple and to the point. Feedback should be immediate and very specific with regard to the player's movement. The more experienced the setter, the more feedback can be delayed and given in general terms.

The availability to train is becoming a greater problem for coaches and players. Gym space is becoming more restricted, and there are more rules and regulations with regard to coaching. In the collegiate game, the NCAA restricts the number of hours per week a coach can train players. Setters need time to train outside of a team practice, whether it's a 15-minute segment prior to practice or during breaks within the session. It's crucial that setters get repetitions setting the ball.

TRAINING FACTORS

Coaches need to be organized with setter training but also should map out season plans for their teams. To what degree the team will train in hours per day, at what physical level, how much teaching will occur, and how much competition to include are all factors to consider when making a practice plan. It's customary to spend more time teaching during the preseason than during the playoffs. Setter training should somewhat mirror the training of the team. A setter doing reps until his or her hands are numb might be good muscle memory training during the preseason, but it's not a good idea the night before a playoff game.

What skills are important to win at the level at which a player is competing? The coach, through research, experience, and data collection, must answer this question. If your goal is to win a running race, you don't practice shooting free throws. Surprisingly, many volleyball teams practice offensive plays and systems far too advanced for their current level of play; evidently, they want to be able to say they can execute these skills, even though they're not necessary. To determine what wins, consider data based on previous matches. When the team won, what was the sideout percentage? What was the hitting percentage? How many times did the setter set outside, in the middle, or behind the setter? How much front row and back row? How effective were the teams when they performed each aspect you're looking at? Were there more kills, digs, or aces, or were there simply fewer errors than the opponent made? Once you've determined what skill(s) correlate with victory, it's time to sit down and block out team and setter training. At this point, for the lower levels, a setter will be paired with an assistant coach for individual training. At the higher levels, a setter coach works individually with setters.

SETTING DRILLS

Harlan Cohen's Footwork Series

Purpose: To be used daily to provide a good warm-up and plenty of touches for the beginning setter

Setup: One setter is positioned on the court near the net.

Execution: Using the sidelines of the volleyball court, the setter sets the ball to himself or herself and quickly shuffles to the next position (figure 3.6a). The setter should stop before his or her hands come up to the setting position. It's helpful for beginners who are new to the drill to stomp their feet before contact. The height of each set should be roughly 9 to 10 feet (~2.75 to 3 meters) to allow the setter to move quickly and stop before getting to the spot. When the setter gets to the spot, have him or her stomp feet and shoot hands from the hips to the setting position. This is done so that the setter understands that running to the ball and setting the ball are two different movements. The setter maintains a heel–toe relationship throughout, with the front foot (right) staying in front of the trail foot (left) the entire time. This movement resembles a gallop but has more control and balance. The direction changes when the setter masters the basic forward movement.

Coaching Points: When the setter has mastered all four footwork drills from the floor, next have him or her jump set from each position. This requires the ball to be set a little higher than 9 to 10 feet (~2.75 to 3 meters) at first and will provide you with instant feedback if the setter doesn't stop before the jump set (because he or she will take off in one spot and land in another).

Variations: The setter faces in the same direction for the entire drill. The set overhead should be only 3 to 4 feet (~91 to 122 centimeters) in length, but still travel the 9 to 10 feet (~2.75 to 3 meters) in the air to allow the setter to shuffle back and stop before setting. Taking two steps forward and one backward allows the setter to proceed across the court in about twice the time it took when he or she simply went forward (figure 3.6a).

Another variation is to include diagonal movements and require feedback when a setter first attempts them. The setter faces the sideline each time and moves on a diagonal (figure 3.6b). A common error is for the setter to turn and face the direction he or she is moving. The movement should be with the same footwork pattern and with the shoulders square to the sideline. In a modification, the diagonal is done similar to the second variation, but is done on a diagonal plane (figure 3.6b).

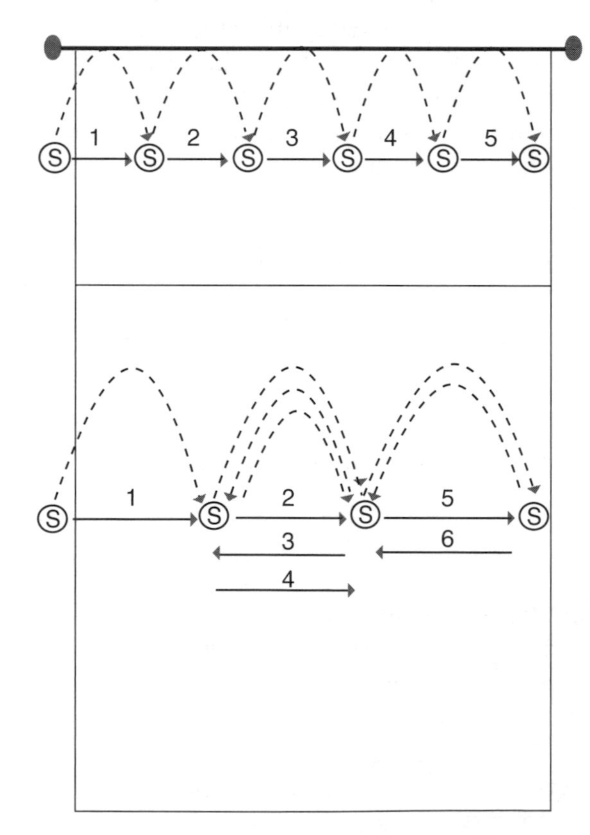

Figure 3.6a Harlan Cohen's Footwork Series: Basic Forward and Two Forward, One Back.

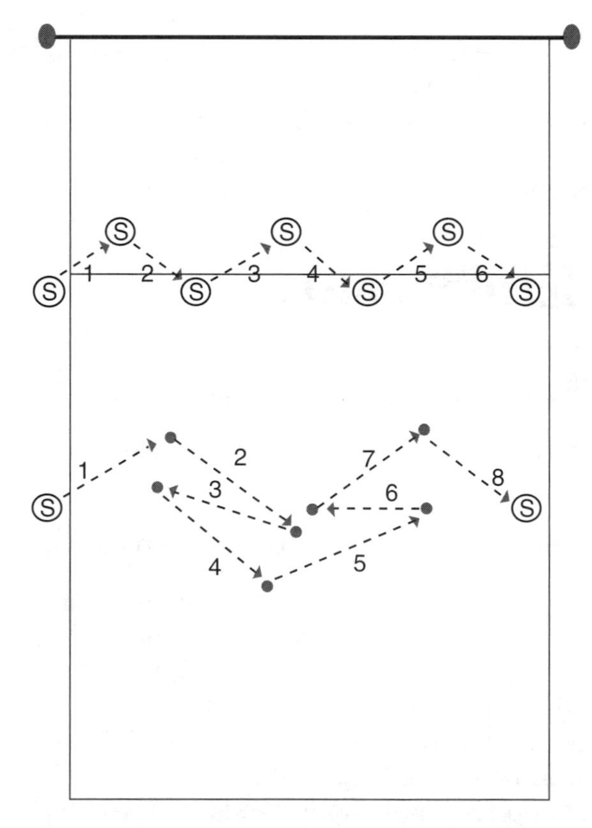

Figure 3.6b Harlan Cohen's Footwork Series: Diagonal Forward and Diagonal Two Forward, One Back.

Location Repetitions

Purpose: To engage in a good number of solid repetitions within a short time

Setup: This drill requires two volleyballs and a catcher (or second setter).

Execution: The setter stands at the target, and the coach tosses a ball to the setter. The setter sets the ball to location A, at which point the second setter catches it. When the coach tosses the ball to be set, the second setter bounces another ball to the coach (figure 3.7). The bounce is important so that the coach can watch the setter contact the ball and give instant feedback. The catcher (second setter) can count the number of successful repetitions before he or she switches positions and gives location feedback to the setter. Examples of feedback on location are "tight," "off," "inside," and "outside" and should be given after every set by the catcher. The catcher should stand on a chair or a box so he or she can catch the ball at the point a hitter would contact it if he or she were to spike. If no box or chair is available, have the catcher move back 7 to 8 feet (~2.1 to 2.4 meters) to a location at which the ball would land if it were set from the target and passed through the hitting zone untouched.

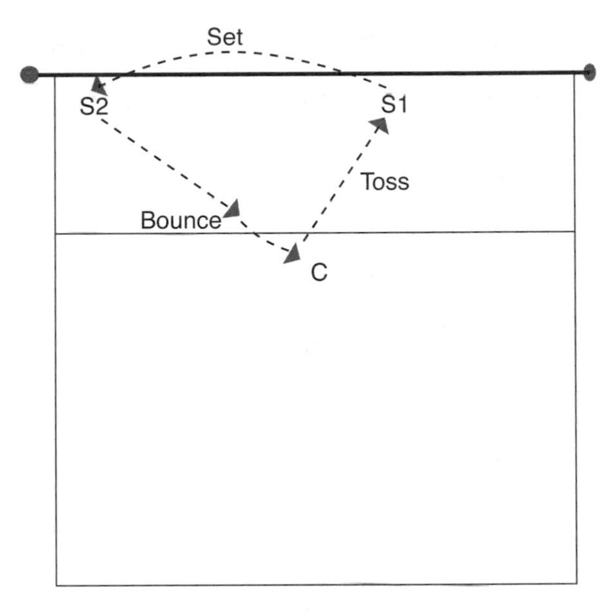

Figure 3.7 Location Repetitions.

Coaching Points: You might want to change position by one step after each toss to simulate passes coming toward the setter from various positions on the court.

Two-Pass Reaction

Purpose: To practice movement patterns in segments

Setup: A coach is positioned behind the attack line to toss passes to a setter. The setter will set to a predetermined target.

Execution: The coach tosses 2-point passes (errant passes that are settable, but not to the target), at which point the setter attempts to move, stop, and set the ball to a predetermined location. It is a good idea to predetermine the movement pattern when players first attempt this drill. Begin with one toss to position A, then one in position B, and repeat position A so the setter is moving forward and backward. The coach can control movement off the net during the drill, allowing the setter to recover on his or her way back to the target and tossing a distance just within the capabilities of the setter (figure 3.8a).

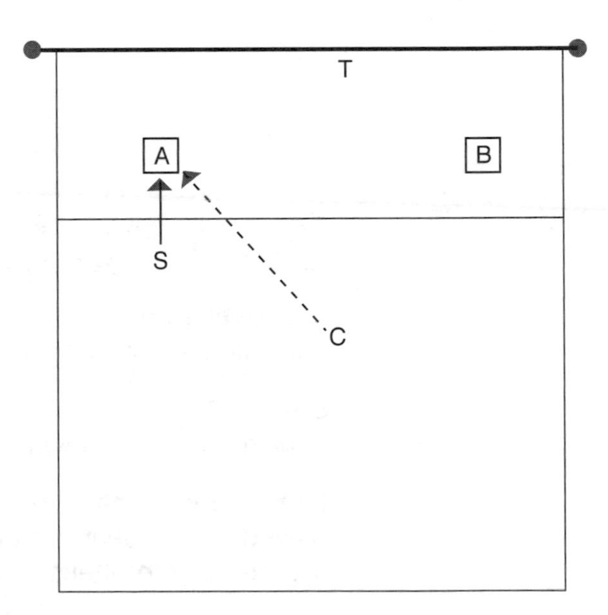

Figure 3.8a Two-Pass Reaction.

Coaching Points: This drill helps you to identify which planes the setter moves better or worse in. Some setters move well across the net, whereas others move more naturally away from it; this movement pattern often dictates the setter's style.

Variations

- With tape, divide the court in two halves and add two catchers. Tell the setter that he or she can set only the catcher on the same side of the divider as he or she is when making contact.
- Allow the setter to set the catcher on the opposite side of the divider from which he or she contacts the ball. This creates what many coaches call a "reverse flow setting trend." It's crucial for the setter to stop before setting either the same side or the opposite side. Extraneous movements such as "floating" make it more difficult for the setter to compensate when he or she releases the ball.
- Add an extra blocker or coach to make a move in the direction of one of the catchers (simulating a blocker releasing early); the goal for the setter is to set to the other catcher. For beginners to this drill, the blocker or coach should make his or her move very early so the setter can get an easy read regarding which direction the block is leaning. As the setter improves in decision-making, the move can occur later and eventually become a rather small twitch (as opposed to shuffling the entire body in one direction). It's important that during this drill the setter give a well-located set to the hitter, not simply "faking out" the blocker with a good decision (figure 3.8b).
- As the setter becomes more advanced in reading the blocker, he or she should then practice identifying blocker movements before contacting the ball. This variation increases the player's decision-making skills.

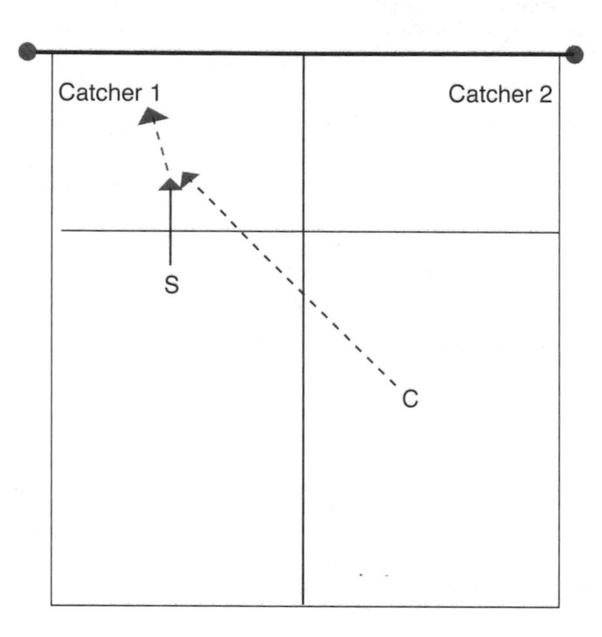

Figure 3.8b Two-Pass Reaction drill with an added blocker.

Offense Versus Defense

Purpose: To give setters practice in making decisions and running the offense in a controlled environment

Setup: The setter and two attackers are on one side of the net; on the other side is a full team of six players.

Execution: A coach or player enters the ball to the offensive side, and the point is played out. Repeat this nine times and, depending on the level of play, you will have a score for the offense (figure 3.9).

Each setter goes through with the same attackers, and scores are recorded. Set a standard for the offense to win each minigame. For example, if you're looking to win the point 70 percent of the time when you're receiving serve, then the offense needs to win seven out of 10 attempts. Each group of 10 plays can be a minigame, and players can rotate through the drill quickly. It is very easy to keep track of big points (the number of minigames won; see the sample score sheet). The first contact by a coach, player, or machine can be as easy or difficult as needed. If the drill is for the setters, they need to be able to set the ball, and the passes need to get to them. If the player serving the first ball to start the drill is unable to serve to a particular passer, the drill becomes an ineffective use of time.

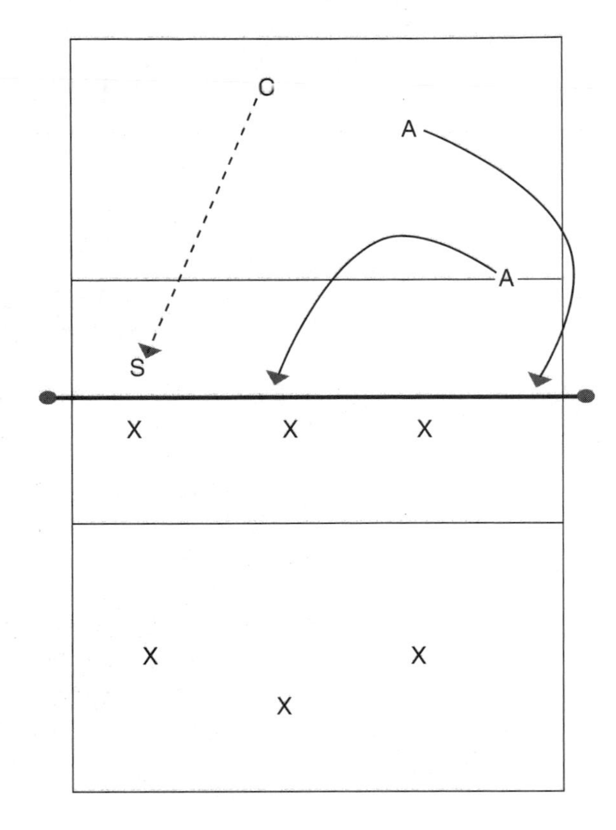

Figure 3.9 Offense Versus Defense.

Coaching Points: It's always better to have players, rather than coaches, enter balls into drills, but the focus of this particular drill is offense and setting, not serving for points. A libero can pass the first ball with each outside hitter, and the coach can add other passers to help serve reception. If the setter needs to practice setting out of system, then make the serve more difficult for the passers to handle. Scoring for various setters can be done by number of minigames won or total points won.

If the setter needs work on setting an antenna and a quick attack, then let those be the only options he or she can set upon serve receive. This drill is great for attackers to focus on one or two specific sets. Setters can practice seeing the block and delivering hittable balls to different attackers. As the setter improves at seeing offenses come at him or her, add attackers to the drill.

Variation: To increase the importance of first-swing effectiveness, the score can be kept with this criterion in mind. The routine of the drill is the same, but when the offense wins the first attempt at a ball, they get a point. If the defense makes an error after a dig or the offense wins the point in transition, then no point or attempt is awarded to either side. See table 3.5 for an example of a score sheet.

The setter Adena won the drill because she won both games and scored 16 out of 20 points. Shaina scored 14 out of 20 points and won only one game. Note that both setters had a chance to play with each pair of attackers.

Table 3.5
Score Sheet

Setter	Score (out of 10)	Win/Lose	Attackers
Shaina	8	Win	Julie, Grace
Adena	7	Win	Mary, Joyce
Shaina	6	Lose	Mary, Joyce
Adena	9	Win	Julie, Grace

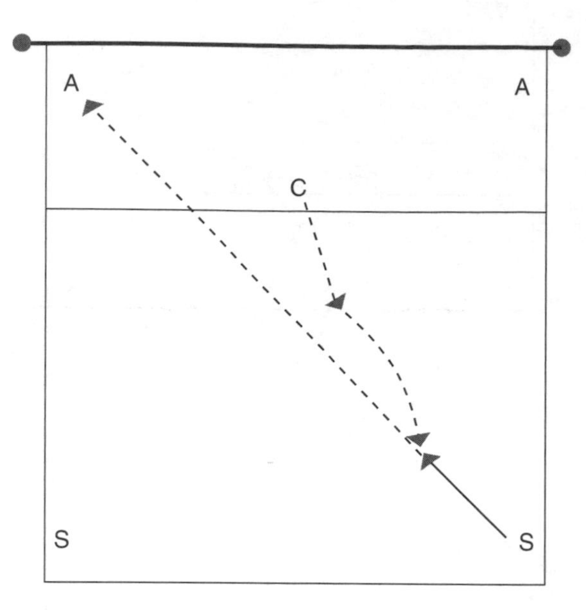

Figure 3.10 Setting Corner to Corner.

Setting Corner to Corner

Purpose: To give setters practice in setting corners while getting the entire team involved

Setup: Players form two lines in the corners of the court on the endline.

Execution: The coach stands on the attack line and bounces a ball for one player to run in and set across the court to a would-be attacker near the antenna (figure 3.10). The setter follows the path of the ball and becomes the next attacker in that line. To keep the number of practice repetitions high, the would-be attacker catches the ball and returns it to the coach and then proceeds to the opposite setting line. Once the setter clears the middle of the court, the coach bounces another ball to the first person in the other line, who sets the ball across the court.

Coaching Points: Be sure to bounce the ball high enough for players to get under and set but low enough to challenge them to move quickly and stop before setting.

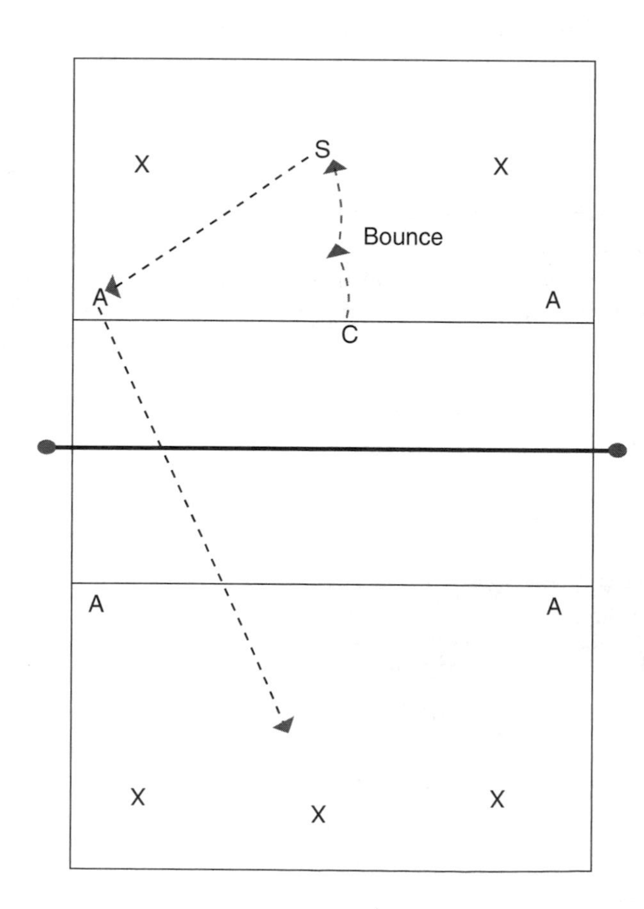

Figure 3.11 Three-Versus-Three Backcourt.

Three-Versus-Three Backcourt

Purpose: To give backcourt players practice in setting to attackers

Setup: Players form two lines in the corners of the court on the endline.

Execution: Similar to the Corner-to-Corner drill, this drill requires players to set the ball to hitters. A coach initiates the drill by bouncing the ball to any of the three backcourt players. That player sets the ball to either attacker, who in turn spikes the ball across the net to the opposing side (figure 3.11). Only the backcourt players can set the ball to their respective attackers. As soon as the point ends, the coach bounces another ball to the winning side. Games are rally point scoring and are played to 11 or 15 points. Players rotate after each game, and the drill is repeated. The first team to win three out of five games is the winner.

Coaching Points: Players should focus on setting a high transition ball that allows the hitter to adjust his or her feet underneath in time to jump and attack.

Variation: Take a point away from the offensive side if the ball is set over the net and deemed unhittable by the coach.

Set or Hit

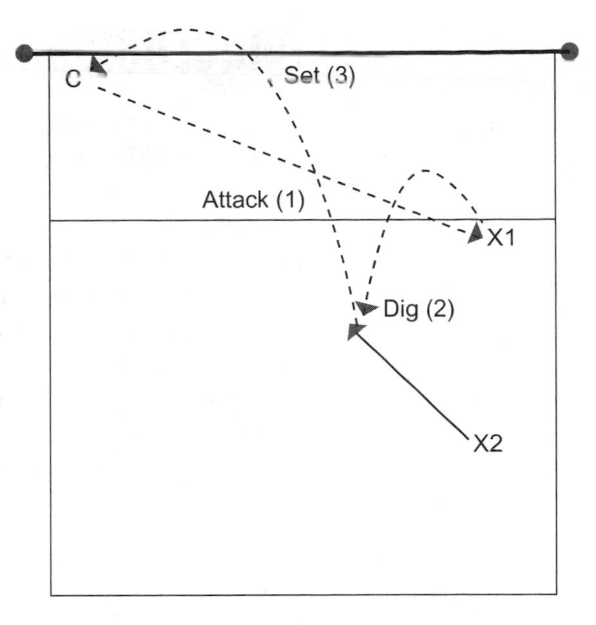

Figure 3.12 Set or Hit.

Purpose: To practice digging and setting in a gamelike situation

Execution: A coach initiates the drill by attacking a ball at either player located on the right side of the court. If player 1 digs the first contact, player 2 needs to move underneath the ball and set it back to the coach (figure 3.12). If player 2 digs the first ball, player 1 needs to take the second touch.

Coaching Points: This drill also helps with reaction time from dig to set. Be sure to allow players to return to their starting position, as the fastest part of the drill should be from attack-dig-set, and not set-attack. Players can switch court positions after one minute or on every other attack.

Neville Drill

Purpose: To practice every skill in volleyball (former national team coach Bill Neville gets credit for this drill)

Setup: A team of six (or more) is on each side of the net; a coach enters the ball to one side.

Execution: The ball is passed to right front, and the player in right front sets a high ball to the player in left front, who attacks into the opponent's court. The side receiving the ball digs to their right front, which, in turn sets it to their left front. The side that wins the point receives the next ball from the coach. The side that loses the point rotates quickly before the coach enters the next ball. This creates a new player in right front and a new setter. This rotation also has a new attacker in left front and everyone playing a different position. It's important for the coach to wait until the losing side rotates before tossing the next ball into play, as there will undoubtedly be confusion the first few times this drill is done. It's a good idea to have a player on each side call out "rotate!" when his or her side loses a point. Rally score games are played to 15 points, which allows enough time for each player to practice each skill. When more than 12 players are in the gym it might help to allow them to rotate into middle back when the team rotates in.

Coaching Points: This is a great warm-up drill and can be modified by allowing only certain sets or by taking away points for true hitting errors (a hit out of bounds or into the net).

CONCLUSION

Fans love watching powerful spikes and monstrous blocks, so setting is often a thankless skill in volleyball. But experienced players understand how critical the setter position is to the team's success. Like no other position, the setter position allows a player to control the flow of the game. Setters need to possess the physical abilities required to set the ball and the mental abilities to comprehend strategy and game planning, but, most important, they must have the leadership capabilities to assess various situations and make decisions on the fly. Setters of every personality type—outgoing or introverted—have been successful at the position. The setter needs to be able to garner the attention and respect of his or her teammates and generate this in his or her abilities. A setter is much more than just a "ball placer"; a good setter is a court thinker, a court leader, and a court psychologist.

4

Attacking

Jim McLaughlin

Photo by Scott Bjornlie

To the casual observer, attacking is the most identifiable skill in volleyball, especially for spectators. To the players, attacking is often the most fun and dynamic skill. Undeniably, attacking is the most explosive part of the game and garners the most attention. To the coach, however, attacking is more than just the excitement of the terminated play. It's about the numbers. In an average NCAA Division I women's college volleyball match, the average number of swings in a 30-point game is approximately 40, and the average number of kills in a game ranges from 15 to 20. That equates to about 50 to 67 percent of points being scored on the basis of a team's ability to kill the ball. When reminded that the average number of kills per game and hitting efficiency are the two highest coefficients to winning, we might ask two questions: What do the truly great hitters do? What are the characteristics of a great attacker?

PHYSICAL CHARACTERISTICS OF A GREAT ATTACKER

First and foremost, elite hitters possess superior eye work and timing. They're able to see a play develop, whether in sideout or transition situations. They're also able to answer the following questions at a moment's notice and make a split-second decision: Is it a fast pass or a slow pass? Is the pass away? Do I have to accelerate? The best hitters can synthesize visual information and quickly choose and make an appropriate movement pattern.

In addition to the ability to see a play develop, elite hitters also have impeccable mechanics. Whenever possible, they use a four-step approach. They jump high, hit hard, and hit with range. They use biomechanically efficient arm work that allows them to jump as high as their bodies permit. They repeat the same mechanics and movements over and over, eliciting the same result: a kill—or at least a ball that opponents can't easily pass to their setter.

So how do we train and learn to be quintessential attackers? Mere activity doesn't equate to progress. You need to develop your coaching eye, too. You need to put your players through sound activities. You need to regulate the stimuli in the activities. As a coach, you must give your players several opportunities to respond; then you provide feedback and give them more opportunities to respond as they learn the fundamentals of the skill.

So what exactly do you look for? Let's begin with the mechanics.

PHASES OF THE ATTACK MOVEMENT

There are six basic movements inherent in any good attack, including the approach, which encompasses the plant or step close; the jump; the armswing; ball contact; the follow-through; and landing. How a player executes each movement during the attack leads either to success or failure. If executed properly, the attack terminates a rally, gains a point, and swings momentum in your team's favor. The object of a good offensive attack is to put the ball where the defense is not. It all begins with the approach.

The Approach

The most tried-and-true method to teach a solid attack is to instruct hitters to use a four-step approach that starts slowly and ends quickly. In serve-receive situations, all hitters (outside and middle) should use four steps. (In transition, this might not always hold true, but we'll address that later.)

For most volleyball teams, no matter the level or gender, the most prevalent attack is made by the outside hitter. In this case, the hitter approaches from the left front of the court. The outside attack is most popular because of the longer approach to the net, a better angle, and the setter is often positioned much closer to the right side of the court. As a result, the set ball travels farther to the outside hitter, providing more time for a proper approach.

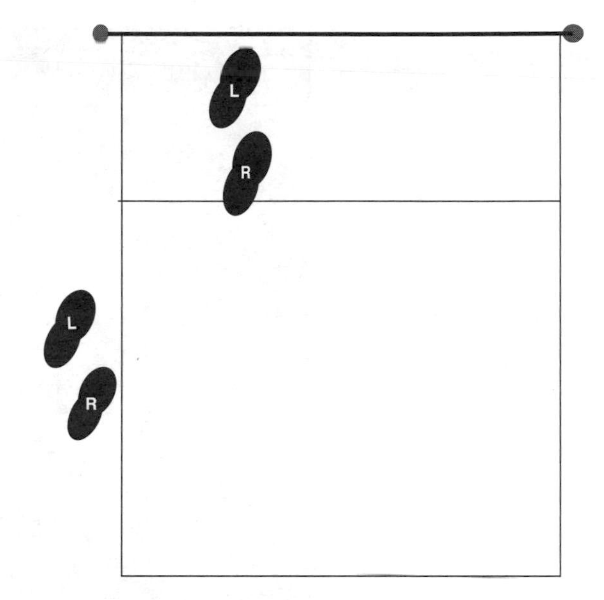

Figure 4.1 Right-handed approach pattern.

If the outside hitter is right-handed, the hit is commonly called an "on-hand spike," in which the player hits the ball before it travels across his or her body. A right-handed hitter's step progression will be right-left-right-left, providing an angular approach (figure 4.1). A right-handed hitter who is hitting offside from the left has a bit more of a challenge because the ball must cross his or her body—which is why all coaches love to have a left-handed offside hitter. For a left-handed hitter, the approach pattern is left-right-left-right (figure 4.2).

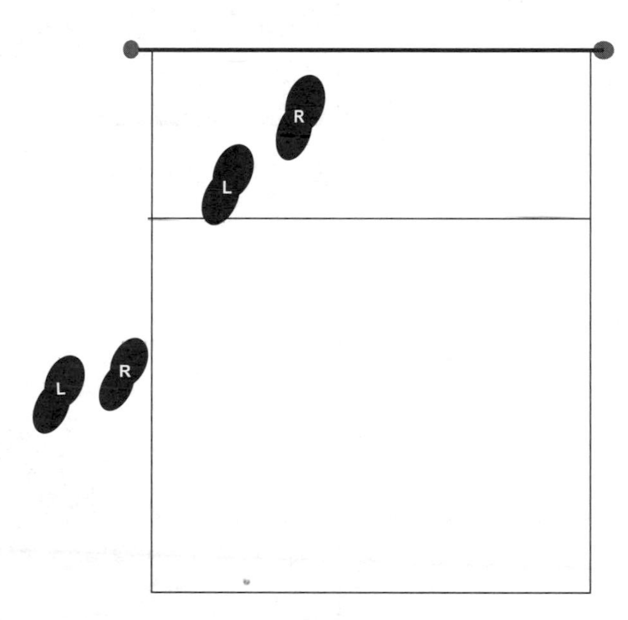

Figure 4.2 Left-handed approach pattern.

Because the goal of the approach is to build momentum, a player must accelerate as he or she progresses through the approach. Building momentum at this point increases speed, which, in turn, converts to a much higher vertical jump. We might then think of the steps of the approach as "slow, faster, fastest" or perhaps even "small, bigger, biggest." The last two steps are the fastest and result in a two-footed approach jump (figures 4.3-4.6).

The first two steps, slower than the last two, help to generate timing as the hitter observes and pinpoints the location of the set. The first step shifts the attacker's body weight forward, allowing him or her to stay balanced and prepare to execute the second step (figure 4.4). The second step should always be quicker and longer than the first, allowing the attacker to adjust to the speed, height, and set trajectory of the ball.

The last two steps, which are often referred to as the "step close," are the fastest and most explosive. It's important that when taking the final two steps, the feet are pointing in the direction that the player is traveling so that horizontal speed is not inhibited (figure 4.5). This enables the hitter to jump up to the ball and create a good relationship to the ball. In addition, during the third step (also known as the "plant" or "hop"), the attacker should be about 12 inches (30 centimeters) from the ball with the hitting arm lined up behind the ball (figure 4.6). At this point, the attacker transfers forward velocity and the resulting momentum into vertical velocity. By the fourth step, where the attacker jumps depends primarily on how far he or she can broad jump.

Indeed, the ability to hit balls that are not perfectly located where you want them at the net is what separates elite hitters from the simply good ones. This is why it's imperative that the approach be slower at the beginning and fastest at the end. A

Figure 4.3 Two-footed approach jump.

Figure 4.4 First two steps.

Figure 4.5 Step close.

Figure 4.6 Plant or hop step.

player at full speed at the beginning has a more difficult time changing direction and adjusting to sets. Also, a player who is slowing down with each step loses horizontal velocity and thereby vertical velocity. Thus, we encourage our players to go slow at the beginning, which allows them to "chase" the ball.

The only variation to the habitual movement patterns just described occurs when time is reduced (i.e., in transition; see chapter 9). Given sufficient time, there should always be the attempt to take a four-step approach. But, lacking time, a three-step approach might be necessary instead. A hitter running from the net after a block or from a 10-foot × 10-foot (3-meter × 3-meter) position will sometimes have to abbreviate the approach. However, most of the time after turning and running, players can make an adequate four-step approach.

Coaching Points for the Approach

- Use a four-step approach.
- Start slowly and end quickly.
- The footwork pattern for a right-handed hitter is right-left-right-left.
- The footwork pattern for a left-handed hitter is left-right-left-right.
- Accelerate as you progress through the approach.
- Think *slow, faster, fastest.*
- Think *small, bigger, biggest.*
- Use a two-footed approach jump.
- The step close (last two steps) should be the fastest and most explosive.
- At the third step (plant or hop) you should be 12 inches (30 centimeters) from the ball
- During the last two steps (step close), feet are pointing in the direction they are traveling as you prepare to attack the entire court.
- "Chase" the ball.

Proper Armswing

Of course, once the proper approach has been executed, the ball must be hit over the net—preferably over a weak or nonexistent block or into an unoccupied area of the opponent's court. Here arm work is the key. Once a player has built speed with the proper four-step approach, the arms become the key to converting horizontal momentum into vertical height. Teach and learn "hands down, not up and not out" on the second step of the approach (figure 4.7). The second step should be on the spiking line, and the swing begins on this step. At this point, the arms should be forward (not facing up), no higher than the waist (figure 4.8). Then, on the third step, the hands go straight back as the arms swing as far as possible (figure 4.9). On the fourth step, the feet are parallel to the net, and the hands and arms go up in front of the body, using a double-arm lift (figure 4.10). As the body ascends, the hitting-arm elbow is drawn back and down to about shoulder height while simultaneously opening the shoulders to the ball. This position resembles a bow-and-arrow shooting position (elbow above the shoulder) and prepares the body to torque rather than pike when hitting (figure 4.11).

Figure 4.7 Hands down, not up and not out.

Figure 4.8 Arms forward and no higher than the waist.

Figure 4.9 Hands go straight back and arms swing as far as possible.

Figure 4.10 Double arm lift with feet parallel to the net.

Figure 4.11 Hitting-arm elbow draws back to shoulder height and opens shoulders to the ball.

Ball Contact

Once the four-step approach has been completed and the hitting arm is in the proper position, teach attackers to contact the ball as high as possible and in front of the body. As the body begins to torque, the hitting hand swings up and over the top of the ball, making contact in front of the hitting shoulder just outside the ear (figure 4.12). The combination of the shoulder rotation, along with some slight hip rotation, generates the torque that produces power. Use a fast armswing with an equally powerful wrist snap (figure 4.13). The hand should be open and firm, with fingers apart, giving the attacker more surface area on the ball. This results in much better ball control.

Landing

Many coaches overlook teaching the landing phase of the attack, but a player who lands incorrectly certainly knows the difference. (Injury to the ankles or knees can

Figure 4.12 Hitting arm swings up and over the top of the ball. Player makes contact with the ball just outside the ear.

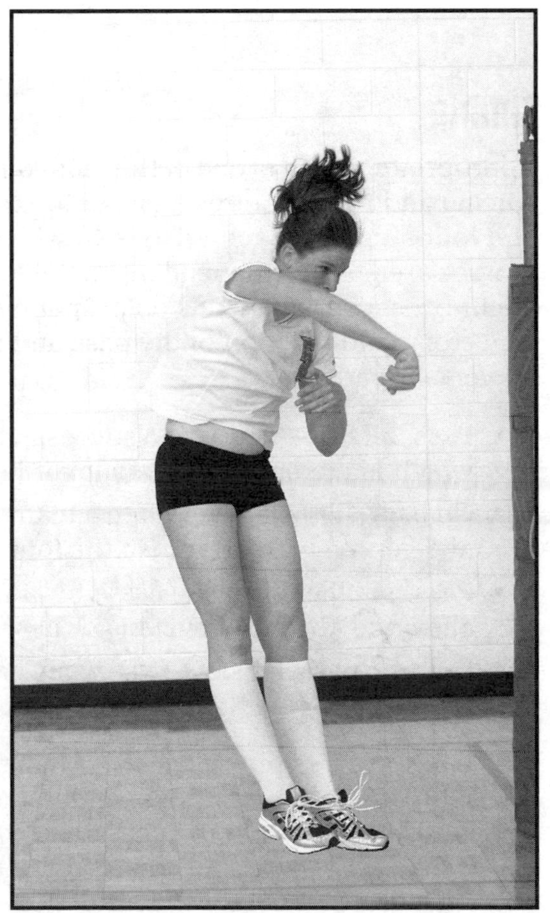

Figure 4.13 Player uses a fast armswing with an equally powerful wrist snap.

result.) The most important thing to remember is to bend the knees slightly to absorb the shock of hitting the hard floor. The attacker should land with the body weight distributed uniformly on both feet and knees slightly flexed. When possible, avoid an awkward, one-foot landing.

Coaching Points for Armswing, Ball Contact, and Landing

- Hands are down, not up and not out, as you begin the approach.
- The swing begins on the second step of a four-step approach.
- Think *bow and arrow.*
- Contact the ball as high as you can in front of you.
- Use a fast armswing.
- Use a powerful wrist snap.
- Use a two-footed landing with knees slightly bent.

Timing

Appropriate timing is one of the most difficult, yet important, factors that regulate spiking and thus requires a closer look. Timing for the act of hitting is a function of a four-step approach relative to when the setter has the ball. Several different tempos are possible depending on the level of play, but no matter what the system might be, success depends on proper eye work. All hitters must track the source, trajectory, and location of the pass and then use one of the following four natural movement patterns:

- Pass, hit fast—use after a successful pass by the player who is going to attack, which immediately allows him or her to begin the four-step approach.
- No pass, hit fast—use when a teammate passes, allowing the hitter to release and get ready to attack via the four-step approach.
- Pass, shuffle, hit fast—use after a pass that's high in trajectory and doesn't allow the hitter to begin his or her approach right away.
- Pass–no pass, hit slow—use when passes are poor; the offense runs at a slower tempo to ensure the hitter gets a good swing.

The best players reproduce these habitual movement patterns over and over and, through countless repetitions, understand which to use at the appropriate time. Above all, it's important to understand what pattern the pass will allow the hitter to employ. Clearly, there's an advantage in running the offense at a faster tempo, but you must first stress that the hitter gets a swing. At the University of Washington, we know that speed can kill, but we also know that when not run correctly, speed can kill you.

TRAINING THE ATTACKER

Individual tutoring, small-group reps, and six-on-six reps are the three phases to employ when training attackers. The three things a coach should encourage are getting a considerable number of reps, passing or digging to hit (rather than a coach tossing balls at the net), and getting enough gamelike practice. In tutoring, then, you might wish to engage in hitting lines. In small groups, run pass, set, and hit drills in which a specific eye sequence and movement pattern is isolated. In six-on-six drills, introduce enough variables so that players must learn to recognize the common situations practiced in the small groups and apply the appropriate movement. Remember, though, the bigger the game, the fewer the reps. The more reps, the greater the development.

Objectives

At Washington, each phase of our training has a focus or objective. Individual tutoring primarily involves cognitive learning, in which basic understanding of techniques and mechanics is emphasized. Feedback given here primarily relates to technical difficulty and technical mastery. In small-group training, we attempt to apply what has been learned in tutoring to common game situations. You can do this by isolating certain parts of the game or constraining the game to regulate the stimuli that you want your players to respond to. This part of training emphasizes developing players' eye work and ability to respond to what they see. Six-on-six action then puts everything together and randomizes the environment. At this point, players apply their ability to recognize what's developing and to reproduce the proper movement patterns.

Today, at all levels of volleyball, players can use several types of attacks to get effective shots and get the best of a defense. In addition to the "generic" outside attack, there are also more advanced attacks, such as "quicks" (short, fast sets used to surprise the defense), which are classified as ones, twos, threes, and slides.

The one is attacked close to the setter. In fact, the hitter is in the air before the setter sets the ball. For a one, the attacker hits the ball as soon as it leaves the setter's hands. (There is also a back one, which is set behind the setter.)

Coaching Points for a Successful One

- The attacker must be able to pass well to the setter. The ability to pass well enables the attacker to judge the speed of the approach.
- The attacker should jump just before the setter touches the ball.
- The attacker takes off on the jump before becoming even with the setter. At this point, the attacker should be lined up with the setter's extended arms. The ball should be hit right out of the setter's hands.
- The attacker should not jump too close to the net or in front of the setter.

For the two, the timing is a bit slower than for the one. The attacker should be on the second step of the four-step approach when the setter touches the ball. For this quick, the ball is also set higher than for the one.

For the three set, the timing is the same as for the one, but the attacker is farther from the setter. (The three is a medium set about halfway between the setter and the spiker, if the setter is in the middle.) Again, for the three, the attacker should be on the second step of the four-step approach when the setter touches the ball.

The slide is a type of attack all its own. In the slide, the attacker actually slides behind the setter and hits the ball off one foot. If the attacker is left-handed, he or she slides in front of the setter from right to left (much like a layup in basketball). The timing is similar to that of a two, and the knee goes up at the same time as the hitting arm (figure 4.14). The slide is used most by middle blockers (but should be learned by all attackers) and is used to catch the opposing blockers off guard so that a two-player block can't be set. With the increased popularity of the 5–1 offense, it has become essential to create an attack opportunity behind the setter to spread the offense antenna to antenna.

In addition to quicks, more advanced teams also use back-row attacks. When hitters can attack from the back row, the setter has three to four attackers to go to at all times. When hitting from the back row, the approach is similar to the front-row attack, but the attacker must jump from behind the attack line (figure 4.15). The attacker will usually broad jump and can then land in front of the three-meter line.

Figure 4.14 The slide attack.

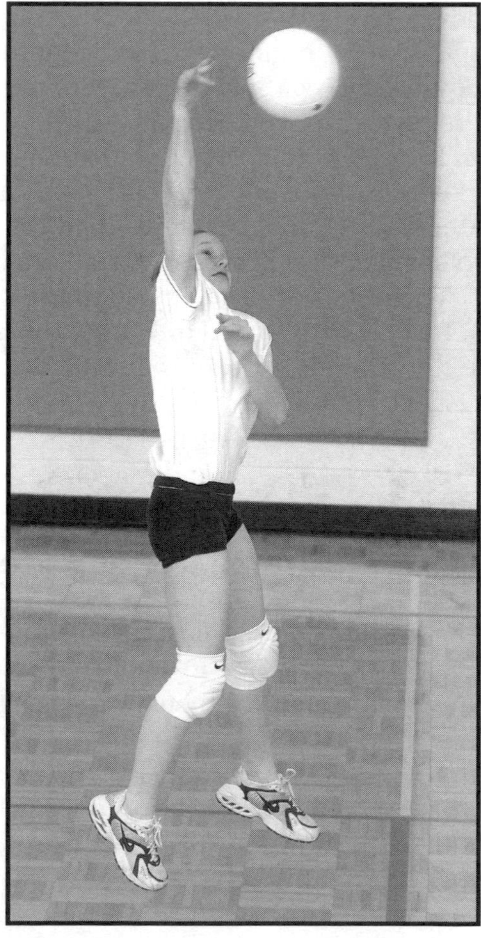

Figure 4.15 Back-row attack.

Once the type of set has been determined—and for whom—it's up to the attacker to use the right kind of shot to confuse the defense. Figure 4.16 gives examples of many types of sets. Of course, the greater variety of shots an attacker uses, the more the opponent is kept guessing.

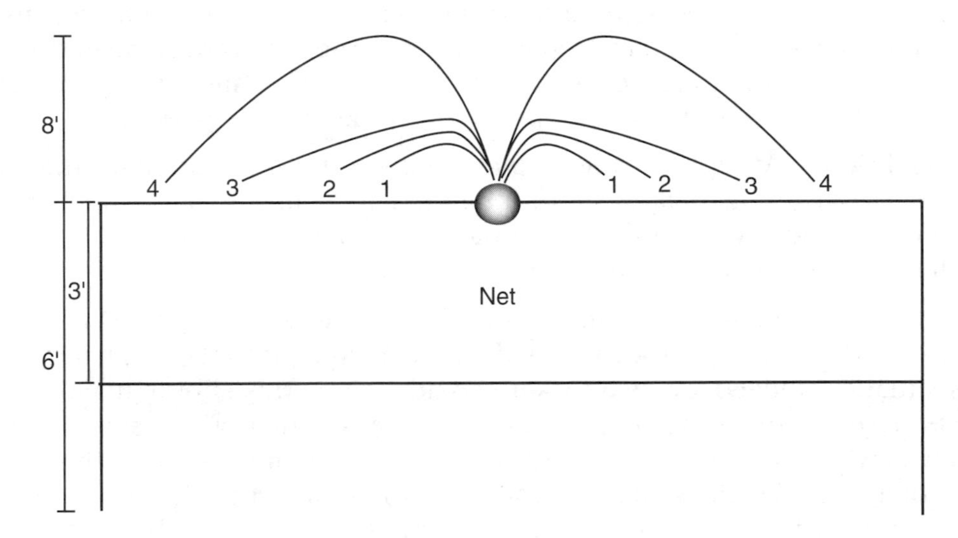

Figure 4.16 Varying types of sets.

TYPES OF SHOTS

Essentially, at the lower levels of play, most setters opt for the zero or "regular" set, which is a high and wide set to the left sideline. The beginning attacker is concentrating more on footwork and timing than placement of the attack, so basically the ball goes anywhere on the court—preferably within the boundary lines. As attackers gain experience, they learn to place shots to various areas of the court and to vary the tempo. Once this occurs, several types of shots are available.

Tip/Dump/Dink. The tip (or dink) shot is used at all levels of play. In this shot, the attacker hits the ball with an open hand, making contact with the finger pads, softly lobbing the ball over the block for an effective attack. The dump shot, most often used by the "live" (front-row) setter, is executed by contacting the ball at its highest point and shoving it down into the opponent's court, catching the defense off guard. Although tip and dump shots are often viewed as defensive maneuvers to use when conditions are poor, they are also great offensive weapons that can disrupt a defense's timing and throw them off target.

Roll (or off-speed shot). The roll is another shot seen at all levels of play and which is used to keep the defense on its toes. In the roll (also called an off-speed shot), the attacker contacts the ball toward the bottom of the sphere with the heel of the hand. On contact, the fingers roll over the top of the ball, and the wrist snaps. The result is a hard-hit shot with a fairly straight trajectory.

High-and-flat shot. When the set is not in the perfect spot (wide, inside, or way off the net), the attacker contacts the ball in the center, swinging hard, high, and flat. It translates into a viable attack without resorting to passing the ball back over on the third hit.

Line hit. As attackers gain experience in placing shots on the court, the line hit becomes a useful weapon. In this shot, the attacker makes a normal approach in the air and then turns to hit the ball down the sideline. When the attacker is crafty, the defense will not recognize the body is twisting to execute the line shot until it is too late and the ball has hit the court.

Deep-corner hit. The deep-corner hit is another shot that can catch a defense off guard. The attacker hits the ball deep into either corner (preferably an unoccupied one). Especially at the lower levels, defenders often creep into the middle of the court and a deep-corner hit often translates into a kill for the offense.

Sharp-angle hit. At higher levels of play (college and international), the sharp-angle hit is a dangerous weapon in the attacker's arsenal. On a sharp-angle hit, the ball lands between two frontcourt and backcourt defenders. When hit perfectly, the ball lands on or in front of the three-meter line.

Wipe-off (or tool) shot. Although many attackers, especially younger ones, are afraid to use the block by hitting into it, the tool or wipe-off shot can be quite useful in this situation. Indeed, every attacker should include this shot in his or her bag of tricks. To execute a wipe-off, the attacker makes contact on the side of the ball opposite of where he or she really wants to hit it. Once contact is made, the attacker hits partially into the block and then follows through with the hitting arm (usually out of bounds). If the shot is performed correctly, the ball bounces off the block and either out of bounds on the opponent's side or just inside the three-meter line.

Seam shot. A good attacker looks for a seam in a block, especially when the block is not formed well. The attacker can then deflect the ball off a blocker and catch the rest of the team sleeping.

Rebound shot. Although it's seen only at elite levels, the rebound shot is effective when the attacker can't hit around, off, over, or through a block. In this case, he or she taps the ball into a blocker's hands and then plays the ball immediately as it rebounds off the hands.

Coaching Points for Attacking Drills

Approach

- Right foot forward
- Four steps
- Small, bigger, biggest
- Slow, faster, fastest

Mechanics

- Arms down on second step
- Double-arm lift
- Bow-and-arrow armswing

ATTACKING DRILLS

Individual Drills

You Go, I Throw

Purpose: To increase an attacker's coordination and timing on the approach

Setup: Each attacker stands in a line in the middle of the court, ready to engage in the approach. A coach positions near the net to toss the ball.

Execution: Individually, each player begins his or her approach with the second step on the spiking line. If the attacker has performed the four-step approach properly, the coach then tosses the ball. Players need to come to the coach, and the coach tosses the ball just as they jump. Players should actually jump a couple of feet back from the net and make sure they're placed directly in front of the coach. The coach ensures the toss is only high enough for the attacker to take a swing, which eliminates considerable problems with timing. The toss can't be too tight to the net (1 to 2 feet away) so that the attacker has room to swing without hitting the net.

Coaching Points: This drill provides feedback, first on the components of the approach and then on the components of the mechanics.

Variations

1. Vary the height of the toss.
2. Toss from far off the net.
3. Run the drill with the middle and right-side hitters as well.

I Throw, You Go

Purpose: To increase an attacker's coordination and timing on the approach

Setup: Each attacker stands in a line to the left side of the court, ready to engage in the approach. A coach positions near the net to toss the ball.

Execution: Individually, each player begins his or her approach. The coach makes an underhand toss to the outside (left front), 24 to 36 inches (~60–90 centimeters) above the net and also 24 to 36 inches away from the net. Attackers begin off the court and use the four-step approach for an outside set. They should begin their approach as soon as the coach tosses or sets the ball.

Coaching Points: As in the You Throw, I Go drill, ensure that the toss is not too tight to the net so that the spiker has enough room to swing without hitting the net.

Small-Group Drills

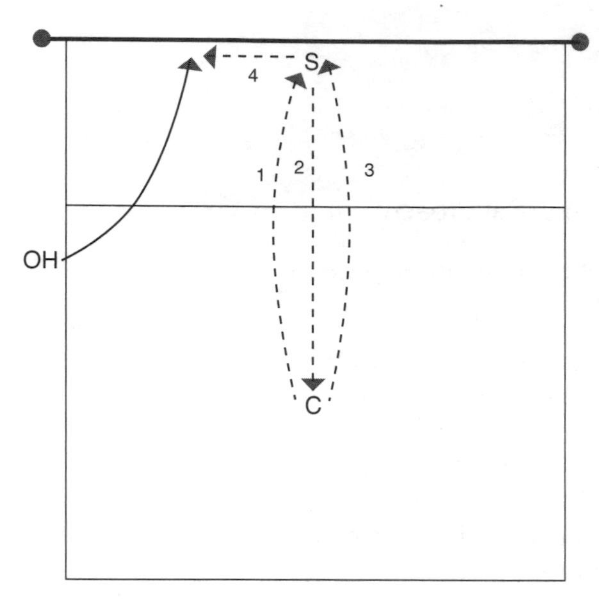

Figure 4.17 Back-and-Forth.

Back-and-Forth

Purpose: To teach hitters to watch the pass before engaging in the approach

Setup: Setters are in the proper front-row position; an outside hitter in area 4 is ready for the spike approach.

Execution: A coach tosses a ball to the setter. The setter then passes the ball back to the coach. As the coach passes the ball back to the setter, the hitter makes the appropriate move while observing the pass and its trajectory and location (figure 4.17).

Coaching Points: Vary the pass location and trajectory so that the hitter has to respond to a variety of stimuli.

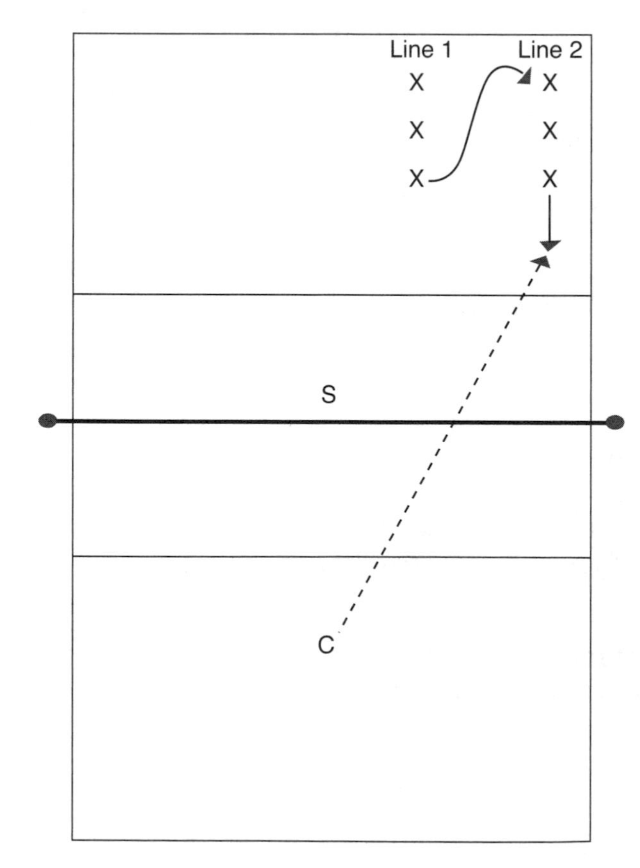

Figure 4.18 Incoming.

Incoming

Purpose: To teach hitters to watch an incoming ball and determine whether to use a *pass and hit fast* or *no pass and hit fast* response

Setup: Set up two lines of three hitters on one side of the net with a setter in proper setting position. A coach positions on the opposite side of the net.

Execution: The coach bowls the ball over the net to the first player in either line. The first person in line 2 uses the appropriate footwork pattern to hit the ball. If the coach tosses to line 1, the hitter in line 2 shuffles and hits (no pass and hit fast). If the coach tosses to line 2, the hitter in line 2 passes and goes into the approach (pass and hit fast). In either case, the first player in line 1 rotates to the end of the hitting line (figure 4.18).

Coaching Points: The ability to make split-second decisions is what separates the truly great hitters from the mediocre ones.

Variations

1. This drill can also be done on the right side.
2. Blockers can be added.

Outside Hitter (OH) Tournament

Purpose: To ensure the outside hitters watch the serve and then pass and apply proper mechanics and timing

Setup: Two outside hitters set up on one side of the court behind the three-meter line, and a setter on the same side of the court sets up in proper setting position. Two additional hitters are behind the endline on the opposite court.

Execution: OH3 and OH4 serve to OH1 and OH2. OH1 and OH2 score a point every time they get a clean hit. After five serves, OH1 and OH2 switch. After 10 serves, OH1 and OH2 serve to OH3 and OH4. After the round is completed, the hitters pair up with someone they haven't played with yet.

Coaching Points: You can turn this drill into a tournament configured this way:

1 & 2 vs 3 & 4

1 & 3 vs 2 & 4

1 & 4 vs 2 & 3

OH1 and OH3 versus OH2 and OH4

OH1 and OH4 versus OH2 and OH3

Six-on-Six Games

The remainder of the drills for attacking should involve six-on-six games. Progress comes as a result of deliberate repetition and meaningful feedback. In six-on-six games, the emphasis of the feedback dictates the meaning of the drill. Coaches need to provide feedback similar to that given during individual tutoring and small-group training, reminding players that the "movements of the game are the movements of the game." Proper emphasis of this concept, along with emphasis on eye work, leads to consistent reproduction of good movement patterns.

CONCLUSION

Great hitters can see what's happening and know quickly how to respond. They can reproduce the same movement patterns and mechanics many times over. To develop great hitters, you need training methods that provide maximum transfer to the game. During training, emphasize proper mechanics and movement patterns. Proper mechanics are generally a result of mindful repetition and meaningful feedback from the coach. Proper movement patterns are generally a result of great eye work and recognition. Once attackers have learned the habitual movement patterns, their success depends on doing the right things at the right time and staying focused on the variables that instruct them on what to do.

The attack is not only one of the most spectacular skills to watch, but also one of the most difficult to learn. The attack requires considerable coordination and body control while the player's body is in motion, beginning on the ground, in the air, and finishing with the landing. Teaching and learning the components of the attack involves using sound teaching principles and drills that allow players to work on timing, footwork, and arm and body positioning. When the attack is performed well, both the players and the spectators truly enjoy the result. I learned most of the principles discussed in this chapter from Carl McGown, former head men's volleyball coach at Brigham Young University. In more than 10 years of applying these fundamentals, we have seen our players realize meaningful and measurable progress. They have developed confidence through knowing what to do and by doing the right thing at the right time. One of the great things about the principles discussed in this chapter is that they can be applied at all levels of the sport.

5

Blocking

Don Hardin

Photo by Scott Bjornlie

As the level of play rises, volleyball becomes more of a power game, and the block becomes a critical factor for success. When opponents can pass the ball with a high percentage of success and accurately set the ball into "attackable" positions, it's important to stop specific players from having a hot hand.

Blocking attackers can quickly create a momentum change in your favor. Many attackers respond very poorly to being blocked, perhaps following a block with unforced errors or significantly reducing their aggressiveness. A great stuff block can both intimidate your opponent and start a fire on your side of the net.

The skill of blocking is one of the most challenging to teach and learn. This is true for several reasons. First, from a motivational standpoint, a player can move into the best position, execute flawless technique, yet not be rewarded with a successful block. Second, the risk factors involved in blocking provide a challenge and can be counterproductive. Last, from a motor-learning viewpoint, skills conducted while airborne often develop more slowly.

The chapter begins by explaining two separate but interrelated sequences of events the blocker should follow for optimal results. The first summarizes how events unfold during a match, providing a solid foundation on which to build solid technique. The second explains the visual cues and processes that should draw the blocker's vision or attention.

In this chapter we'll look at the basic fundamentals of blocking. For example, here we'll examine posture, positioning, and how to move. We'll leave system work for chapter 8 on team defense. System work would cover blocking strategies, schemes, and matchups.

SEQUENCE OF EVENTS

Let's look at the four actions a blocker should perform before every serve and throughout the opponent's offensive attack. This will identify and provide an understanding of responsibilities of an effective blocker, which have implications for technique, training, and designing drills.

Identify the Attackers

As the team lines up to serve at an opponent, frontcourt blockers should be busy identifying the attackers on the other side of the net. Even more important, they should communicate to one another about their responsibilities, perhaps with a "blocking captain" designated in each rotation to facilitate this communication.

Knowing which attackers are likely to run a quick attack dictates the posture a blocker will employ against them. In addition, players who know they'll be blocking solo might line up differently and initiate a different hand position to stop the attack. Being able to use proper visual technique is also much easier because the opposing attackers and their likely approach patterns are clearly identified. Great blockers identify their assigned hitters and keep them in their vision, even if only peripherally. Each blocker will likely have at least one attacker who will approach his or her designated zone of responsibility.

Move Into Base Position

If an opponent's attacker is running a low quick set, it will be imperative that the base position of the blocker move to "front" the quick attacker before the set, as he or she makes an approach (figure 5.1). Taller blockers with longer reaches might be able to move their base without completely fronting the hitter, enabling them to react quickly to other sets.

As the opponent passes the ball, blockers must be prepared for an overpass. An overpass might occur only a few times each match, but these are sure points and will boost the team if managed properly.

As the pass comes to the setter, someone must keep an eye out for a setter attack or "dump," should the setter be in the front row. For example, if the hitters are "split" in this situation, the responsibility goes to the middle blocker.

Or, the hitters might be "stacked" to one side or the other of the setter, as shown in figures 5.2 and 5.3. In these cases, the appropriate outside blocker has setter dump responsibility.

Often, attackers line up in one formation and move to another. Blockers, if they continue to keep the approach of the attackers in their peripheral vision, might be able to identify when a stack to one side can quickly change to a split situation, thereby demanding a different response regarding who blocks the setter on a tight pass (figure 5.4).

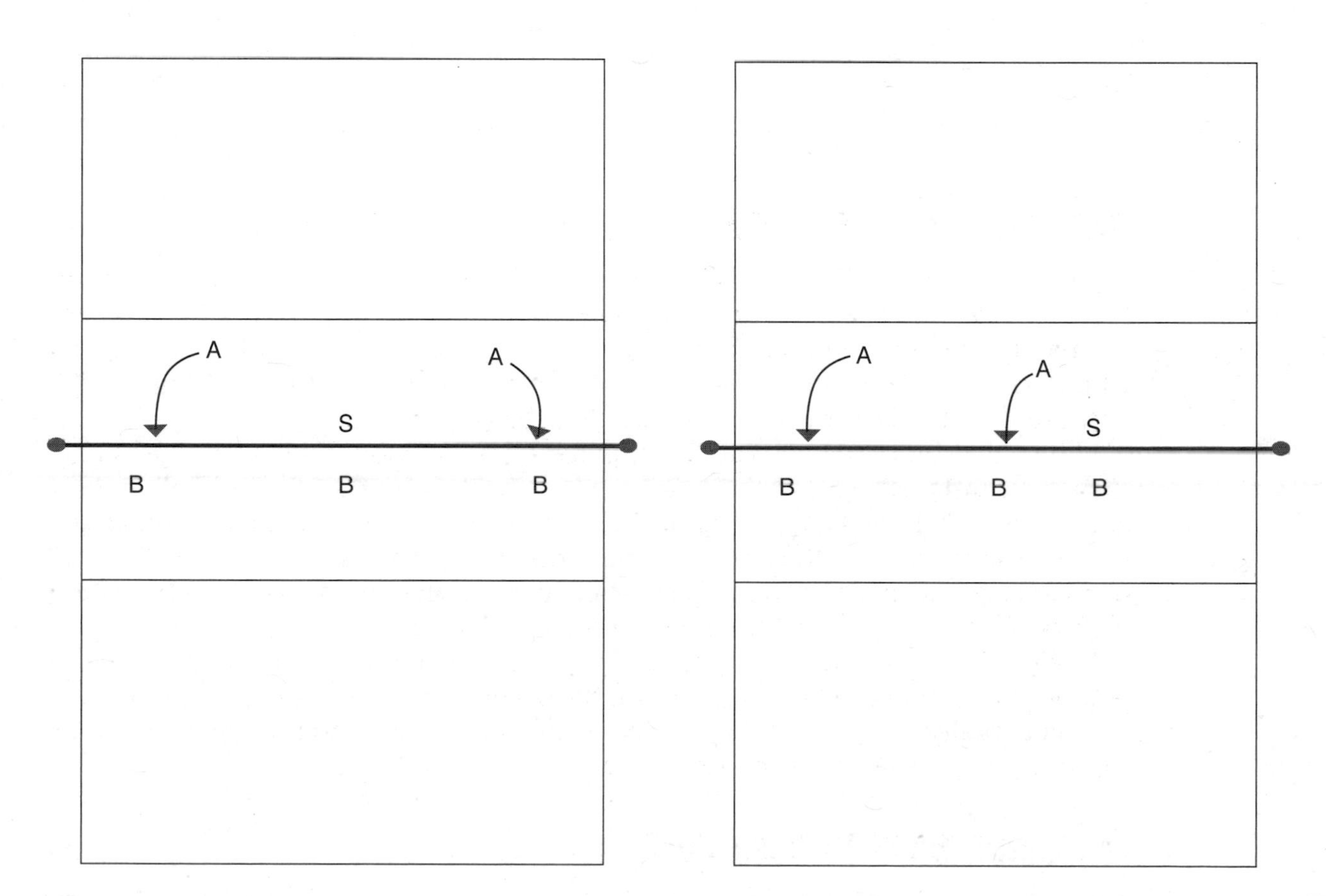

Figure 5.1 Move into base position.

Figure 5.2 Stacked blockers, right side.

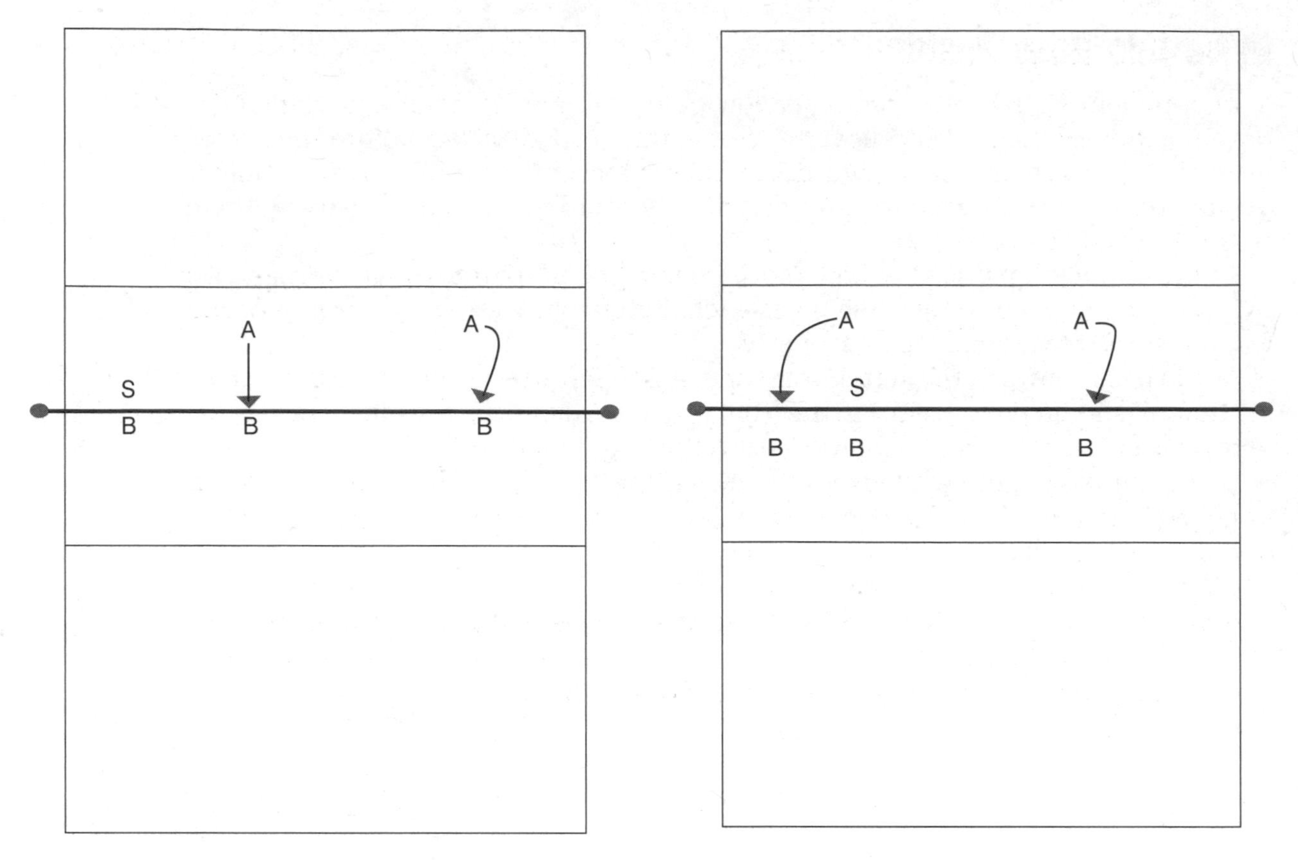

Figure 5.3 Stacked blockers, left side.

Figure 5.4 Split situation.

Move Into Read Position

As the setter sets the ball, blockers must move from base position to read position. The block is executed during this position (named because of the emphasis on reading the action on the other side of the net to determine who, where, and when to block). Following the set, blockers move to read position by "fronting" the appropriate attacker in preparation for their block jump.

If the ball is blocked back into the opponents' court, blockers land and remain at the net in anticipation that the opposing team will cover the blocked ball and set another attack. If the ball goes by the block or deflects off the block, blockers must land and transition off the net in anticipation of their own set. Since this is a vital part of the game, it's important to practice blocking in conjunction with transition responsibilities so that the training is more specific and gamelike.

It should be noted that sometimes, to gain a transition advantage, players will land on one foot in an effort to land with the other foot already stepping off the net. This is actually not quicker. In fact, by using a proper first step (explained later), it's quicker and safer to land with both feet before making a first step.

Transition Back to Base Position

After a missed block attempt in which the ball remains on their side of the net, blockers will transition off the net and back into their approach. They immediately assume an offensive role and after attacking the ball into the opponent's court, quickly return to their base positions and repeat the process. In this return phase to base, however, there's less time than before on the serve to read, make decisions, and communicate. This phase of blocking must be practiced and simulated as an educating process for the blocker, since the ball often crosses the net several times before points are scored.

VISUAL TECHNIQUE

To become an outstanding blocker, training the eyes is just as important as training the rest of the body and should become a regular part of blocking practice. This vision and movement pattern can and should be trained.

Peripheral vision is an important skill in blocking. With peripheral vision, you glance up at the ball and perhaps still see opponents moving into their approach patterns. Blockers also need to be able to watch the setter and see the attackers from their side peripherally.

Sequence of Visual Cues

Just as there's a specific sequence of actions blockers should perform before and during each rally, there's also a series of actions a blocker's eyes should follow during the blocking sequence to facilitate optimal performance.

Look at the hitters. Before each serve, identify which of the opposing players are eligible front-row hitters, from what area of the court they will be attacking, and if the setter is in the front row.

Glance at the pass. To be prepared for an overpass, a quick glance at the pass is necessary. Don't look at the ball too long or you'll miss other information.

Look at the setter. Specifically, look at the hands and arms of the setter and his or her body posture. Look directly at these areas and cues on the setter.

Glance at the set. Only a brief moment is required to gain an understanding of the direction and flight of the set. This information will dictate the important first-step response in the direction of the ball and give some indication of how far the ball is traveling. In addition, you'll gain knowledge regarding how far off or how tight the set is to the net, which affects the timing of the block.

Look at the hitter. Upon moving into read position in front of the hitter, looking directly at the hitter will provide the blocker with a tremendous amount of information about the hitter. Great blockers watch the hitter to gain information on jump timing and attack direction.

Coaching Points for Recognizing Visual Cues

- Identify the attackers (hitter).
- Glance at the pass (ball).
- Look at the setter (setter).
- Glance at the set (ball).
- Watch the hitter (hitter).

Many players close their eyes at the moment of attack or even earlier. With some of the controlled drills covered later in this chapter, it's a good idea to watch for this problem and emphasize keeping the eyes open and relaxed.

BLOCKING TECHNIQUE

Once blockers are trained with their action and visual sequences, they can begin practicing proper physical technique. Teaching and learning the skill is most effective when done in reverse order of how it takes place on the court. In other words, it's much more effective to first learn the end position in a more controlled environment and then learn the complex movements required to get to the end position. Thus, I'll begin by explaining hand position at the time of contact before explaining the movement prior to the jump.

Hand and Arm Position

As we examine hand and arm position, we can first look at proper technique and then study proper responses upon hitter contact. Poor responses and habits during hitter contact comprise some of the greatest challenges in maintaining proper hand and arm position as a blocker. However, on some occasions these blocking problems are symptoms of poor technique that occurs much earlier as the blocker prepares to jump.

After the jump. On the way up and during hitter contact, the blocker should have the thumbs pointing up and fingers spread to the outside (figure 5.5). This accomplishes many things. First, this position protects the fingers from injury as the attacker pounds the ball into the block. If fingers are straight up in the air (especially if the wrists and fingers flex forward on hitter contact), they become very vulnerable (figure 5.6). Second, this thumbs-up "posture" of the hands provides for more

Figure 5.5 Thumbs out and fingers spread.

Figure 5.6 Fingers become vulnerable to injury if straight up in the air.

frequent deflection opportunities. After all, a successful block is not only defined as a stuff block. If a blocker can turn a hard-spiked ball into a high deflection, he or she has neutralized the attack and provided an opportunity to counter with a point swing (assuming ball control and transition skills). Third, proper lateral hand posture covers more area than when fingers are pointing up. The several inches gained in lateral zone coverage make for more deflections.

Still another reason for proper positioning of the hands is that the angle and location of the hands play a vital role in the direction the reflecting ball will travel. Each of the blocker's hands has a different responsibility in this regard. As the blocker faces the net, the hand closest to the center of the court is called the "inside hand." The hand closest to the antennae is the "outside hand." The inside hand, on hitter contact, should be extended over the net, and the adjoining arm should reach back to the center of the court in order to cut off the available angle shot of the attacker (figure 5.7). For a middle blocker, this takes away the sharp cross-court angle, whereas an outside blocker will find that this method will assist the middle in closing the seam or gap between the blockers. The middle blocker will also reach back to center court and over the net with the inside hand to cut off an even sharper angle. The thumb remains pointed up and the fingers extended out. The inside hand should reach this position on the way up, or as the blocker elevates. Reaching straight up and then dropping the hand to this inside position can create the same complications as "batting" creates. The attacker might send the ball into the angle before the blocker gets his or her hand in position.

Reaching back to the inside with one arm obviously creates a large space between the blockers' arms. However, if the attacker is not directly in front of the blocker, this angle might be spread without a danger of the ball passing through. In contrast, when directly in front of the blocker, the arms should be closer together (figure 5.8), but the inside hand can still penetrate and reach back to take away the angle. Note that reaching to the inside alone doesn't take away the angle shot. The blocker must also penetrate the net plane with this inside hand (figure 5.9).

Figure 5.7 Proper hand technique for blocking.

Figure 5.8 Angle of hands for deflection by middle blocker.

The outside hand should be angled (the palm angled toward the center of the court) with the arm straight up and in front of the attacked ball (figure 5.10). Should the ball contact the outside hand (nearest the antenna), this angle will deflect the ball back to the center of the court instead of out of bounds.

Figure 5.9 Penetrating the net plane.

Figure 5.10 Spread angle reaching back.

Figure 5.11 Inside-to-out position.

Twitching or sweeping the arm on hitter contact won't direct the ball. It's the angle of the hand and arm that make the difference. Sometimes it's difficult to ask a player with such a habit simply to keep his or her arms and hands still. Learning the thrust is something else on which to concentrate. The small shrug or thrusting motion (described soon) will be more than adequate.

During the jump phase. When executing the jumping phase of the block, blockers should jump while spreading their hands from an inside-to-out position (figure 5.11). During the jump, hands and arms are close together. The hands spread as the blocker rises and comes closer to the point of potential contact with the ball.

Many blockers do just the opposite. In other words, their hands and arms come from wide to closer as they jump and anticipate hitter contact. Obviously, this outside-in movement will cause the hands to cover less area as they come close together. In some cases, blockers' hands will even overlap on the moment of hitter contact. Sometimes this is exaggerated with good intentions by the player who knows that the hands must be apart. In an effort to accomplish the task, some blockers begin with the hands and arms apart. The problem in doing this occurs as they jump with their arms apart. While using their arms for jumping momentum and while positioning their hands, their arms and hands naturally must come from an outside position to an in position as they block. This motion is similar to a "jumping jack" and actually presents the attacker with a nice angle shot to the inside of the court (figure 5.12).

Figure 5.12 Jumping Jack preparation.

On the way up, blockers (of ample height or jumping ability) should keep their hands close to the net. It's vital that the blocker seek to penetrate the plane of the net as he or she rises and not after the jump has peaked. In other words, the block should "seal" the space between the top of the net and the arms as the blocker ascends. As the blocker jumps, the elbows and the arms should be in the frontal plane of the blocker. However, just prior to the jump, it's acceptable for a blocker to bring the elbows—and in some cases, even the arms—behind the frontal plane to gain jumping height assistance. In fact, this "swing-blocking" technique is becoming very popular, especially among players who need the extra inches on their jump to be effective. However, on the way up and off the floor, the hands, arms, and elbows should be in front of the blocker's frontal plane.

Batting. As they leave the floor, players who start with their hand coming up from behind will have a tendency to "bat" forward with their arms (figure 5.13). This is one of the most common problems in blocking. Unfortunately, batting might be dramatically successful on rare occasions, thus giving some false positive feedback. When the arms and hands aren't "sealing" the net, the attacker has more of an angle open for the attack (figure 5.14).

Figure 5.13 Batting.

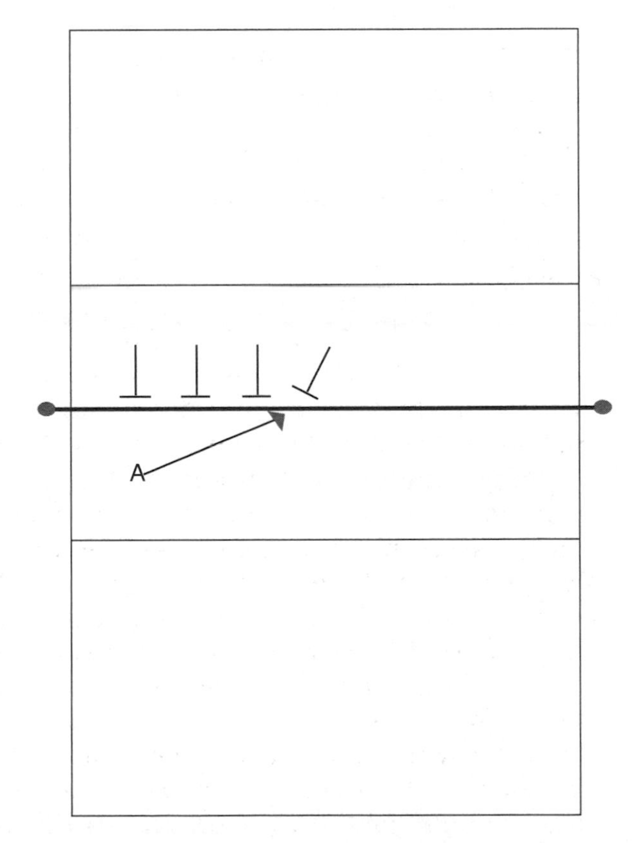

Figure 5.14 Leaving an open angle.

Batting on hitter contact might also create unnecessary net violations. Sometimes players will bat forward with one arm only as a poor habit. They do this in anticipation of the attacker hitting the ball into their hand. This is a frequent cause of net violations.

Thrusting. How, then, does a blocker generate any force or strength for a stuff block? This is accomplished through a motion I call "thrusting." Imagine the thumbs turned up in the air and over the net in the proper plane. Instead of batting forward as contact is anticipated, blockers thrust their thumbs toward the ceiling and continue through the blocking plane.

Think of the thumbs being tied to a string and someone from above pulling on the string upon hitter contact. This motion aligns the arms and hands, creating a solid force. The ball will come off with more force. Also, this alignment creates a more solid deflection, sending more "playable" deflections into the back court. Often when the ball hits the top of a well-formed block, it deflects upward and converts the attack into somewhat of a free ball.

Drawing out the block. The last point of focus on the arms and hands involves "drawing out the block" as long as possible while in the air. Some players do a nice job of shooting their arms up into the proper plane with great arm and hand posture, but as they peak and begin their descent, they pull the arms and hands down just as quickly. Because the arms and hands in such cases are only up there for a flash, the window for timing accuracy is reduced. Holding the arms up as long as possible—even landing with the arms still extended—provides a much longer time period for potential blocker contact.

Position of the Block

The position or setup of the block depends on your blocking strategy. As a result, most blockers would be smart to move in somewhat on the block and give some space in order to tempt a high error shot down the line.

A good starting point for positioning is with the outside foot and outside arm on the ball. In other words, because the blockers will be watching the hitter as he or she jumps, they attempt to set their feet up with the outside foot on the attacker's right shoulder (left for a left-handed attacker.) Outside blockers can be taught to adjust inward from this position, depending on how much line they wish to "give." At the high school level, it would be recommended to move in about 12 inches (30 centimeters) from this position. Make an attacker prove that he or she is able to hit effectively down the line before adjusting to the outside. At higher levels, the outside hand is on the ball and the inside hand reaches over and to the middle in order to cut off the cross-court attack.

From the middle of the court, the attacker can hit at both angles, so the blocker must line up directly on an attacker and watch him or her closely as he or she jumps to spike the ball. This will often give an indication for hand and, if time permits, foot adjustment. As described later with timing, the blocker jumps shortly after the hitter, permitting a small time for adjustment.

Blocking the slide attack (one-foot takeoff approach) of an opponent can be accomplished with these same techniques. The blocker moves with the slide attacker and looks for where the attacker will plant for the spike jump. The blocker hits his or her slant at this point and jumps "outside-in," reaching with the inside hand (usually the right hand versus a slide attacker) back to the center and over the net for the likely cross-court attack.

Timing of the Block

Ideally, blockers should contact the ball as they peak or even on their way up. This is because on their way down, they must retract their arms slightly to avoid a net violation (especially if they penetrated well over the plane of the net.) If the ball is contacted as the hands are retreating, it might go between the blocker's arms and the net, or not deflect with any force. To contact the ball with the best hand position, blockers watch the hitter and wait until the hitter jumps. The blocker can use this valuable time to read any directional cues from the attacker. For example, maybe he or she has turned as he or she leaves the ground to hit line. With this short window of "waiting time," the blocker can make a minor foot adjustment—or at least jump and take initiative with the hands to block more angle or line. Too much reaching won't be beneficial for reasons discussed earlier (twitching), but a player can adjust the arms and hands into a good position prior to hitter contact.

Most beginning blockers jump too early, usually because they're staring (instead of glancing) at the ball during the flight of the set. Obviously, timing will vary according to the depth of the set from the net. As the opposing setter delivers the outside set, the blocker glances at the ball to determine whether he or she must wait longer in the slant position until after the hitter has jumped. If the attacker is hitting a ball that's very tight to the net, it will take less time for the ball to get to him or her, and the blocker will need to jump slightly earlier or even in conjunction with the attacker. If the ball is set even a few feet off the net, the blocker must wait until the attacker has left the floor before initiating the block jump.

Movement to the Block

Once a blocker learns the proper position of the hands and arms during the block, he or she can begin learning the movement required to get to read position. Because volleyball is such a quick and explosive game, being able to perform the movements quickly and efficiently is key to success.

It's very important to understand that players need to focus on their center while training movement. Most players lean and react with their upper body. However, for greatest efficiency, movement must be initiated from the floor. The energy from the floor should transfer to move the core or center of the player with as little lapsed time as possible.

The first ingredient to great movement is attaining a posture from which you're prepared to respond quickly and in multiple directions. Although most movement requirements are targeted at the middle blockers, the outside blockers may have similar demands placed on them. For example, if outside blockers are asked to have a base position that's farther in from the antenna in order to tandem or solo block a quick attack, they'll need good movement skills to get back outside if necessary.

Coiled posture. The posture that best facilitates quick movement is the "coiled" posture. The term "coil" implies being ready to strike, similar to a snake uncoiling to attack. Most offenses attempt to freeze the blocker or slow him or her from executing a well-formed block in tandem with an outside blocker. Thus, the coiled blocker must be ready to strike in both lateral directions, as well as up. So there are three potential coiled responses. It's extremely important to resist being pulled out of coiled posture or faked into a false direction, which costs valuable time in recovery.

Figure 5.15 Push step posture.

Push step. On setter contact, the blocker should bend slightly at the knees and waist. The feet are positioned just outside of shoulder width. The weight is distributed slightly on the inside of the feet, slightly forward, and the toes are pointed slightly out. This posture allows a very important component to efficient movement called the "push step" (figure 5.15).

The push step implies pushing before stepping. The push step is also called a "jab step," which is a good term because jabbing implies speed over a short distance. To initiate quick movement, the player makes a quick push off of the inside of the opposite foot (the foot opposite the desired direction of movement). This push starts from the floor with the intention of quickly budging the player's core or center in the desired direction. The movement foot—or same foot of direction—lifts slightly and makes a short but quick step (figure 5.16).

At the same moment as the push, the hips open to the direction of movement to enhance speed. The first step by the movement foot should be short and very quick, keeping the knee over the toe and the center over the knee—perhaps even past the knee. This puts the blocker in the best possible position to amplify the speed of his or her movement with the next power step or "drive step." Blockers who step out past their center or who step past the knee will block their speed for the next step (figure 5.17).

Figure 5.16 Making the quick step.

Figure 5.17 Improper first step.

Drive steps. Drive steps can be thought of simply as run steps. Obviously, we're looking for speed and efficiency with these steps. Hips should open to the movement direction to facilitate speed. During this phase, the player is driving his or her center in the desired direction. The arms should relax during these steps and work together as they would in a running motion. There's no longer a need for the player to keep hands high and parallel to the net because the quick set option has already passed.

The drive step phase should be kept simple. Sometimes people refer to drive steps as "crossover steps," but actually they are simply running in a lateral direction from where they originally faced. It confuses a player to think in terms of "right step–left step–cross over" and so on as they're moving. They should simply push and run to the desired direction. Drive steps and run steps should be made with the center remaining low. If the center arcs up and down as the steps are taken, time is lost.

Players should take as many fast drive steps as needed to get to their setup position for the block. This could mean meeting to close with an outside blocker. For an outside blocker, this could mean moving to a position that properly fronts the hitter. Some methods for helping players to feel this movement are described in the drills. For short distances, a player might need only one running step or drive step after the initial push step. In most cases, two steps are sufficient. Experiment with these running steps to determine how many are necessary. This varies from player to player, depending on strength and size.

Slant (or plant). With push and drive steps, the blocker runs to a specific setup point for the jump and the block. Just as with the approach on the spike, the player is running into a jumping position and posture. This important phase of stopping the feet in preparation to jump from a specific spot and with proper hand and arm posture (as described earlier) is called the "slant." This name is perfect because "slant" describes what needs to happen with the body posture and position.

During the slant (or plant), players are very low in preparation for a jump. The final drive step into the slant should keep a player's center low. Raising the center slows down the slant and reduces the player's ability to maximize his or her jump. The feet stop in a position parallel to or facing the net with the body slanted back toward the center of the court. This abruptly stops the movement so that the blocker can jump toward the center of the court as he or she reaches back toward center with the inside hand.

As the blocker hits the slant position, the elbow of the inside arm should be tucked in so that the arm can shoot back to the center, as described earlier in the chapter. The slant should include these important components:

- Contact of feet should be nearly simultaneous.
- Weight distribution on the feet is toward the inside of the court.
- The outside foot comes around to parallel position with the inside foot (which aligns the hips and upper body).
- The feet are past the blocker's core or center to stop movement and help him or her to reach back with the inside hand.
- The inside elbow is tucked in, with arms and hands in front on the way up.

If the blocker gets his or her center past the feet or the outside foot doesn't come around to parallel position, he or she will "drift" toward the outside of the court or into the outside blocker. This basic concept is a big problem at the fundamental levels of volleyball.

The slant by the feet and the reach back to center by the inside hand is critical for the outside blocker, as well as for the middle blocker. Drifting by the outside blocker opens the gap that the middle blocker worked so hard to close.

The other important feature for a good slant by the outside is that it puts both feet in position quickly. Some outside blockers tend to drag their inside leg as they move to the outside, which impedes the inside blocker from closing. A good drive step, even if it's short in distance, gets the inside foot out of the way and plants both feet quickly as a cue for the middle blocker.

ALTERNATIVE BLOCKING METHODS

What about players who are too short or don't possess the necessary jump to block with hands penetrating the net plane? In every case, a player's jumping height should be assessed when determining the best method to use on the block. In some cases, it might be an intelligent choice not to have a player block at all.

How high do blockers need to be able to jump? This depends on the opponent's ability. Take the time to analyze opponent attacks. Without taking exact measurements, this can easily be accomplished during an attack warm-up. You might be surprised to find that in many cases the ball doesn't clear the top of the net by much. It has been suggested that players sometimes jump too high or reach too high on the block. Actually, the latter may be partially true. Jumping high is a great asset if blockers know how to use their reach properly. An outstanding jump and reach permit a player to reach further over the plane of the net and sometimes even surround the ball with the hands before the hitter makes contact.

Swing Blocking

If players can't reach the height they need to block effectively, there are a few options. One advanced technique for achieving a higher block is referred to as "swing blocking." Simply put, this means using a full backswing or a modified backswing of the arms to gain additional height on the jump. While this might accomplish additional height for a blocker, it also causes some problems in stabilizing the hands and arms in a good position for the backcourt defenders to read. At more powerful levels of play, this might not be as important, simply because fewer balls are actually "diggable" because of their extreme power. When playing at a level at which the velocity of most attacks would permit a dig (especially a controlled dig), a more stable block is recommended.

Another factor determining whether a player wants to use the swing block is his or her vertical jump. The time and distance spent off the floor permits a great jumper to "right" one's arms in the air. A modified version of the swing block can be executed by drawing the elbows back and out and then forward and in with a circular motion. This motion enables a blocker to incorporate upper body assistance for the jump without as great a need for correcting in the air.

Soft Blocking or Deflection Blocking

Another option for a shorter player is to use a technique known as "soft blocking" or "deflection blocking." In a soft block, the blocker deflects the ball up rather than blocking it down. Because many attackers love to hit the ball down, the soft block can be effective and very frustrating for a taller attacker who finds trouble scoring against a much smaller blocker.

To execute a soft block, the blocker uses much of the same arm and hand "posture" as in a typical block but adjusts arm and hand position. The position of the hands and arms in the soft block is slightly distanced from the net, with no penetration of the net plane on hitter contact. The posture of the hands changes slightly, with palms facing slightly upward and toward the ceiling. The thumbs remain up and slightly pointed back, and the fingers are spread wide and stiff. The thrusting motion on hitter contact is employed, but in the soft block the thumbs extend and pull up instead of extending over the net plane (figure 5.18). The distance from the net will vary depending on the blocker, but generally about 12 inches (30 centimeters) or slightly less will do the trick. Should the attacker hit down, this distance can provide a greater opportunity for a deflection.

Figure 5.18 Soft block.

Blocking the Quick Set

The "base position" for blocking the quick attack is different from that employed against higher sets. Because the quick set is hit directly from the setter's hands, there's very little time for movement or adjustments. The quick-tempo attack can be stopped by the blocker only if the hands are in front of the ball very quickly. Most often—but not always—the quick set is executed somewhere in the middle of the net in an attempt to freeze a middle blocker from getting outside. For this reason, many coaches put their tallest reaching blocker in front of the quick attack. A shorter blocker who jumps very high might reach the point of contact, but the time needed for the jump might cause him or her to be too late and take more time to land and recover for an outside move.

Blockers can gain an advantage against the quick attack by using the coiled posture, as described earlier. Holding the hands high and just above the face is also very important. The time in which it takes the hands to get to the point of contact is critical, and this greatly reduces that time. If the blocker identifies the quick attack and lowers the hands in anticipation of a jump or to incorporate the arms in the jump, it takes too much time to get the hands in front of the ball. Fortunately, compared to most high sets, the quick attack is often contacted fairly low to the net. In addition, most teams set this ball a little tightly to the net. These factors help a good blocker get to the stopping point more readily. Learning to hold the coiled posture while fronting the quick attackers in base position is a challenging skill to learn. Much patience is required in this learning process. Remember that blockers are watching the setter at this point and see the quick attacker from the peripheral. As they watch the setter with this proper posture, they can wait until they actually see the quick attack before jumping. This is sometimes referred to as "read blocking" because the blocker is waiting to identify the set.

Jousting

For balls extremely tight to the net or even part way over the plane of the net, the ball often becomes "trapped" between the blocker and attackers' hands. This is known as a joust and requires some training for success. Usually, in a joust, the player who gives the second push or last push on the ball wins. However, there's a little trick to the second push. Even the strongest person can be deflected if he or she is pushed off the line of force instead of directly into it. When your players are jousting at the net, teach them to trap the ball with some force into the opponent on the first push, then have them push over and to the side (either right or left, whichever is convenient) on the second push. You'll want to practice this technique with your middle blockers against your front-row setters because these are the players who are most often involved in jousts.

BLOCKING DRILLS

Visual Response

Purpose: To practice blockers' visual sequence of glancing at the pass, watching the setter, glancing at the set, and watching the hitter

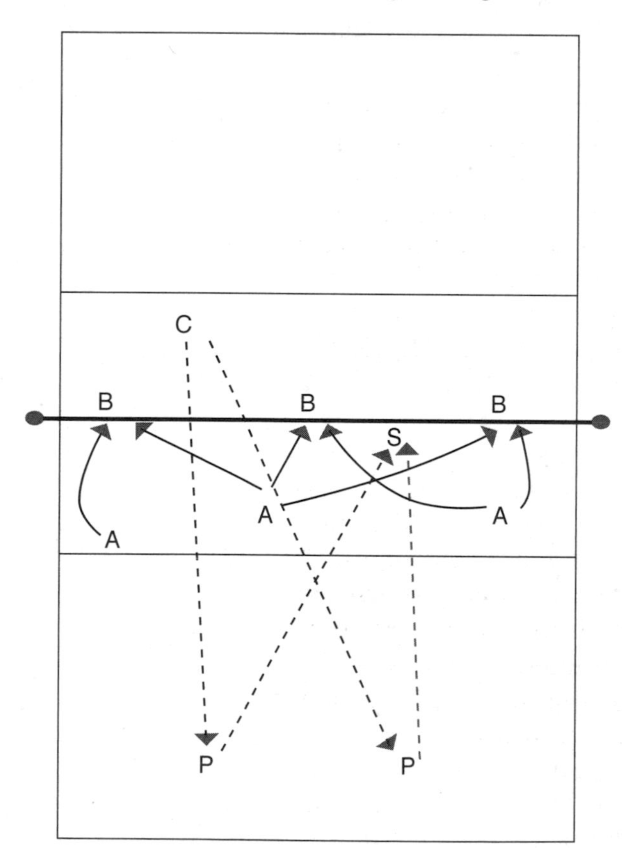

Figure 5.19 Visual Response.

Setup: Blockers line up in position opposite the net from a setter and passer(s). Coaches serve controlled balls to the passers from behind the blockers. Attackers or simulated attackers catch the ball from the setter (figure 5.19).

Execution: A ball is served from behind the blockers to a designated passer on the other side of the net. The setter sets the ball to the simulated attackers, who can line up in any of the attack zones. As the setter sets the ball, the blockers use the proper footwork to either set up the block if it comes to their zone or pull off the net on defense if it goes to the opposite zone. Blockers practice the proper visual sequence:

1. Glance at the pass to determine if it is an overpass or if the middle is no longer an option.
2. Watch the setter to determine direction of the set in order to get a good first step. This is especially important for the middle blocker, who will be involved either way.
3. Glance at the set to determine the setup point for the block. Blockers watch for the depth and location of the set to determine where to set up.
4. Watch the hitter for cues on timing and direction of attack. Blockers wait to jump after the attacker jumps.

Coaching Points: The blockers' visual responses are practiced in conjunction with foot reacting, proper setup, and blocking technique. This drill might be conducted as a warm-up activity before practice.

Variations

1. Attackers simulate different plays. A quick attacker moves to different zones, or crossing patterns are simulated. Assignments for who will help with different situations are discussed in advance as part of the blocking strategy.
2. Passers are instructed to occasionally pass the ball over the net to keep blockers alert for overpasses.
3. Instead of catching the ball, coaches or players attack into the block. (This is to be conducted after the warm-up).
4. Instead of catching the ball, coaches or players tip the ball over the block for the "off blocker" to play on defense.

Coil and Reaction: Three Directions

Purpose: To enable blockers to hold a dynamic position and respond quickly to different situations

Setup: Opposite a single blocker, line up three attackers and a setter. A coach tosses the ball into play. One attacker hits a quick set directly in front of the setter. Another attacker hits a higher set several feet in front of the setter. The remaining attacker hits a higher set several feet behind the setter (figure 5.20).

Execution: All attackers are prepared simultaneously; the setter chooses which set to make as the coach tosses him or her the ball. The blocker must hold his or her coil, watch the setter, front the quick attacker, and respond appropriately to whichever set occurs. Emphasis is placed on proper posture for blocking the quick attack and, if the set is delivered to one of the other hitters, a good first step. As the blocker's reactions become efficient, increase the distance between the two outside sets. Crossing patterns may also be employed to train the blocker to recognize different situations.

Variation: If this activity is too advanced for your players, blockers can begin with a two-direction drill. This can be done with a quick attack and a single hitter in either direction. Or the quick hitter may be eliminated and attackers placed on either side of the setter.

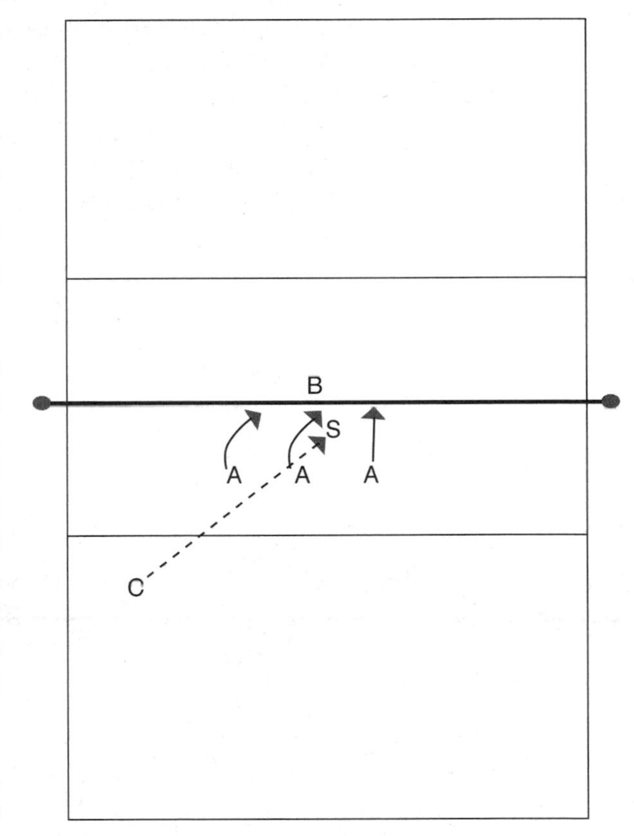

Figure 5.20 Coil and Reaction.

Block–Counterattack

Purpose: To train players to block the opponents' serve-receive offense and, when unsuccessful, to transition off the net for offense

Setup: It's very important to train blocking with the distraction of transition offense. Serve-receive patterns are set up on one side of the court, opposite three blockers and a back-row setter (or one of the blockers can be the transition setter).

Execution: The serve-receive team is served, and the blockers attempt to stuff-block the opposing attackers. If the block is successful, blockers remain at the net, and another serve is immediately introduced. If the ball is attacked by the block, the coach immediately tosses a transition pass to the setter. This simulates a very fast dig and transition requirement for the blockers. The attackers on the other side attempt to block the counterattack of the blockers, but without digging so that the drill can be controlled (figure 5.21).

To provide goals for each blocking group, points may be scored. Two points are awarded for a stuff block. One point is awarded for a successful counterattack kill. If the block creates a deflection, resulting in a "free-ball" and then gets a kill from the counterattack, two points may also be rewarded. However, if the deflection doesn't result in a successful counterattack, no points are scored. This promotes finishing the point. Ten points per blocking group is a suggested starting goal, before a new blocking group comes in.

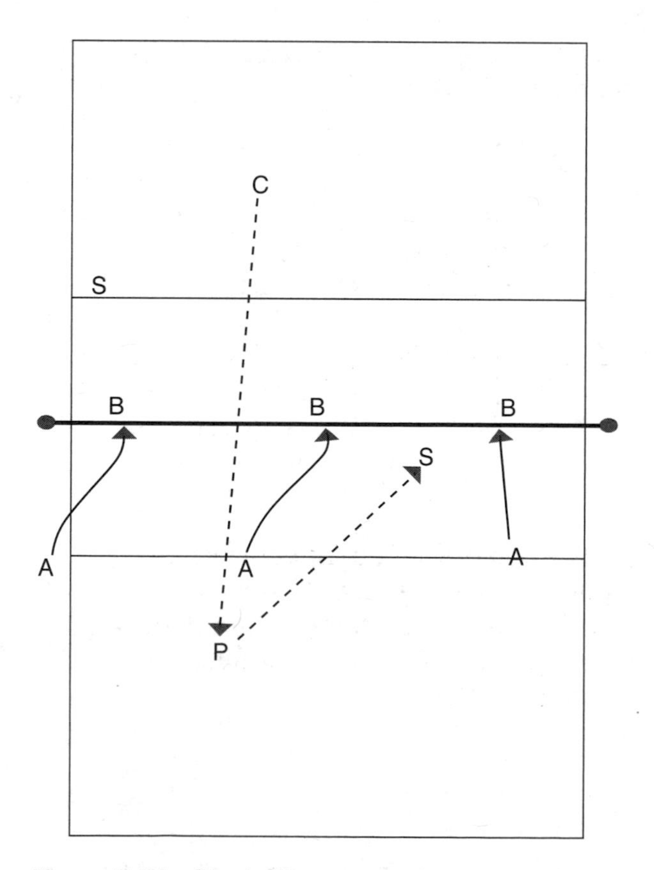

Figure 5.21 Block–Counterattack.

Quick Recognition of Offense

Purpose: To enable frontcourt players to immediately recognize and react to offensive patterns of the opponent

Setup: Assign a blocking team with a setter for transition attack. On the opposite side of the net, line up a team of hitters and a setter who are secretly assigned a sequence of offensive plays.

Execution: Begin with three to four offensive plays and work up to six. Some of the plays may be repetitive, but the idea is to force a mix of situations for the opposing blockers. Toss the first ball for the offensive sequence (figure 5.22). If the ball goes by the block, blockers will pull off of the net for transition attack. A coach on that side tosses a ball to the setter for the attack. The offensive team on the other side lets the ball go, and another ball is immediately tossed to their setter for the next offensive sequence. This continues for the entire set of three to six attempts.

Coaching Points: Be sure to mix in some overpasses to keep players alert. Toss bad passes to the opposing setter so that the blockers can identify and react to out-of-system situations, including free balls.

Variation: This drill might be run in conjunction with a sideout or serve-receive drill so that players learn to attack the ball out of serve receive, make their switches at the net, and immediately recognize the position of the opposing attackers.

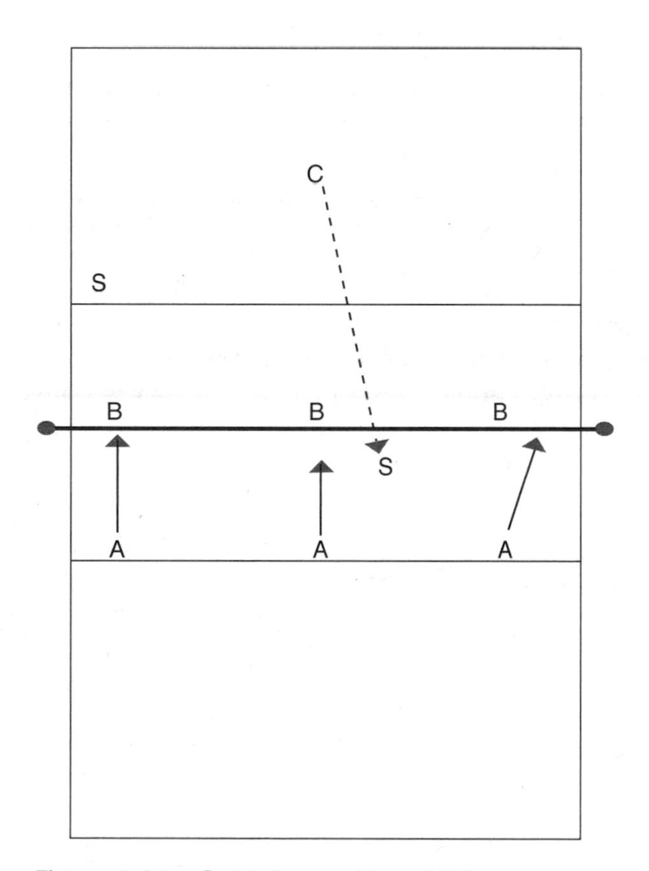

Figure 5.22 Quick Recognition of Offense.

Blocking Progression to Enhance Timing and Hand Position

Purpose: To assist blockers in feeling proper hand position and timing against the attack

Setup: Coaches or attackers stand on a platform to attack balls into the blocker.

Execution: Coaches practice the following sequence to help blockers feel their proper hand position on hitter contact.

Step 1: On a platform, a coach tosses a ball to him- or herself and hits it into one of the blocker's hands as the blocker jumps to block the attack. The blocker glances at the toss and times the jump to block the attack. Proper hand position is reinforced.

Step 2: The ball is tossed higher, and the blocker moves from a base position to the proper setup position before jumping to block. Movement prior to the jump often causes problems for the blocker. Proper hand position must be reinforced with this movement requirement.

Step 3: The ball is tossed or set to the coach on the box. Blockers learn to glance at the set and move from base to read position, moving their hands and arms into optimal blocking position. Keep the toss a short distance from the coach to ensure accuracy.

Step 4: Finally, the ball is tossed or set to a line (ideally three) of attackers, who hit into a blocker for about six repetitions.

Coaching Points: Players may help each other by watching what happens with their teammates' hands on contact by the attacker. Players provide teaching cues to one another as they learn not to "twitch" or "bat" at the ball on hitter contact. Hands may also be videotaped for immediate review. Blockers learn to glance at the set, make foot adjustments, and focus on attacker.

Variation: For players who have trouble taking their eyes off the ball in order to watch the attacker, steps 3 and 4 can be conducted with the toss or set coming from the other side of the court and behind the blocker. The toss is coming over the net for the coach or the attacker. This requires blockers to focus only on the attacker and adjust their feet and timing accordingly.

Queen of the Net

Purpose: To create competitive blocking and incorporate transition attack

Setup: Three blockers line up at the net opposite another team of three blockers. A setter comes from the back row on both sides of the net (figure 5.23).

Execution: A coach tosses balls to the setter on each side of the net. Play begins with a toss to the setter on either side. As the ball is tossed, blockers transition back from the net and attack the ball into the opposite court. The side of the net the ball lands on dictates the next toss. If side A attacks the ball and it lands on the side of B, then the coach for the B team tosses a transition pass to the B team setter. If side A attacks the ball and it is blocked back into the court of team A, then the coach on team A tosses the next ball. Even if the ball is attacked or deflected out of bounds, whatever side the ball lands on becomes the next attacking team. Games can be played to a set number of points. Start out playing to 10 points per game. Points are awarded as follows for each team:

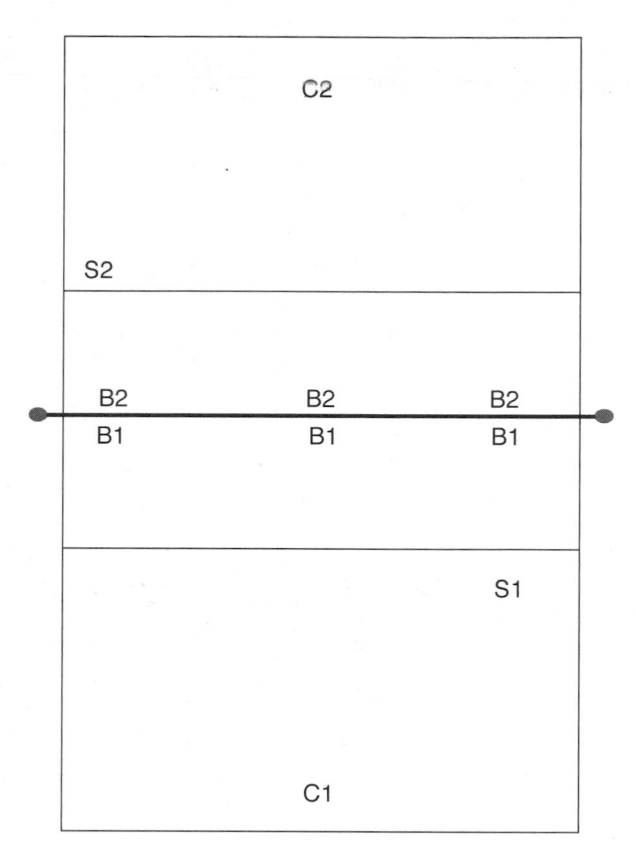

Figure 5.23 Queen of the Net.

Stuff blocks = 2 points
Kills = 1 point
Attack errors = subtract one point
Net violations = subtract one point
Tips, roll shots, or deflected balls = wash (no points)

A coach on each side of the net keeps track out loud as his or her team scores points. Begin this game very slowly in between points to minimize confusion. Pick up speed as coaches and players become familiar with the drill and its scoring. Once coaches understand which setter to toss, this is an excellent drill for competitive blocking and transition. The winning team may stay on the court and be challenged by new teams.

Coaching Points: Setters may also block, creating a "two-hitter" situation. Encourage players to be creative with their offensive calls to confuse the opposing block.

CONCLUSION

Always remember that safety comes first as you teach these blocking techniques. All players must watch their feet for problem landings. Blocking is an aggressive skill that is strengthened when the blocker is more confident. In today's game, the best blockers are not necessarily the highest jumpers or the tallest players. The best blockers must have great vision, anticipation, and intensity, which can be developed only through practice.

6

Digging

Joan Powell

Courtesy of FIVB

Defense is an attitude that begins with the coach. This is the transcending attitude throughout practice and into competition. Not all teams are blessed with or are guaranteed to have a big, domineering offensive team year after year. Coaches are continually reminded in clinics and books to showcase their strengths and hide their weaknesses. Tenacity can be any team's strength, unless the team possesses an overriding lethargic attitude and is uninterested in a productive work ethic. The coaches' expectations, along with their levels of involvement and motivation, are key. A passion to perform is contagious and will spread among the players.

If a coach sets the bar and states that defense is an important ingredient for the team's success—and then follows up in practice—the team will begin to take on a defensive attitude. Then, if players agree collectively and buy into the process, a defensive attitude becomes second nature. Practices must provide the venue in which players are continually being challenged, are willing to step out of their comfort zones, and are willing to push their teammates to become better. Coaches need to provide this well-balanced environment and cushion it with some fun. Players should look forward to and relish the time to practice defense. As players begin to reap the benefits of their labor at practice, the coach must reinforce those efforts during actual competition and again during the practices that follow.

DIGGING TECHNIQUE

Teams that "dig everything" frustrate their opponents by keeping the ball in play and by consistently defending what normally goes down for a point. Successful defenders not only dig but also control the ball better than their opponents. The ball is controlled and returned at such a high rate that opponents often make errors caused by their own frustration. These successful defensive teams don't panic when they play the game predominantly "out of system." (Being "in system" means that the pass or dig is perfect and the setter has the maximum number of offensive options to pursue.) Although being "out of system" is never the desired norm, a great dig—although not necessarily to the setter—is still a fantastic play, which may be followed by scrambling or an offensive opportunity with a controlled attack. Patience is the key here; many times it's better to hit the ball smart than to hit the ball hard. In any case, the idea that the ball is kept alive is critical. If the dig is under control, the defense has just given the offense another chance to reload. A great dig can also spark a change in momentum.

Volleyball is a contest of momentum. More to the point, though, it's a simple rebound game in which the object is to keep the ball from hitting your side of the floor. For success in the game, players need to know how to protect their floor. With this in mind, coaches need to make the floor a friendly and safe place to land, fall, roll, sprawl, collapse, or dive. Coaches are responsible for teaching sound techniques but also for allowing players to experiment freely. Although performing a defensive skill with correct technique is preferred, situations occur when time doesn't allow for the preferred technique—only reaction. Reactive skills can be unique and replicate odd form, but they should be welcomed if the result is safe and successful. There are reactive movements in self-defense or last-ditch efforts not taught in practice but rather are learned in the "line of fire," and such moves, when successful, should be applauded. Such moves might not follow the textbook or look very pretty, but when a player makes a great move with relentless pursuit, the move can inspire further exciting efforts and bring the spectators back for more.

On today's volleyball court, the shorter players are no longer relinquished to the back row as a specialist or a libero. Rather, today's defensive players are fearless hustlers, determined and feisty. They have a "nothing falls" attitude.

Although a coach might have assigned players to serve in a defensive role, all players must learn the fundamental techniques associated with digging and floor defense. Having all team members involved in defensive drills is important for team morale, and there's a practical side as well. Defense is not just played in the back-row positions; front-row players are engaged defensively and need to acquire the necessary tools to protect their territory. There are limitations to the substitution rule, and in a long game in which the coach has reached the maximum number of subs, the players who normally are replaced by the better defensive specialists must stay in the game and play defense. For players to attain the defensive skills necessary to become good or even great defenders, they must master some fundamental concepts.

Ready-Position Posture

When the opposing team begins its offense, defenders are in "base" position. Base is the position assigned to each back-row player (right, left, or middle back) and constitutes a ready position in which a player is anticipating the opponent's attack. If the opponent's setter is in the front row or the opponents use a quick attack, the back-row players' base positions should be on or in front of the attack line. As an opposing attacker reaches the height of his or her jump, the digger might have to shuffle to a better spot after reading the attacker and his or her own blocker(s) to prepare to dig by lowering his or her body into a stable ready position (figure 6.1).

To establish a base position, a player needs to be balanced with feet shoulder-width apart. Body weight is on the balls of the feet in a low, stable position. Arms should be bent at the elbows in front of the body, ready to dig overhead or underhand. The hands are relaxed and unclasped. Eyes are focused on the attacker. Attackers

Figure 6.1 Ready-position posture.

sometimes telegraph their shots by their positioning or their technique. When a digger can recognize these hints, he or she is "reading the attack." For instance, the attacker's shoulders might assist the digger in determining the best positioning from which to dig the attack. The digger might be able to read the attacker and the type of shot to be hit and anticipate his or her move before contact or shortly after the shot is made. The defender must also be alert to his or her blockers' positions as they front the attacker. Blocks that don't close cause a hole in the front line of the defense, forcing the digger to cover that gap.

Coaching Points for Maintaining Proper Ready-Position Posture

- Feet are shoulder-width apart and stable.
- Weight is on the balls of the feet.
- Arms are bent at the elbows in front of the body.
- Hands are relaxed, not clasped together.
- Eyes focus on the attacker.
- Observe the attacker's approach and shoulders.
- Read teammates' blockers and their positions.

Movement to the Ball

Depending on the type of attack, the digger must decide whether movement is necessary and what type of reception is needed to dig. The velocity of the ball dictates how much the digger needs to absorb the ball or provide impetus to the ball. The harder the attack, the more the digger needs to cushion the ball. If the attacked ball is a slow impact ball, the digger might need to add impetus by lifting the legs or raising the arms slightly to add to the desired flight. Ideally, a defender wants to take the ball low at the midline with contact made under the ball.

Coaching Points for Efficient Movement to the Ball

- Move quickly to the ball.
- Remain on feet as long as possible.
- Position the body to take the hit directly.
- Take the ball low and from the midline.
- Contact is made under the ball.
- The more the velocity, the more the give (rebound or cushion).
- With less velocity, provide movement with the arms and legs, as in the serve receive.

Players need to be trained to stay on their feet as long as they can before and during a dig. Running through the ball, bending the elbows to get the proper angle of deflection, and turning the thumbs in an upward motion (J stroke) to ensure the ball remains on the digger's side of the net requires considerable practice (figure 6.2).

Figure 6.2 J-Stroke.

THE FOREARM DIG

If the ball is hit low with velocity, the digger needs to use his or her forearms to cushion the contact and allow the ball to be absorbed (figure 6.3). (All rule codes disallow the ball to come to rest, resulting in an infraction whistled by the official; thus, too much cushion can cause an illegal contact.) Ideally, in digging a hard-driven ball, a player wants to allow the ball to rebound from the platform in such a way that it remains on the digger's side of the net and the setter can position himself or herself near the net, allowing him or her to set more than one attacker. If a ball is coming toward the digger in a servelike fashion, the digger would choose to use the forearms to pass the ball, as he or she would do in receiving a serve (figure 6.4). Also, it would be disadvantageous to dig a ball so low that the back-row setter has insufficient time to meet the ball and make a decent attempt to set a hitter. (In practice coaches should always provide a "target," whether it's another player, a cone, or a hula-hoop, so that players are trained to dig to the desired area of the court.)

Figure 6.3 Digger cushions the ball by allowing the forearms to absorb the ball on contact.

Figure 6.4 Server uses forearms to pass the ball.

Figure 6.5 One-arm dig.

Ideally, the same forearm pass used to receive serve should be the first priority when digging a ball. But there are times when a defender simply can't bring his or her hands together to perform the proper forearm pass technique. Because of this lack of preparation time, players are often lucky to get the heels of their hands together. A one-arm dig is certainly not a conventional or desired technique, but it might be the best or only method to use under such circumstances as a last-minute deflection off a blocker or an unexpected contact from another digger. A quick change of direction by the digger leaves only one alternative (figure 6.5).

Difficult attacks from the opponent might be directed outside the midline of the digger's body. Coaches should encourage players to continue their efforts with two arms outside their midline, followed by an adjustment. The furthest foot from the ball should pivot slightly to align the shoulder to the desired target.

A ball that doesn't provide much velocity, such as a roll shot, a tip, an off-speed shot, a deflection off the block, or even a missed hit—which slows the attack down—should be pursued with two arms when possible. Quickness and agility are two important attributes for a digger to possess. The topspin from the opponent's hit—or the fact that a slower attack was delivered—actually forces the digger to react quickly and shuffle his or her feet or even run to the ball to retrieve it. This is precisely why it's so important for diggers to be on the balls of their feet, prepared to move in any direction.

Coaching Points for the Forearm Dig

- Use the forearms to cushion contact for an easy dig.
- Dig a hard-driven ball by allowing it to rebound from the platform.
- When possible, use the same forearm pass to dig as to receive serve.
- Dig the balls high to the setter.

Common Mistakes

- Inexperienced or overzealous players have a tendency to add impetus by swinging their arms or standing up on contact, causing too much of a rebound effect. Players need to feel the difference between playing the ball and the ball playing them.
- Depending on the team's offensive pattern, if the setter is coming from the back row, the digger doesn't want to dig a ball that jams the setter into the net.
- Some coaches do a disservice to players by continually training them to dig balls directly hit at them instead of challenging them with a variety of shots.

DEFENSIVE FLOOR MOVES

There are times during practice and competition when the ideal forearm dig is impossible to execute. Players need to be exposed to a variety of alternative floor moves. By practicing many options, players become more comfortable going to the floor and over time learn to execute the most efficient moves to save a variety of shots. In a game, diggers make an effort to retrieve every ball, focusing on making it playable, so in practice they need to see all kinds of shots coming at them. The more they see, the better they'll get.

The Collapse

When staying on one's feet is virtually impossible for a digger, some techniques are handy for a player to have in his or her repertoire. The collapse is one such technique. The player might choose to cushion the ball in a manner that causes him or her to sit down on either side and rock backward. Sometimes the digger anticipates a certain type of ball coming at him or her, but it "dies," and the only move the digger has is to collapse forward. In this case, the digger is in a low posture and simply collapses to the floor on his or her kneepads and extends both arms forward to get under the ball. The body follows in a sprawling fashion (figure 6.6).

Figure 6.6 The collapse.

The Sprawl

When a defender anticipates that a ball is falling short in front of him or her, he or she lunges toward the area in which the ball will land. The sprawl is comparable to the collapse, except that there's enough time to take a large step toward the ball, extend one hand, and attempt to get under the ball (figure 6.7). Contact is made on the back of the hand. Timing is of utmost importance. Often the defender sprawls and makes contact, but the ball gets very little trajectory and ends up going under the net.

Figure 6.7 The sprawl.

Figure 6.8 The dive.

Figure 6.9 The pancake.

The Dive

The dive is similar to the sprawl and the collapse, but here the player is actually airborne before contacting the ball. Players must have sufficient upper body strength to accept their body weight as they return to the floor. Without proper strength, the chin is often the body part that absorbs the weight, which can have obvious negative consequences. Only players with upper body strength should execute the dive (figure 6.8).

The Pancake

A player might choose to employ a pancake maneuver to retrieve a slower ball. Some coaches view the pancake as a last-ditch effort to be used when a player can't play the ball any other way. Other coaches accept the technique as a viable option. The pancake is similar to the sprawl except that the fingers are spread firmly and placed on the floor early. The hand provides a surface for the ball to rebound from rather than off the floor. The opposite hand serves as a buffer, helping to lower the body to the ground (figure 6.9). The pancake, if executed correctly, gets a good bounce. One drawback is that referees often have difficulty seeing the contact and determining whether it was all hand or floor—or part of both. Players and coaches get frustrated when a ball is whistled down after a player makes a legitimate save using the pancake. By the same token, however, there are times when an unsuccessful pancake is followed by a silent whistle, even though the ball has hit the floor. In general, players should be encouraged to stay on their feet as long as possible to dig. Still, the pancake—like the collapse, sprawl, and dive—is an emergency method that works for many diggers.

Shoulder Roll and Barrel Roll

Shoulder (figure 6.10, a-d) and barrel rolls (figure 6.11) are used following a defender's extension right, left, or forward in an attempt to play a ball close to the floor. The body is almost prone in a reaching posture to retrieve the ball; after contact, the body's momentum is dissipated by rolling over, and then the player regains balance and takes a proper ready position. By extending to the right, left, or forward, a player can cover more court and thus reach more balls. Rolling after making a defensive move helps reduce the chance of injury and also facilitates a quicker recovery so the athlete can get back on his or her feet. When using the extension or shoulder roll, the player moves toward the ball and drives the lead knee forward (figure 6.10a). He or she attempts to play the ball with both hands while both feet are in contact with the floor. Then he or she pushes off with the legs and cushions the sideways fall to the floor. When both hands can't be used, the player extends just one arm to the side of the ball, and it's as if he or she has a magic wand—he or she can extend further with the single arm than with both arms. The knee of the extended leg is bent and turns inward, eliminating contact between the kneecap and the floor. As the digger touches the ball, his or her weight moves over and past the front, extended foot. He or she flicks the wrist in an attempt to lift the ball up. (In practice, coaches must train their players' right and left hands. If players are right-hand dominant, when they attempt to save a ball to their left, they might end up making an errant dig and recover by facing the wrong direction. This is particularly evident on the left sideline of the court.)

After contact, the player's hand slides along the floor as the body eases to the ground (figure 6.10b). The head actually rests on the extended arm, and the chin is tucked. The opposite leg goes over that shoulder (figure 6.10c). After the roll is completed, the player uses his or her opposite hand for support in returning to his or her feet (figure 6.10d).

Figure 6.10a Player lunges toward the ball.

Figure 6.10b Player's hand slides along the floor as the body eases to the ground.

Figure 6.10c Player rolls to soften landing.

Figure 6.10d Player returns to ready position.

Figure 6.11 Barrel roll.

For the novice, it takes many repetitions to learn to pursue the ball and smoothly and sequentially perform the roll as designed. At first, the beginning player might be too concerned about the mechanics of the roll and forget to make contact with the ball. Coaches might have to manipulate the opposite leg over the shoulder to give the player the feel for the sequence. When players perform the roll slowly, they can get stuck and flop over, unsure of which way they're facing. The key is to get the body as low as possible, then extend and reach out (figure 6.11). With practice, players will roll automatically.

The barrel roll is very similar to the shoulder roll. This defensive move became more popular as a safer and quicker means of recovery. The player makes the same moves as in the extension roll by lunging toward the ball. After contact, the leg with the bent knee (on the same side as the ball) leads the body into a more compact roll. The bent knee forces the body to roll over, and the toes of that foot support the player back onto his or her feet. The head is less likely to hit the floor in the barrel roll. The barrel roll is a good roll to teach beginners.

Overhead Pass and Beach Dig

Figure 6.12 Overhead pass.

Sometimes a ball is coming toward a digger too high for the defender to play with the forearms. Now that all rule codes allow multiple hits on the first team contact, players are able to use overhead skills more freely. Since the rule has been relaxed, there have been many more saves and longer rallies—which, of course, was the reason for the rule change (figure 6.12). See chapter 2 for more information on the overhead pass.

The same techniques as the forearm dig can apply when digging a ball overhead; however, caution should be taken because of the velocity of the attack. Hard-driven balls taken with the fingers can result in injury when fingers are jammed or extended back too far. Players need to experiment with taking balls overhead.

When balls are hit too hard to use an overhead pass, players might choose a safer means, known as the "beach dig." In the beach dig, the hands are formed a bit differently than usual. Proper defensive posture, in which the elbows are bent and in front of the body, allows a player to make a split-second decision to dig underhand or overhead (figure 6.13). When the decision has been made to go overhead, the player lifts the opened, cupped hands in front of his or her face. Some coaches advocate the thumbs being overlapped in front of the face as the player looks at the back of the hands, providing a wide contact area, whereas others prefer one hand cupped in the other with contact made on the outsides of the hands. Regardless which technique is used, control is the key. The player must not add force to the ball; rather, he or she provides a surface from which the ball can rebound.

Figure 6.13 Beach dig.

Juggling

Sometimes volleyball players have no other choice but to stick a fist in the air to keep a ball alive. Juggling refers to a player using a fist to punch the ball into the air to continue play. Juggling can be an underhand action or an overhead action (figure 6.14). For example, when a blocker attempts to block, but the ball remains in the air, close to the net on one's own side, and the blocker doesn't have time or space to pass the ball, he or she might use a fist to pop the ball up to a teammate. There are also plays in which bodies are on the court, and the only way to keep the ball from hitting the floor is to use a one-handed poke. (High school rules allow legal contact above the waist; all other rule codes allow legal contact anywhere on the body—that is, the ball can even be kicked.)

INFORMATION NEEDED BEFORE TRAINING DEFENSE

There are many ways to defend the court and several techniques to use in myriad situations. It's imperative that coaches fill their players' arsenals with as many options as possible to keep the ball from hitting the floor, provide repetitious opportunities to experiment and improve, teach the proper means to keep their players safe, and continue to make the game exciting for everyone. If a coach accepts this responsibility and embraces the philosophy that defense is an attitude, his or her program will foster a proud and rich tradition and a distinguished reputation that will help cultivate younger players to embrace the attitude.

Figure 6.14 Juggling.

As mentioned at the beginning of the chapter, the coach has an obligation from day one to set the stage. Before attempting any of the defensive drills, there must be an underlying charge established to which all players commit. One such mission is the "Relentless Pursuit Policy," which is as follows: "For every ball that goes to the floor, there needs to be a body or bodies accompanying it." No ball goes uncontested or there will be a team consequence. Team consequences might be floor moves such as barrel rolls—three to the right, three to the left. Sit-ups and push-ups are also common team consequences. Encourage players to reaffirm their commitment by initiating the team consequences, with no word from the coach, if a ball falls without a sincere effort to save it. Bill Neville, successful international and collegiate coach, author, and one of the most outstanding volleyball clinicians in the world today, says, "[There must be] a total commitment to the fact that every ball is playable until proven otherwise after a sincere, maximum effort fails. No value judgments whether a ball is unplayable during play are tolerated. As long as the ball is in the air, it is assumed playable and the players react accordingly." Every ball is an opportunity to get better. Players should not permit themselves to give up or become spectators. Instill in your players the idea that when one player pursues, a teammate follows and communicates.

Nothing is more disconcerting for a player than making a great effort, only to find that no one is "on help" to make the play over the net or that the effort is late and half-hearted. Mike Hebert, PhD, head women's coach at the University of Minnesota, explains his pursuit rule this way: "A player may stop pursuing the ball only if the ball strikes the floor or an out-of-bounds object, such as a standard, antenna, wall, or ceiling; continued pursuit of the ball would risk injury; the referee's whistle stops play; or a teammate clearly calls, 'mine.'"

Philosophical differences that surround the training of volleyball players revolve around the two different methodologies that coaches choose: random versus block. Those advocating random training prefer that skills be taught while playing the ball over the net in gamelike situations. In block training, a specific skill is trained in a repetitive manner. To train defense, both methodologies are needed. Some techniques call for an abundance of repetitious opportunities so that players get a feel for the number of ways the ball can be directed and rebounded. According to past Olympian Laurel Brassey Iversen (1980 and 1988), "For every ball I dug in a game, I have dug a hundred in practice." Regardless of your philosophy, it's crucial that defensive footwork and technique be demonstrated and taught with cues.

DIGGING DRILLS

The following drills are a combination of footwork and agility drills and individual, partner, and team drills that help develop defensive-minded players.

Footwork and Agility

Purpose: To increase agility, coordination, and speed

Setup: The team lines up behind the endline. No equipment is necessary. (Footwork and agility can be practiced daily with jump ropes, agility ladders, cones, or sequential floor patterns.)

Execution: When the coach says "go!" players run to the attack line, shoulder to the net, and do 10 ski hops over the attack line. They immediately go under the net to the opposing attack line and do 10 jumping jacks without arms. They then run to the endline and do quick steps over the line in groups of three: right, left, right, over the line with left, right, left, repeated 10 times. They then return to the attack line and do forward and backward steps 10 times (right foot forward, left foot back, bring the feet together, left foot forward, right foot back, bring feet together, and repeat). Finally, players return to the first attack line and do crossover steps 10 times before sprinting to the endline.

Coaching Points: Ensure that players are executing correct technique and that they're not miscounting. You might choose to repeat the exercise if players don't follow directions.

Variation: You can use this drill as a warm-up or as a relay race. (Sometimes form is sacrificed when competition is added.)

Juggling

Purpose: To improve ball control

Setup: You'll need one ball per player.

Execution: Each player juggles a ball from one hand to the other 25 times in an underhand fisted motion, followed by 25 fisted juggles at head level.

Coaching Points: Do this drill every day after warm-ups before the first water break.

Variation: Depending on the rule code for your team—add foot, knee, shoulders, and head juggling.

Rolling With Socks

Purpose: To encourage safety and build confidence

Setup: Players bring extra pairs of long socks and put them on their hands and forearms.

Execution: When you're first teaching floor moves, the socks allow players to slide and feel safe from floor burns. Demonstration is followed by practice. For the barrel roll, you might say, "Ready position! To the right! Step! Lunge! Dig! Roll!" Then have them repeat to the left.

Coaching Points: Ask experienced players to be role models. They are in front of the others and facing the same direction so that new learners can mirror the veteran leaders.

Variation: Have players partner up. One partner rolls the ball to the right of his or her partner. The partner must step, lunge, lift the ball with the wand hand, and roll. Repeat to the left and center. By rolling the ball at first, you take away the timing of when to contact and when to roll. Advance to a tossed ball and eventually remove the socks.

Base Roll Series

Purpose: To practice the barrel roll with commands to better understand posture and sequential actions better

Setup: Three players are on a half-court in their assigned defensive positions (right back, center back, and left back), with no ball. (The remainder of the players are in groups of three in waves, behind the endline and ready to go.)

Execution: The center back communicates the commands. "Base, retreat, roll right. Base, retreat, roll left. Base, retreat, roll middle." That group then goes to the end of the line, and the next wave of three enters the court; the center back starts the group.

Coaching Points: Reinforce proper technique. Remind players that this is not a race.

Variation: Add other floor moves (e.g., collapse, sprawl) or add partners with balls.

Partner Series

Purpose: To encourage ball control

Setup: Players pair up, each pair with a ball.

Execution: One partner is on the attack line, and the other is inside the endline. Balls always start with the player with his or her back to the net. The ball is tossed, and partners pass 25 each, followed by setting, followed by passing to self and setting to partner, then setting to self and setting to partner, setting to self and hitting at partner, and adding jump sets and back sets. Then have players hit balls at their partners, who will dig. Then assign a number and switch. Add the collapse—five attempts and switch, followed by four barrel rolls, two to the right and then two to the left. Add the overhead pass and the beach dig. Have players challenge their partners by giving them a series of tough balls, such as hard hits right and left, interspersing tips and off-speed shots.

Coaching Points: There are no limits here. Whatever skills need additional practice and attention can be drilled. Some players tend to attach themselves to the same friends, so change partners periodically. Add variety. For novice players, hitting may be disastrous at first. Partners can throw the ball at each other (using two-handed, overhead, and one-handed throws) until they gain control hitting. Give instructions on the number of contacts before switching partners and switching skills.

Pepper With a Digging Emphasis

Purpose: To promote good ball control; to practice floor moves

Setup: Players pair up, each pair with a ball.

Execution: Players are about 13 feet (4 meters) apart. Player A starts with a toss. Player B passes. Player A sets, followed by a spike from player B. Play continues using all the players' digging techniques.

Coaching Points: If a ball is errant, both partners chase it.

Variation: Time the drill and rotate players so that each player gets a variety of partners. You can do this many times. Add competition by starting everyone at the same time to see which group can keep the ball alive the longest. Players can vary their shots (tips, off speed, roll shots, and so on) to provide a variety of opportunities for digging.

Repetitive Digging

Purpose: To encourage communication among players, as well as proper movement

Setup: Position two or three players in right back and two or three players in left back. Coaches are in right front and left front. Each coach has a cart of balls and a player to hand balls. All other players are shagging.

Execution: Each coach hits a variety of shots at the players cross court from him or her. The player gets into ready position; if he or she digs the ball successfully, that player moves off the court behind his or her teammates and the next player steps onto the court. The coach determines the number of successful attempts before the players are out of the drill. The next three players then replace the first group. Repeat (figure 6.15).

Coaching Points: Ensure that players are entering the court with proper defensive posture. Encourage players to cheer for their teammates. Reinforce great moves and digs.

Variation: Players can run the drills as well. Coaches and players should hit at all positions on the court. Using one coach, have players positioned at left front and left back. Balls can be hit at both or in between the defenders. Communication and movement are key.

Coaches and players should hit from a box on the other side of the net. Also, coaches could add blockers and three defenders to make the drill as gamelike as possible.

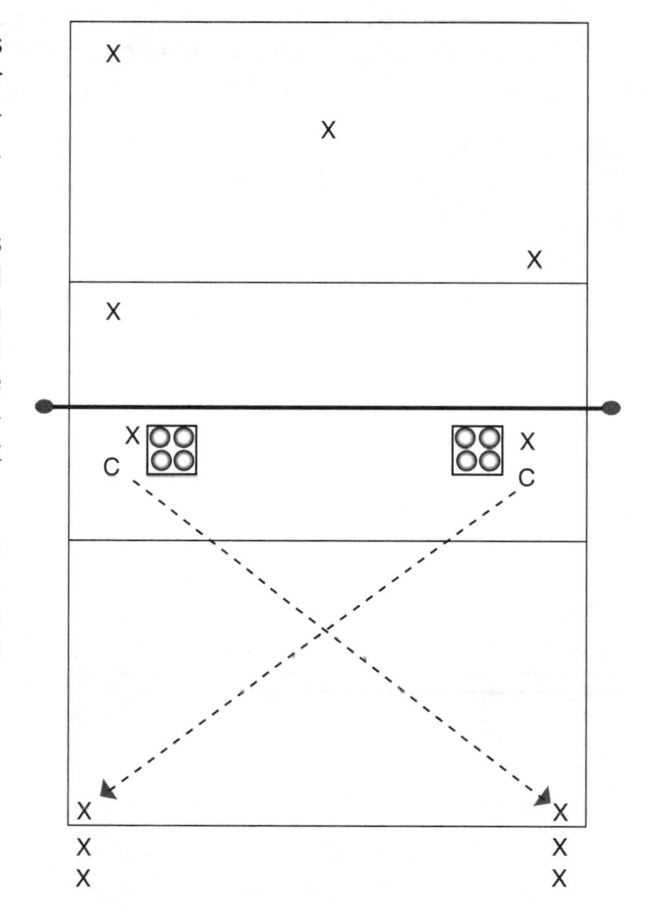

Figure 6.15 Repetitive Digging.

Dig, Tip, Chase

Purpose: To develop various response opportunities

Setup: Three players participate at once: one in right back and the other two behind and ready to enter the court. A coach is on the same side of the net with a cart of balls and someone to hand them to him or her. All other players are shagging and enthusiastically cheering on their teammates.

Execution: The coach hits the ball hard at the first player. He or she must dig it successfully or the coach gives that player another chance. Immediately following the dig, the coach tips a short ball to the middle of the court at the attack line. The same player pursues the ball, with whatever floor move is necessary. Right after that, the player is given a ball that he or she must chase down and save over the net (figure 6.16). As that player goes to the left-back position, the second digger gets his or her dig, tip, chase series. Then the third player follows. After each has gone through once, each gets to go again from the left-back position. After the first group has gone, the next three come onto the court.

Coaching Points: If executed properly, this drill can become a team's favorite drill. Players love to get down and earn your positive reinforcement, as well as that of their teammates.

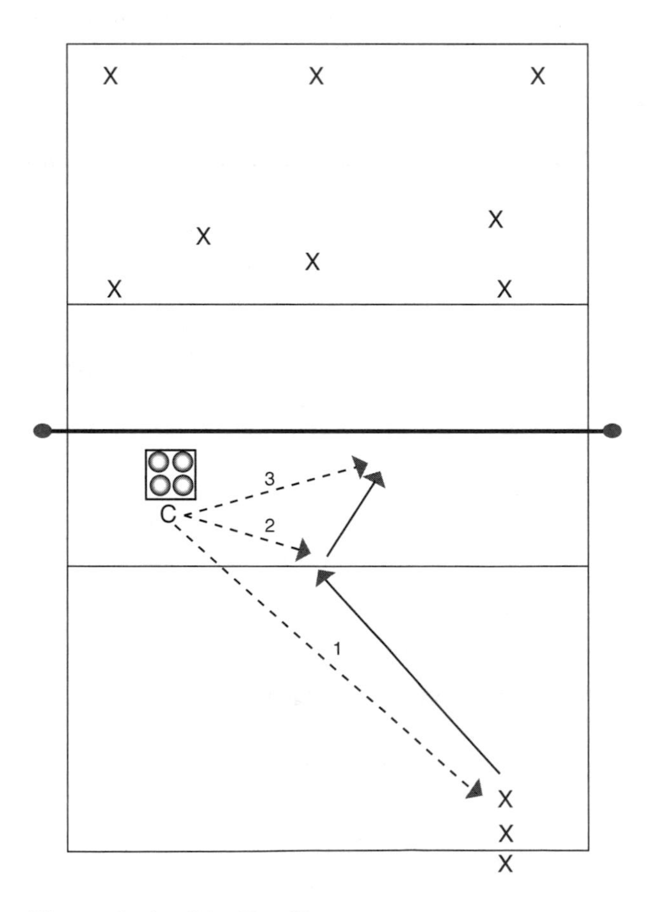

Figure 6.16 Dig, Tip, Chase.

Variation: You can make the opportunities difficult and have players stay in the drill until they complete the attempts to your satisfaction. A player could have many attempts before moving on. For instance, during the tip attempt, give players balls while they're on the ground. During the chase, make some impossible, but keep feeding them more balls.

Russian Pepper

Purpose: To promote continuous ball control to target and good communication

Setup: Four or five players participate at once; a coach is on one side of the net with a cart of balls and players to act as shaggers.

Execution: Three back-row players take their designated positions in right back, center back, and left back, along with a setter as the target. A coach is in right front. Start with a toss to the setter. The setter sets to the hitter (coach), and the hitter attacks balls in numerous ways to challenge the back-row diggers. The defenders must dig the ball to the setter. Repeat, dig, set, hit. Time the drill and bring in three more diggers (figure 6.17).

Coaching Points: This can be a frustrating drill if it gets out of control. It's a good drill for warming up if a team has only half a court available.

Variations

1. Add another coach in left front and have the setter set each coach while alternating.
2. Have two courts going at once, and have the players initiate the drill. When it's time to rotate, the setter becomes the hitter.
3. Add a left-front player.

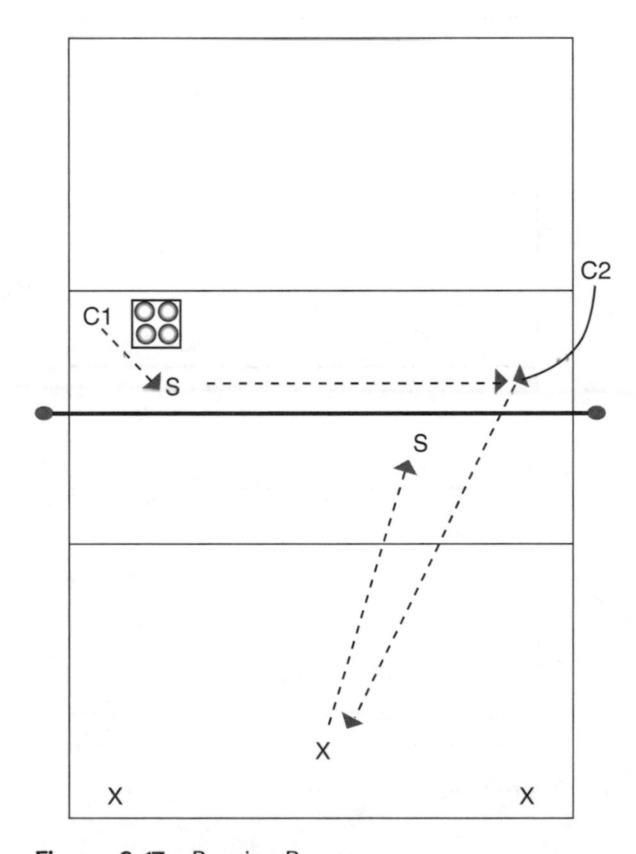

Figure 6.17 Russian Pepper.

Two Versus Four

Purpose: To give doubles partners many opportunities to contact the ball

Setup: Arrange two players on one side of the court and four on the other. The coach is on the doubles side, off the court with a cart of balls. Provide a flip chart and someone to keep score.

Execution: The coach always initiates the ball on the doubles side of the court with an attack, tip, ball into net, chase, and so on. The doubles team digs, sets, and cooperatively attacks the ball (figure 6.18). The team of four passes, sets, and cooperatively attacks the ball from the backcourt and returns it to the doubles team. The doubles team now has the opportunity to put the ball away for a point. Play continues with rally scoring. The four-person team can only attack from the back row, but the doubles team can hit on the net. (Cooperate, cooperate, then hit away.) After a point is scored, introduce another ball to the doubles team. Mix up the shots. Teams play to six points. Change teams; bring on a new doubles team.

Coaching Points: You need to work the doubles team very hard. They should be exhausted after a six-point game. Encourage defensive moves.

Variation: Have both teams take three hits.

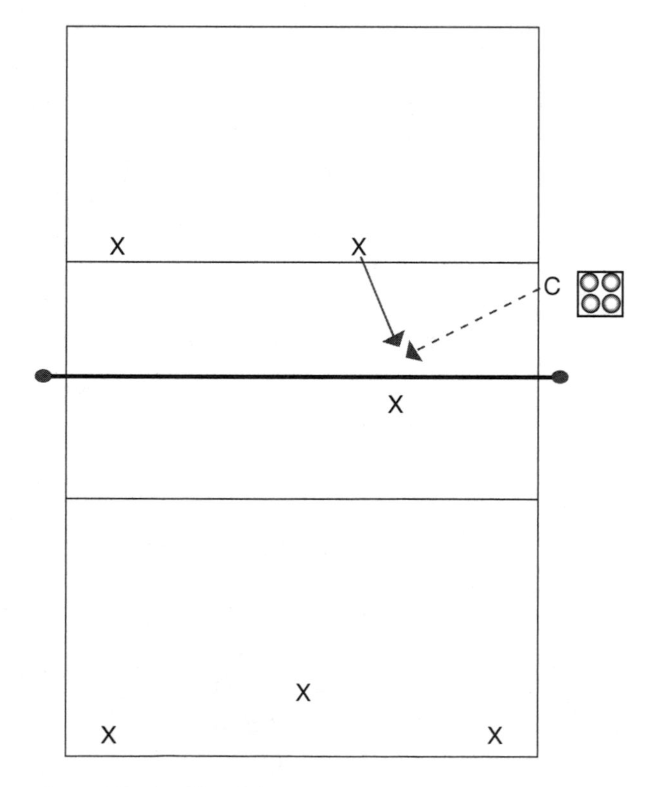

Figure 6.18 Two Versus Four.

Six at the Net

Purpose: To cause a team to play out of system; to force players to make the best of a chaotic situation

Setup: Players play six on six with one team at the net facing the same direction and holding onto the bottom of the net.

Execution: A coach hits the ball to the floor, and the team at the net scrambles to get to the ball and play it three times. Opponents respond to their play, and the game continues. The coach changes sides and has the other team scramble from the net. Play to a set number of points (figure 6.19).

Coaching Points: This drill calls for considerable communication and effort. Be sure to vary the bounced ball—low, high, far, on the court, off the court, and so on.

Variation: Allow the scrambling team only two hits. The bounced ball simulates an errant pass, and the team gets two more hits to get the ball over the net. Or set the score at 20 to 20 and play to 25.

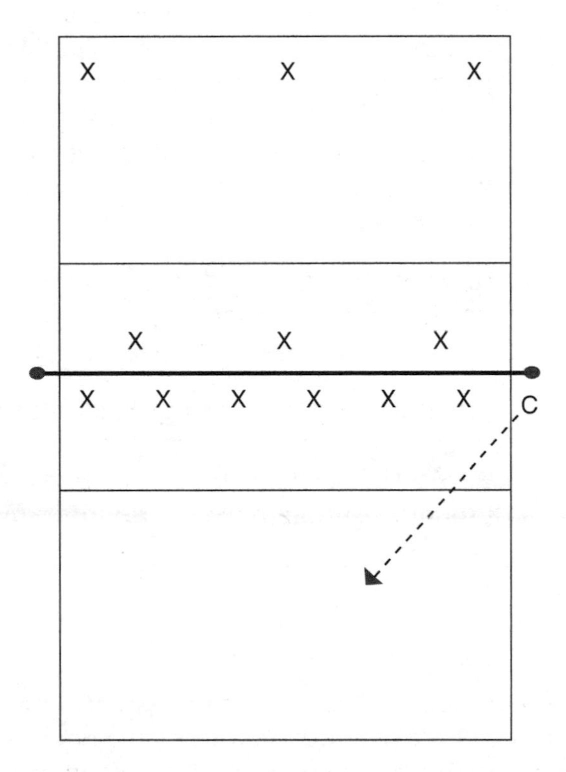

Figure 6.19 Six at the Net.

Chaos

Purpose: To expose players to a variety of situations within one series

Setup: Players play six on six; you'll need a cart of balls at each endline (figure 6.20).

Execution: Determine who is serving. The serving team must win its serve to earn the next five balls. If they don't win the serve, the ball is given to the other team, and it must win the serve to get the next five balls. The five balls are free ball, down ball, joust, Omaha, and chase. After a team wins the serve, the coach introduces a free ball from the other side of the court. The serving team plays it out, as do the receivers, until a point is scored. Immediately following is a down ball, which is played out until a point is scored. Then the coach tosses a ball between two front-row opponents at the net, who will jump and fight it out (legally) until a point is scored. The Omaha is a ball tossed very low to the ground that is allowed to bounce so that the defender has to use a floor move to save it; then, the team plays the ball two more times until a point is scored. Finally, the serving team is given a bounced ball off the court; players are given only two chances to get the ball over the net. Five points are possible in the series; the serve doesn't earn a point but does earn the right to the next five balls. The team that wins three, four, or five of the points wins that series. A team has to win two series before rotating.

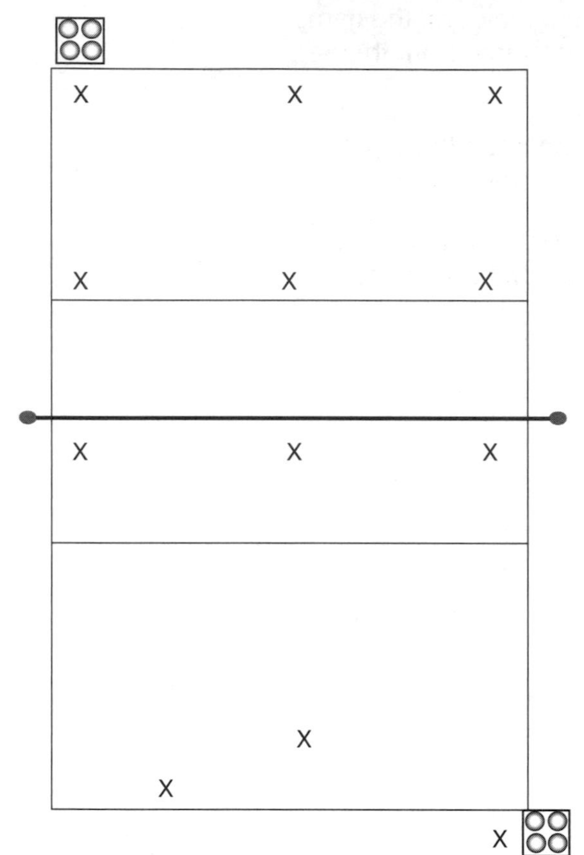

Figure 6.20 Chaos.

Coaching Points: This drill provides different types of opportunities for players that happen in a game but which normal play and coaches can't replicate in practice.

Variation: Instead of having the starters play the nonstarters, have players with even jersey numbers play against players with odd jersey numbers. If the game takes too long to rotate through six rotations, omit the front row and back row.

CONCLUSION

The familiar quote "offense sells tickets, but defense wins championships" is true. However, defensive-minded teams do not just happen; coaches and players do not simply will it to happen in their pre-season goals. As a result, a considerable amount of time must literally be spent on the floor, digging balls coming at various speeds, trajectories, and locations on the court. Indeed, a good defensive move is just as contagious—sometimes more so—as a spectacular kill, simply because play now can continue.

7

Playing Offense

Joe Sagula

© Human Kinetics

In volleyball, as in most sports, defense is simple and offense incredibly complex. In offense, there is always a high risk factor and pressure to score on easy plays. The mission of the defense, however, is to force the offense to make errors and disrupt timing, increasing the pressure even more. As a result, offense needs power, creativity, and autonomy; it must evolve because the defense will always find a way to counter any offensive action. A team's offensive game plan is in a constant state of flux.

Offense requires excellent strategic planning, coupled with a strong work ethic. It needs a good tactical scheme with consideration of matchups, which are linked to strategy, situation, and team potential and underscored by the team philosophy. The programmed attack must allow for a number of prioritized choices for each attack based on the situation at hand. This requires planning because there's no time to establish these choices during competition.

Indeed, the aim of the offense in the game of volleyball is to put constant pressure on the opponent. The offense must increase the defense's uncertainty via speed and acceleration, through fakes, feints, power, and the use of the cumulative effect. In other words, every act or series of plays leaves a mark or an effect that must be taken into account in every succeeding point of the game or match. For example, when an offense attacks two or three times in a row from position 4 (outside hitter position), the defense remembers this effect (play) and is biased toward this action. When a middle attacker jumps to attack a quick set, the defense tends to focus on that point of attack and is thereby kept off balance. Over time, these actions leave a mark or image that begins to accumulate and make it difficult for the opponent to read, anticipate, or understand an individual's attack or the team's attack patterns. As a result, actions by the defense will always be late and will be reactive rather than aggressive.

The offense is the chain made up of links in passing, setting, and hitting capabilities. These elements are interdependent and cannot be considered alone. In considering team offense, it is crucial for a team to have two or more players who can score either in precise or completely random, out-of-system situations (usually resulting initially from a bad pass). Offense is complex because space (use of the length of the net), time (speed and setting tempo), and depth (play from off the net, the back-row attack, and so on) must all be considered. In addition, the set height also creates more space and attack angles, which are important factors in creating power in the offense and which create more work for the defense. Essentially, how you combine these three factors determines your offensive capabilities. A good offense is efficient; and along with this efficiency, players must see the entire offense as a picture in their minds with various attack patterns and teammates' positions linked to the opposition's defense. A good offense uses different "pictures" and subtle variations, which amount to a squad's "team movement" and incorporates many factors, especially the patterns of timing.

A good offensive action requires investing power, creativity, and a positive mindset into the play, along with good ball control and a knowledge of when and where to begin the attack. A good offensive action also requires a good starting point, creating space and time to allow for fakes, acceleration, and speed. Offense needs to use the flow of the game to its advantage; knowing when to go with—and when to go against—the flow of the ball can make all the difference.

Essentially, offense can be broken down into three areas: free-ball offense, transition offense, and sideout offense.

- Free-ball offense is a counterattack (pass–set–hit) from a nonattacked pass or set received from the opponent. The free ball is received with an overhand or underhand pass, depending on the player's or team's skill. Whenever possible, the back-row players should receive the free ball, allowing the front-row players to prepare for the offensive play or attack. Generally, the offensive play is predetermined before the pass to the offensive side. Free-ball offense should be a high-efficiency attack situation in which a team is in system after a quality dig or pass.
- Transition offense occurs when a team moves from defensive play (ball attacked by the opponent) to offensive play in counterattack (dig–set–hit). In transition, offensive plays are generally called as audibles by the attackers as they evaluate the pass. Attackers are given options within zones based on their court position and quality of the dig or pass.
- Sideout offense immediately follows a serve receive. Because play is initiated by the serve, there is ample time for the offense to be called just prior to the serve. The setter or hitters usually call these plays. Transitioning from receiving the serve to executing a successful offense must have a high efficiency rate. The goal of serve receive is to direct the served ball sufficiently to the net or target area so that the setter has multiple options of setting the ball to any of his or her attackers. Receiving the serve with high efficiency allows a team to run an offense that is "in system." Poor passing results in fewer options for the setter and thus fewer options for the attackers, which puts the offense "out of system." Advanced offensive systems attempting precise patterns and quick-tempo sets require a lower, extremely accurate pass. Less-skilled teams require passes to be high enough for the setter to run under the ball and have time to set the attackers.

ORGANIZING SERVE RECEIVE AND THE OFFENSE

Of course, a team's offense is only as good as its players' skills in passing, setting, and attacking. Let's look at the five key positions that make up the offense: outside hitter, middle hitter, opposite, setter, and the libero.

An outside hitter has the ability both to express power and project stability. This player can analyze situations and make intelligent choices in attack (such as when facing two blockers versus one blocker, seeing openings in the defense, and so on). For good team balance, one of the primary outside power hitters should also be a good passer.

Because of the number of fakes required to set up their teammates' attacks, middle hitters must possess speed and a willingness to self-sacrifice. A key for middle hitters is the ability to interact with the setter and to position based on the quality of the pass (first contact).

The right-side hitter (usually called the "opposite" because he or she positions in the rotation opposite the setter) is one of the more difficult positions to play in today's sophisticated offenses. In this position, a player should be able to engage in multiple offensive tasks and have competency in passing and setting (important, though not critical) and attacking various types of sets. This player must be powerful and have the ability to score in difficult situations.

The setter is the key to coordinating the offense. Much could be written on the qualities and characteristics required to be a successful setter. To simplify, the setter is the player who needs to understand the game at the highest level. He or she is the one player who can make quality choices, communicate them to the team, and execute the play at a high level. The setter is the team leader; more than anyone else, he or she determines the quality of the team's play.

The libero, although originally created with defense in mind, is a position with considerable offensive implications. The libero's ball-handling skills must be at the highest level on the team, with primary dedication to passing. The libero is the player who can improve the quality of the first contact made (the pass) in all offensive situations. The libero significantly improves a team's serve-receive capabilities in the following ways:

- He or she takes away the need to make decisions on how to hide bad passers (that is, placing a potential passer in the back row where he or she is unlikely to receive the serve on a consistent basis).
- He or she simplifies the difficult rotations in serve receive.
- He or she allows for more tactics and ways to use other players in offensive patterns.
- He or she increases the team's ability to cover the hitter, thereby improving the hitter's confidence levels, because he or she is dedicated to coverage and passing.

Obviously, you create or modify your offensive system based on the personnel and talent level on your team. When developing your offensive system, ask these questions:

- What is the individual skill level of our players?
- How many setters are there (one or two) to play on the court?
- What is the ability of our hitters?
- What is the level of our passing? How well do we use our specialists (defensive specialist and libero)?
- What tactical applications are necessary to win at our level?
- How much time do we have to practice?

And always remember the principle that overrides all others: Never attempt tactically what you can't execute technically.

In organizing a team's serve receive, the coach must answer these four questions: How many passers are needed? Should the players be in their specialized front-row positions? Where should the setter be placed? How should we use the libero for passing solutions and tactics? Just as a setter is key to running a successful offense, a team's ability to receive serve is critical to running a team's offensive system. An offense cannot be triumphant without a successful serve receive.

A team's proficiency in passing likely determines how many passers the team uses in the serve receive. The team with good passers reduces this number considerably. Fewer passers allow more specialization and simplify the offensive patterns. Front-row passers not included in the serve-receive formation move easily into their attack positions. The team chooses among four possible serve-receive formations or patterns: five passers—W-shape serve formation (figure 7.1), four passers—U-shape serve formation (figure 7.2), three-person serve-receive pattern (figure 7.3), and two-person passers (figure 7.4).

Figure 7.1 W-shape serve formation.

Figure 7.2 U-shape serve formation.

Figure 7.3 Three-person serve-receive pattern.

Figure 7.4 Two-person passers.

Coaches and players must remember that player positions are determined and judged by the placement of the players' feet on the court (figure 7.5, a-b). According to the *Official FIVB Rules as Presented by USA Volleyball,* "Each front-row player must have at least a part of a foot closer to the center line than both feet of the corresponding back-row player" and "Each right- (left-) side player must have at least a part of a foot closer to the right (left) sideline than both of the feet of the center player in the corresponding row. The server is exempt from the application of this rule." The player position is judged according to the position of the foot last contacting the floor at the time the ball is contacted for the serve. Of course, once the ball is served, players can move to any position on their playing area.

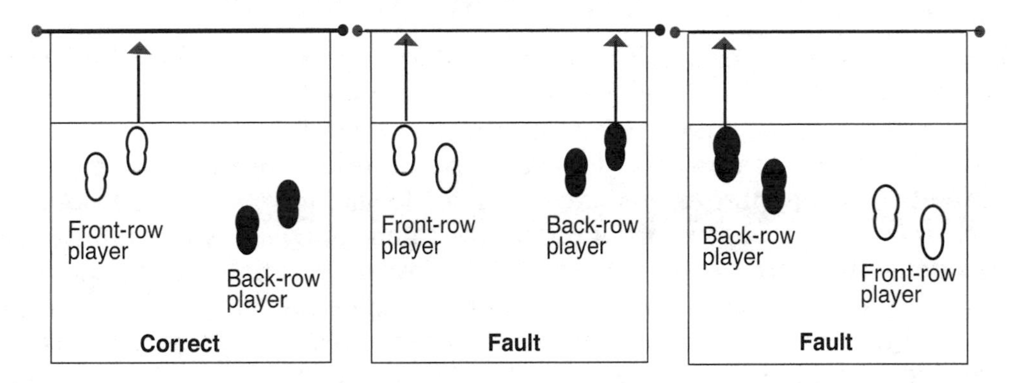

Figure 7.5a Front-row player positioning.

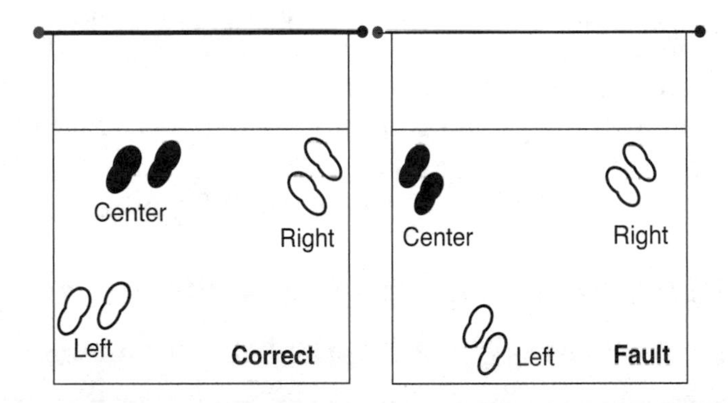

Figure 7.5b Back-row player positioning.

Traditionally, the highest-level teams use fewer primary passers. Using four passers is not unusual, but most top-level teams use three or two passers. In general, a team chooses the formation that allows the ball to be delivered to the setter with the fewest number of passers.

Here are a few principles for the serve receive:

- Expose the best passers to pass a bigger area of the court and hide the weaker passers.
- A good passer usually performs better with a larger area of responsibility; he or she tends to be aggressive and needs room to pursue the ball.
- The player whose priority is to attack a quick or fast-tempo set should have a small area of responsibility for serve receive.

- Serve-receive patterns should be formed to get the setter into the predetermined target position as quickly and easily as possible.
- Hitters should be near—or have the ability to move into—their optimal starting area for attack from the receive pattern.

Serve-receive patterns often use the same patterns but vary by rotation and position of the setter. It's possible for the serve receive to appear to be in one pattern while actually being in another. For example, a four-player (U-shaped) receive pattern might actually be a two-player receive because two primary passers retain the majority of the court and take most of the passes. To be able to make necessary changes or to improve attack routes, the setter must know the various patterns and overlap rules.

Once a team has determined the number of receivers in its formation, it must answer the second question: Do we want our front-row players to play in their specialized positions? The answer is almost always a resounding yes.

Often a team will assign a play (specific attack patterns) for each rotation. This is simple and doesn't require extensive communication among players. The alternative is for the coach or a player to call the plays. Calling allows flexibility and variety in the offense but requires the coach or the players to communicate constantly. Usually, it's the responsibility of the setter to determine the offensive plays in coordination with the coach and the team's offensive philosophy. Serve receive charts the passing formations and determines the play that delivers the hitters into their specialized positions.

A team need not restrict itself to one of the four serve-receive patterns but might use different formations in each rotation. This means the team receives serve with four passers part of the time and with three or two the rest of the time.

"Organizing the offense" refers to deciding which plays to run and when to run them. Team communication is important in this regard in that each player must know what other players are doing. The primary goal of a good offense is to look for efficiency and simplicity and link them to player capabilities.

Offensive Systems Based on Setter Location

The advantage of a frontcourt setter system is that it promotes ease of movement and is less difficult in transition. When the setter is in the front row, the passers have a larger target area, and the setter has an easier path to the target area. In transition, the setter is already in the front row, and there is an additional passer in the back row, so the passing base is more balanced. In the following offensive formations, the first number indicates how many players have front-row attack responsibilities, and the second number indicates how many players have setting responsibility. So, in the 4–2 formation, four players have front-row attack duties and two players have setting duties.

The 4–2 offense. The 4–2 offense is the most elementary of the competitive offensive systems. It uses two setters from the front row arranged opposite each other in the rotation lineup (figure 7.6a). The setter sets from the middle-front position (position 3). The international 4–2 is a variation of the basic 4–2. The difference is that the setter sets from a target area in the right front zone (figure 7.6b). With the arrival of the backcourt attack and bigger blockers and setters who jump set, hit, or dump, this system has become more common and allows for greater attack options.

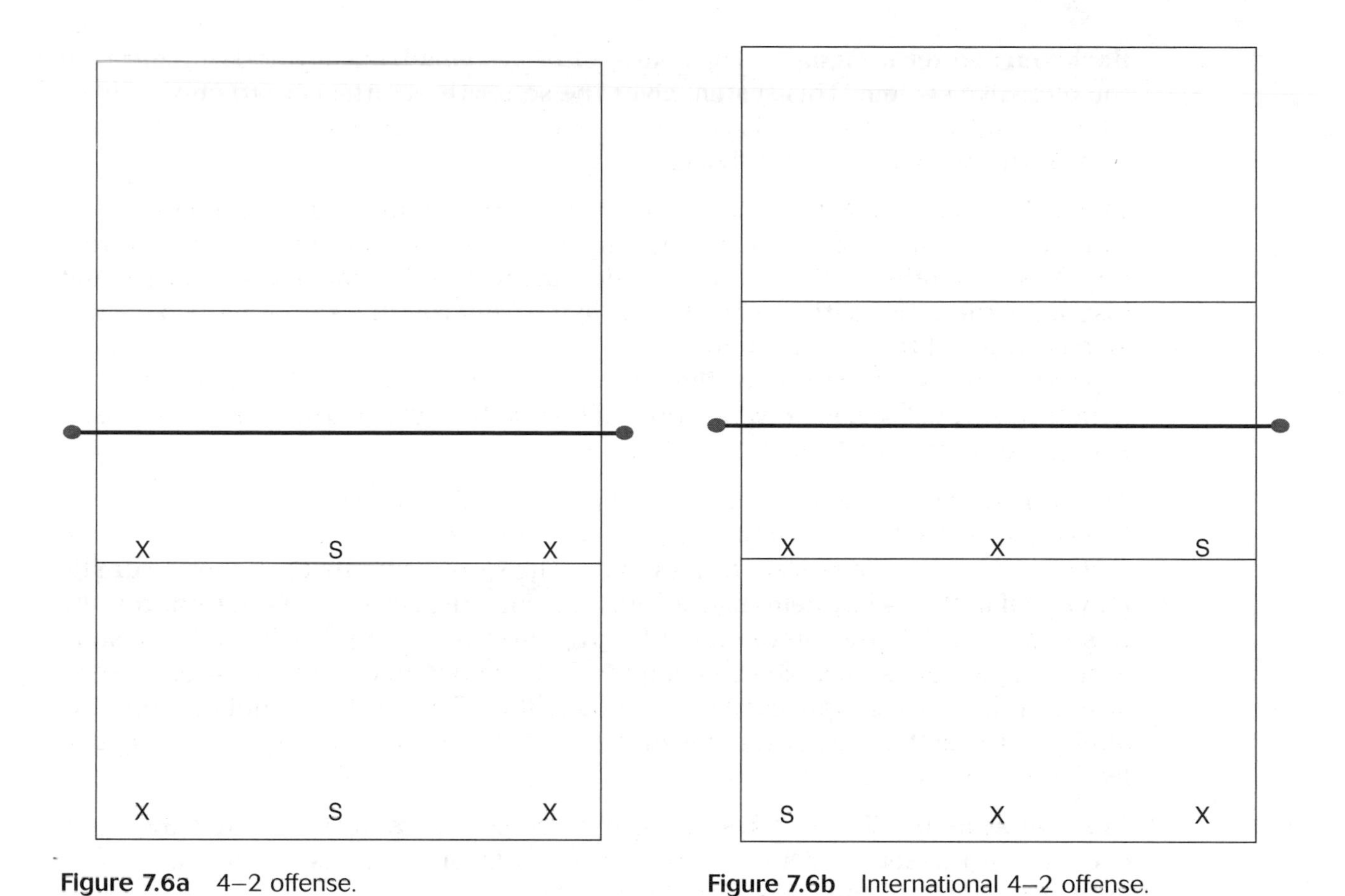

Figure 7.6a 4–2 offense.

Figure 7.6b International 4–2 offense.

The 3–3 offense. The 3–3 offense system uses three setters located in a triangle in the rotation order with a hitter between each setter (figure 7.7). All six players are hitters in this system. In this system, when the setter rotates into positions 2 and 3, he or she becomes the primary setter in the offense and hits in only one front-row position when in position 4.

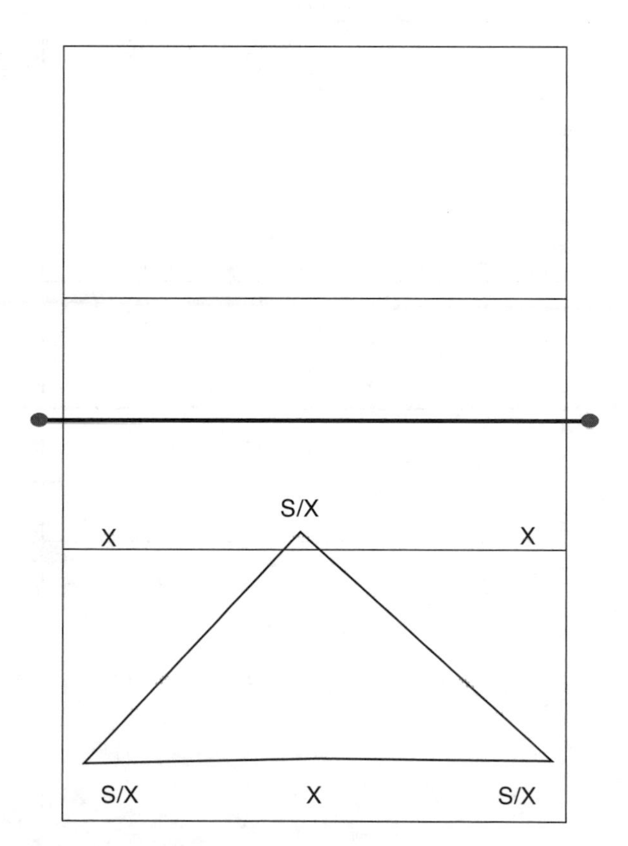

Figure 7.7 3–3 offense.

Backcourt setter systems. Backcourt setter systems basically add one hitter to the offensive system. This system gives the setter three attackers to choose from when setting the offense. It also allows for more tactical planning in designing ways to beat the defense (block and backcourt).

The 6–2 system. The 6–2 system uses three hitters attacking from the front row using a backcourt setter. The 6–2 is similar to the 4–2 but employs two setters opposite each other in the rotational order (figure 7.8). The major difference is that instead of the active setter being the one in the front row, the setter in the back row also carries out the setting chores.

All six players get to hit when their position is in the front row, because the setter penetrates from the back-row position. In this system, the two setters are opposite each other in the rotation lineup.

The 5–1 system. The 5–1 system is the most widely used offense among most levels and is used exclusively by higher-level teams. The system uses one setter, and the other five players are hitters. When the setter is in the back row, he or she plays as if in the 6–2 system (figure 7.9), and when the setter is in the front row, he or she plays as if in the international 4–2 system (figure 7.10). The basic 5–1 system is simple yet can be flexible and complex. This system makes the most of players' strengths and also simplifies their responsibilities. This system is built around the ability of the setter. The advantage of the 5–1 system is consistency in setting and leadership by one player.

The 6–3 system. The 6–3 system uses three setters, similar to the 3–3 system except that the setters set out of the back row from positions 6 and 1, and there are always three front-row hitters (figure 7.11).

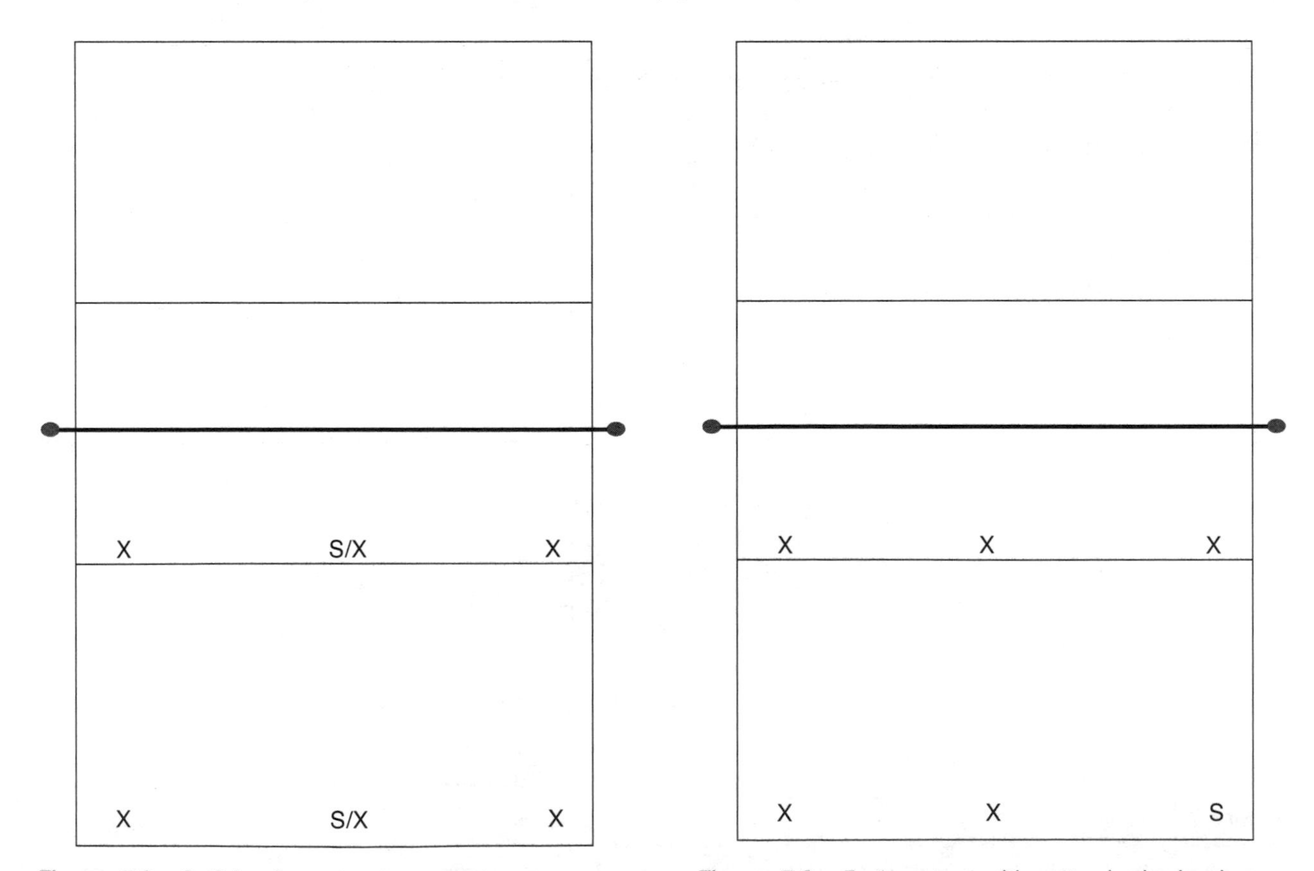

Figure 7.8 6–2 backcourt setter system.

Figure 7.9 5–1 system with setter in the back row.

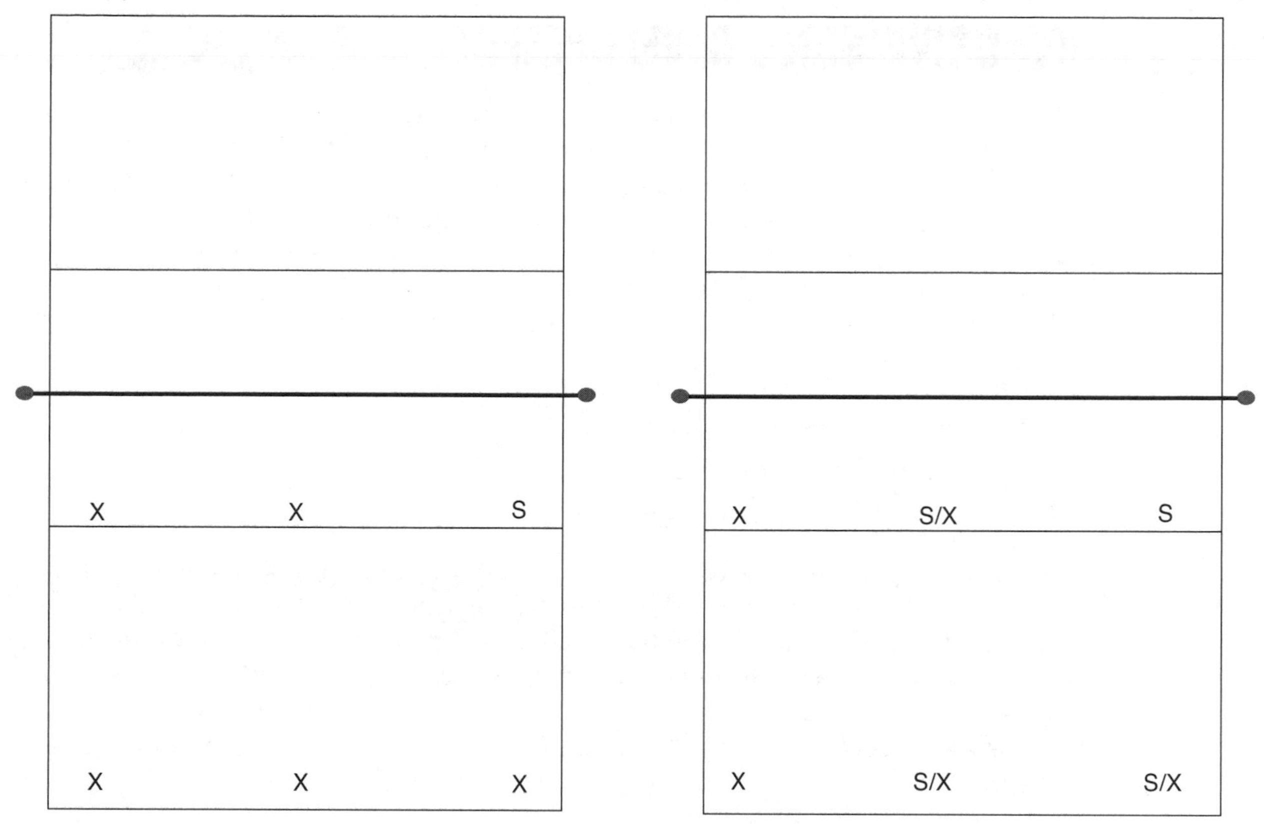

Figure 7.10 5–1 system with setter in the front row.

Figure 7.11 6–3 system.

Offensive Communication

For an offense to coordinate properly, team communication needs to be clear and to the point. The problem with many team systems is that the players neglect their responsibility to communicate to teammates. Along with their volleyball-specific physical skills, players must also practice their verbal skills. Their words to each other should be concise and easily understood. Coaches need to teach their players to communicate their intentions on every play. Here are some suggestions:

- Players should call "mine!" or "ball!" for every ball they will contact.
- When doing simple drills, the player who plays the ball calls the name of the partner or teammate that he or she is playing the ball to. For example, when passing the ball to a setter, the passer calls "mine!" before contact, and after contact he or she calls the name of the setter in the target area.
- Setters must verbally communicate their position and intentions at all times.
- Develop key words to describe sets, directions, or teamwork, such as "mine," "out," "in," "long," "short," "high," "deep," "down," and so on.
- Always communicate what a player intends to do, not what another player should do (that is, don't call "yours!" or "your ball!").

OFFENSIVE SKILL DEVELOPMENT

Offensive skills are determined by attack patterns from serve receive, from defense, and from free-ball or down-ball situations. In turn, the attack patterns all depend on the type of first ball that is passed. Basically, the first ball that is passed can be divided into two distinct and simple categories: good passes (in system) and bad passes (out of system). If the first pass is good, the team runs a particular type of pattern or play set; if the pass is bad, the team runs a different pattern.

There are four major components of offensive play in team development:

- Offense from serve receive
- Transition offense from defense
- Transition offense from free ball or down ball
- Offense from hitter coverage

Normally, a good pass is to the setter's predetermined target zone and allows a multiple attack to take place—the setter has a choice in set selection. The speed, height, and direction determine the quality of the pass. If you have other criteria for a typical good pass, these should be communicated to all players. In essence, all players should think as one. Initially, the setters might be responsible to call a good or bad pass, but eventually all players should recognize whether a pass is in system (good) or out of system (bad). Of course, this can only happen through practicing within gamelike drills.

Some teams like to make the target area even smaller. The more accurate the pass, the more options available. An in-system pass allows for a lower or faster tempo set to be attempted. A bad or out-of-system pass usually means a higher set offense, or a "safe play" in which the sets are high to all the attackers. The key to out-of-system passing is to set the player who has the widest angle to attack the ball (figure 7.12, a-c).

As a team progresses and skills improve, the coach might introduce multiple serve-receive plays for each rotation, including one defensive play per rotation

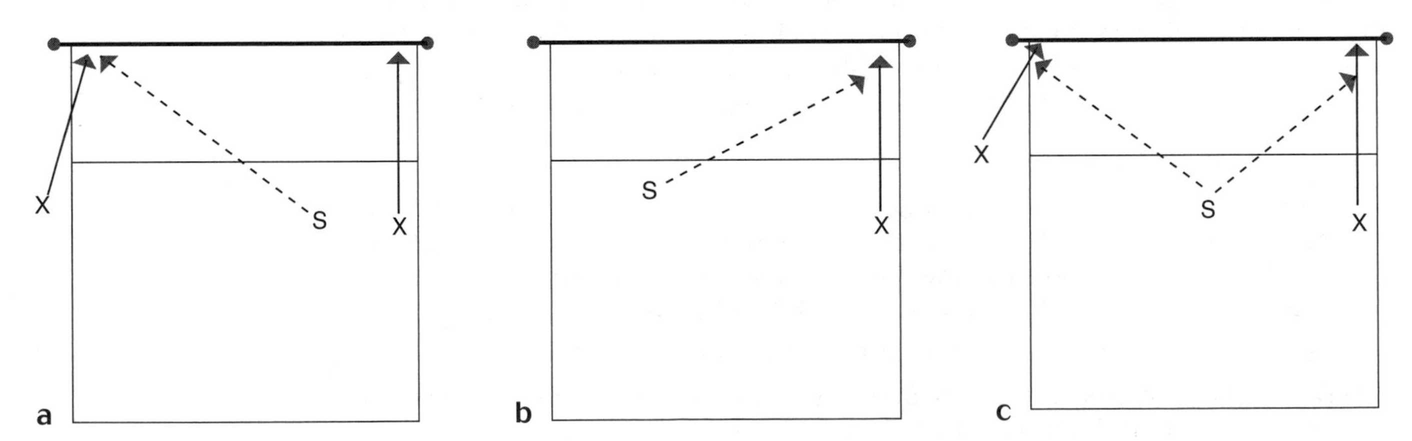

Figure 7.12 Out-of-system passing. *(a)* best angle of attack; *(b)* best angle of attack; *(c)* equal angle of attack.

(this might be the same as the serve-receive plays) and one free-ball play and one down-ball play. Each of these might be the same as—or variations of—the serve-receive play in a particular rotation. Plays are determined by each player's skills and capabilities as an attacker.

Three examples of serve-receive plays are the free ball, the down ball, and hitter coverage.

The free ball. The free ball is a ball the opponent sends over the net with either a forearm pass or a standing overhead pass. The free ball is the easiest ball-control play in volleyball. As soon as players recognize that the opponent won't attack, they should yell "free!" The setter releases from his or her defensive position to the setting area. The blockers back off the net and get into position to attack the ball, and back-row players get into position to pass the ball to the setter. The best passers should handle the pass (usually from the back row). The setter needs to get in the target area as quickly as possible. The ball should be played with an overhand pass for quicker tempo and better control. Attackers must know if they should pass first before going into their attack patterns.

The down ball. The down ball is one that is attacked by the opponent from a standing position, by an off-balanced hitter, or from deep in the opponent's court. The down ball is usually not worth blocking because it is not attacked with power. The blocker should call "down!" and usually won't have enough time to get back into a ready hitting position. The difference in coverage of a free ball and a down ball is that in a free-ball situation, blockers or setters (or both) have time to move to their attack positions before the ball crosses the net. On a down ball, they move to attack position after the ball crosses the net.

Hitter coverage. Try to keep the coverage of the hitters as simple as possible because the action occurs too quickly for much adjusting to occur. If a team attacks a blocking defense, the offense must cover the court behind its hitter in case the ball is blocked. Most teams try to position three players closely around and behind the hitter and two players deeper in the court. Basically, coverage should include all players not involved in the attack. (The quick-attack hitter is often too far from the play). Players must assume a low posture. The setter, the back-row player directly behind the hitter, and the next closest back-row player are usually the three most important players covering the hitter. Many coaches often use the libero as the key player to all hitter coverage. When in doubt where to cover, players should fill in the open space around the hitter.

However, these formations won't cover all serve-receive possibilities, especially if a team has complex patterns of attack. In such cases, the coach must adjust accordingly. Coverage is also combined with players switching in their back-row specialized positions. There are two basic philosophies: (1) cover first, switch second and (2) switch first, cover second. Which offensive coverage system you use depends on your philosophy. Normally, the attacker should be concerned only about balls played in front or to the side of him or her. Practice and communication are the keys to coverage on the confusing or overlapping areas of the court. The concept of coverage is an important skill to train during all offensive team development. Figure 7.13, a-c, illustrates three options for hitter coverage.

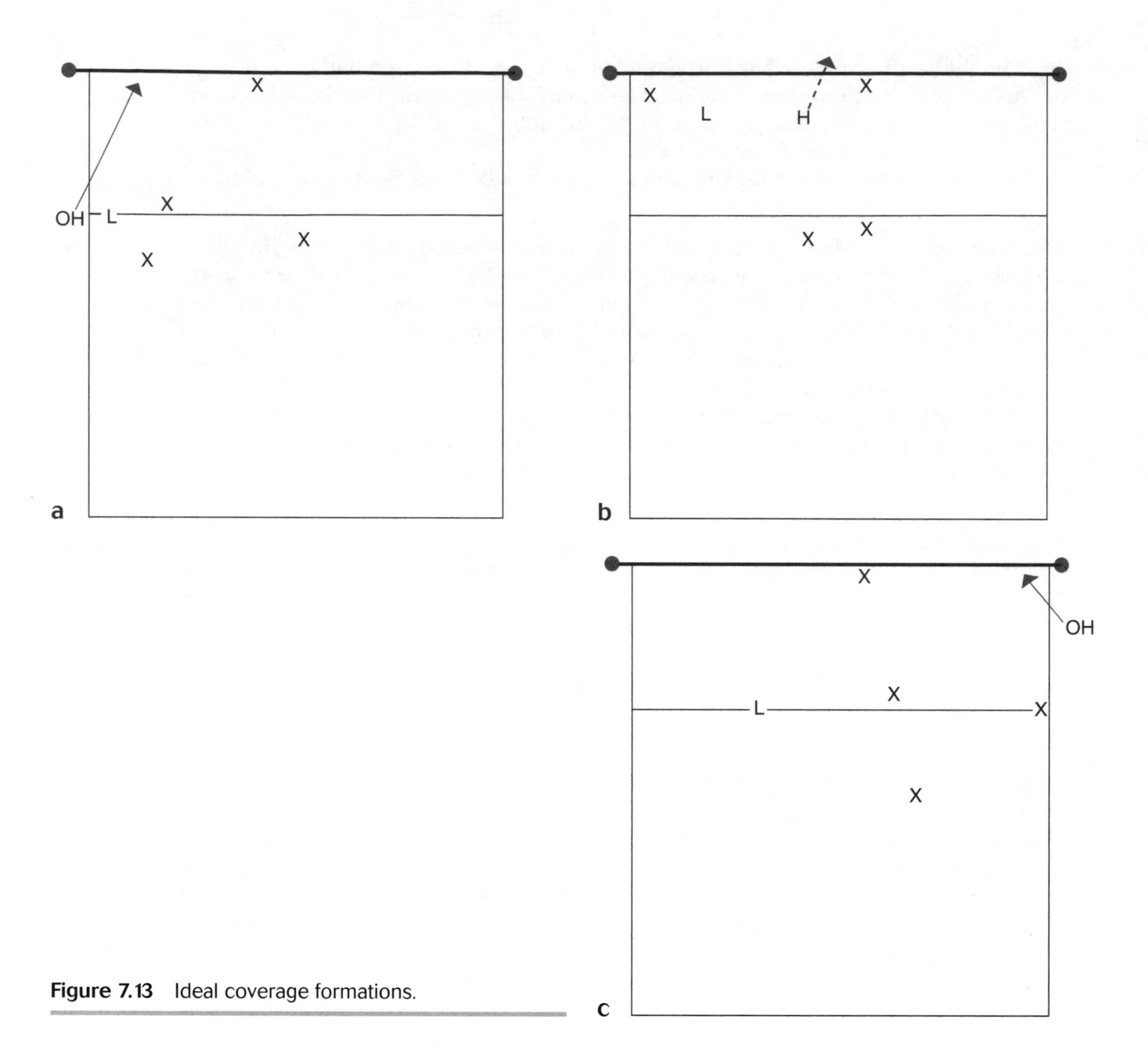

Figure 7.13 Ideal coverage formations.

OFFENSIVE DRILLS

Receive Serve for Points

Purpose: To work on basic serve receive, helping players understand the quality of a pass for in-system (2 points to 3 points) and out-of-system passes (1 point or zero points) and allowing players to pass in different receive patterns (two-player, three-player, four-player)

Setup: From one side of the court, players serve to the opposite side.

Execution: The non-serving side begins in its serve receive pattern (two-, three-, four-person receive). The passers on the receiving team communicate with the setter and pass to the target. The setter penetrates to the target area after the serve and must set the ball in order for the passing points to count (figure 7.14).

- For every perfect pass (inside the 3 zone), the team receives +3.
- For a good pass (inside the 2 zone), the team receives a +2.
- Passes off the net or outside the attack line count as +1.

All other passes count as a zero, or if the setter does not set the ball, the team does not earn the point. The coach determines the team goals (e.g., 30 points total) and then passers and servers switch.

Coaching Points: Since this drill starts with control being initiated with a serve, you can provide feedback to players on technique after each play (as needed). Emphasize the team receiving serve with all players moving on every pass. The coach should demand communication on every pass: call "mine," "long," "short," and so on.

Variations: Score the drill by awarding points for perfect passes in a row (three "3 passes" in a row earns bonus points). To increase difficulty, a coach or assistant may serve. To increase the level of difficulty, determine the number of passes needed to earn 30 points (e.g., 10 passes to get 30 points would be a 3.0 average). The setter penetrates to the target area from different areas of the court. Change the scoring system. Set the point goal higher. Have players pass then hit.

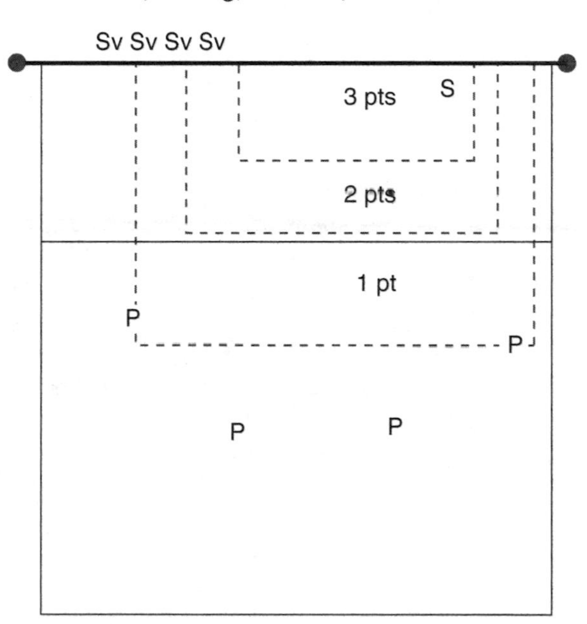

Figure 7.14 Receive Serve for Points.

Receive Serve, Attack, and Cover

Purpose: To work on basic serve receive, preparing to attack after receiving serve and coverage of hitters

Setup: From one side of the court, players serve to the opposite side.

Execution: The non-serving side begins in its serve receive pattern (two-, three-, or four-person receive). The setter penetrates into the target area after the serve. The passers on the receiving team communicate with the setter and pass to the target. The setter sets to a specified hitter, who attacks the ball (figure 7.15), while the remaining players cover the hitter. Goals are determined for each rotation and are specified by the coach.

Coaching Points: Have the libero be the leader of the hitter coverage and call "cover." The libero is in the key position on the court to cover the attacker. Since this drill starts with control being initiated with a serve, you can provide feedback to players on technique after each play (as needed). A coach can also initiate this drill with a controlled serve.

Variations: The setter sets only outside hitters, only the passer, only the non-passer, only the quick-attack hitter, only the backcourt hitter, and so on. Score the drill by awarding points for running particular plays or sets.

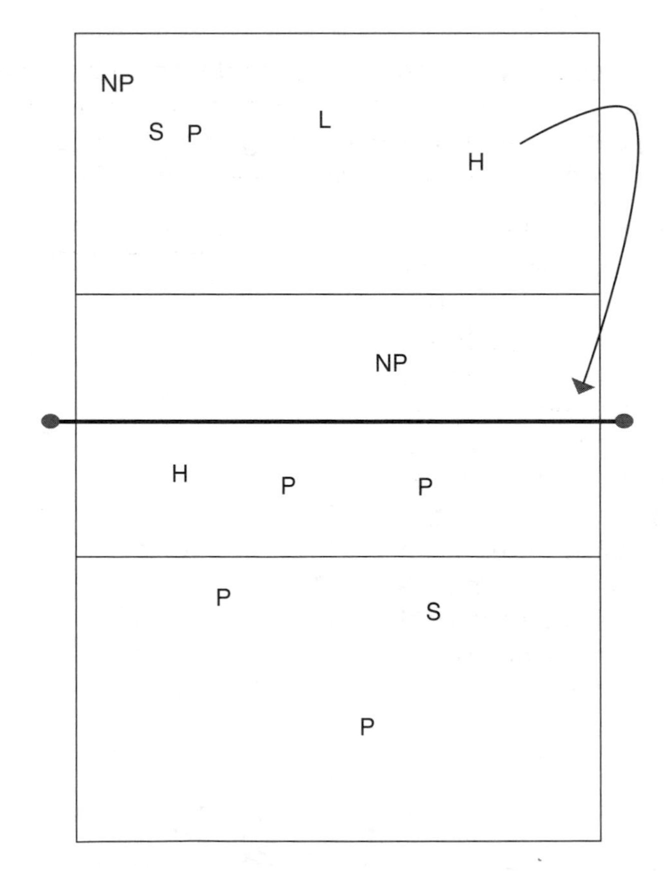

Figure 7.15 Receive Serve, Attack, and Cover.

Serve Receive With Hitter Versus Hitter

Purpose: To encourage serve receivers to attack; to prepare free ball/down ball attack; and to prepare a specified attack pattern after receiving serve and coverage of hitters

Setup: From one side of the court, players serve to the opposite side.

Execution: The non-serving side begins in serve-receive pattern (two-, three-, or four-person receive). The setter penetrates to the target area. The passers on the receiving team communicate with the setter and pass to the target. The setter sets to the designated outside hitter, who attacks the ball, while the remaining players cover the hitter. Goals are determined for each rotation and are specified by the coach. Score the drill by awarding points only for a successful attack by the hitter (see "Variations").

If the first swing is not terminated, the teams play the ball until one side wins the rally. A team can only score by the designated hitter winning the point with a positive kill (points are not earned for the opponent's error).

Coaching Points: Have the libero be the leader of the hitter coverage and call "cover." The libero is in the key position on the court to cover the attacker. A coach can also initiate this drill with a controlled serve and/or free ball/down ball. Be sure to give specific feedback to the designated hitters.

Variations: The setter sets only outside hitters, only the right side (opposite) hitter, only the middle (quick-attack) hitter, or only the backcourt hitter, or a combination of hitters for the first swing and then the second attack, and so on. Change the point scoring system by tossing in a free ball to the receiving team, where the team must earn two rallies in a row to score a point. Either team serves. Teams alternate serving after a specific number of serves.

This drill may also be done as a five versus five (eliminate one player on each team [middle blocker or a back-row player]). This allows for hitters to find the open area of the defense.

Serve Receive Full Rotation

Purpose: To practice the serve receive and full rotation in a gamelike situation that emphasizes team play

Setup: Six players are on one side of the court, and six players are on the opposite side (figure 7.16).

Execution: A team stays in the same rotation for 10 serves, and then the opposite side serves.

Scoring Example: The serving side must score 12 sideout points before the opposite side scores eight points. Each serve is worth a point, and the offensive team earns a point for a service error. In order to rotate, a team must earn 12 points from serve-receive offense. The first team to win 12 points from all six serve-receive rotations wins the drill.

Coaching Points: Coach may initiate the drill with a serve or have the players serve. This is an excellent drill for rotation work and focusing your team's sideout (serve receive) percentage. When winning 12 out of 20, the team's percentage is 60 percent; we want our team to earn above 70 percent in each rotation. This also allows for the coach to work with the setter and develop sideout tactics needed for matches. Setters work with all the hitters and develop creative play-sets for successful rotations.

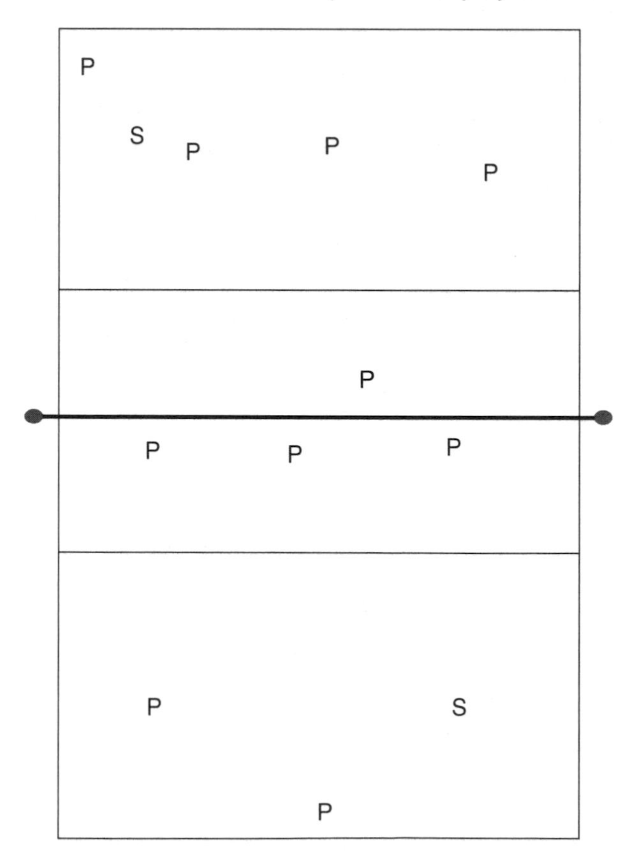

Figure 7.16 Serve Receive Full Rotation.

Variations

1. Change the point scoring system by tossing in a free ball to the receiving team or the defensive team. The team must earn two rallies in a row to score a point.
2. Have the defensive team rotate every three serves in order to create a variety of servers and defensive personnel. At the same time, the offense works against a different blocking scheme (defensive personnel).

Six Versus Six

Purpose: To put emphasis on offensive efficiency and developing strong rotation

Setup: Six players on one side of the court, and six players on the opposite side.

Use a large chalkboard divided into six rotations and three areas for score per rotation (figure 7.17).

Execution: A team stays in the same rotation for five serves, then the opposite side serves five times.

Coaching Points: This is an excellent drill for understanding strong/successful rotations and focusing your team's efficiency in sideout (serve-receive) percentage and in transition offense.

The chalkboard must be visible to the team members so that they can see and understand the good and bad rotations that need work. This drill also allows for the coach to work specifically with the setter and develop and practice game tactics in pressure situations.

Variation: Serve 10 balls per rotation as time allows. Vary the starting rotation each time you begin this drill in order to change the team's focus. Change the point scoring system by tossing in a free ball to the receiving team or the defensive team. The team must earn two rallies in a row to score a point.

Score per Rotation		
Rotation	Sideout	Defense
1		
2		
3		
4		
5		
6		

Figure 7.17 Six Versus Six chalkboard.

Drilling Philosophy and Practice

Preparing for Team Competition

- To prepare an individual or a team for competition, a coach should plan a cyclical training program that integrates long- and short-term units relevant to their competitive targets. The training program should foster learning and physical development, as well as the development of players' mental capacities, decision-making abilities, and tactical awareness. The program should be loaded in such a way that individually and collectively, the players and team are at their peak and are focused to perform at their best at the most critical periods in the cycle. The coach achieves the growth and development he or she wants through training and drilling. Here are some points to consider when developing a series of drills for training offense, for example:
  1. Establish a purpose.
  2. Make all learning and development relevant to an objective, whether it is in the context of a specific opponent or for more generalized volleyball education.
  3. Decide on goals for each drill.
  4. Select the variables to be emphasized in the goals.
  5. Design the drill structure to accomplish the desired results.
  6. Execute the drill as planned.
- Before developing a drill or a series of drills, coaches should identify their teams' needs and what they would like the drill (or series) to achieve. A coach's decisions on drills will depend on several factors, including the skill level of the upcoming opposition, the current skill level of his or her team, the skill level of each individual, and how players match up with the opposition. Based on this information, the coach and staff identify the goals, accents (how the input is being highlighted), and targets of the drill. During drill preparation, coaches should respect the "logic of the duel"—meaning that the essence of any drill should be to create awareness in their players of the need to manage themselves in both ordered and disordered environments. Players must understand the dichotomy between risk and security and the relative value of points and effects of their actions while making their own decisions on the court.
- After establishing a purpose and relevant objective for the drill, the coach will be ready to determine the specific goals of the drill. The context for a drill must be framed by determining the criteria for success. The coach must know what level of efficiency is required of the passing unit for the team to be able to side out often enough to prolong a game. Next, the coach must decide on the accents to incorporate in the drill and on the focus of the feedback given to reinforce the desired behavior of motor patterns. Players should be made aware of what they are being asked to absorb and learn from a drill and what the relevance of this information and learning might be. They need to be aware of the target(s) of a drill and must understand the accents. For example, if it is an offensive coverage drill, the players must understand not only the importance of where the hitters/setters are but also where everyone transitions once the ball crosses the net from their side to

the opponent's side. The following list offers some examples of the variables a coach might choose to emphasize in the goals of the drill:

Intensity—the relative relationship between the volume of work being undertaken in a given time period and the time interval between exercises
Quantity—the total number of contacts
Quality—the degree of precision
Movement—both static and dynamic action

- Ideally, the structure of the drill should condition players to deal with the notion of flow. Sequences should be built to systematize patterns of play and highlight strengths or expose weaknesses. Physical learning must be built from the top to the bottom (i.e., from ball contact to the preparation and anticipation) and vice versa, especially for the setter. Furthermore, the setter, above all players, must be drilled to understand and respect not only the physical aspect of a drill but also the meaning of his or her own actions and the actions of others. Gamelike conditions and match-preparation situations can be used to highlight and give meaning to the actions and to instill team unity by building "rituals." These same rituals help players manage the stresses that they experience within the game. This, in turn, builds confidence. Control games can also build motivation. How coaches integrate and execute a series of drills will determine the character of the learning and the subsequent development that they are expecting from their players.

CONCLUSION

In general, today's volleyball game is a mix of height, speed, timing, space, power, and variation. You need to take risks and be aggressive to score. In other words, players must be taught to "Put the ball on the floor." Additionally, players must be good physically and technically in order to hit high with power for all sets.

Although the modern offense in volleyball is approaching parity when it comes to the men's and women's games, there are still some differences. In the women's game, the backcourt attack is being used more and more, especially from the pipe position. To win today, however, you need one or two star players who can put the ball away in difficult situations and stabilize the offense. One particular aspect is the ability to use the slide. The difference between the men's and women's game is that women attack more in this space because it is more difficult for the defense to deal with or adjust to. Men's teams use the speed of the set as the more important factor. Despite any differences, however, the main principles for organizing specific and well thought-out systems of offense remain the same for coaches of men's teams and coaches of women's teams. An effective team offense should be simple, practical, efficient, and adaptable.

There are more opportunities to make unforced errors in an offense because the offense has the ball first. You must have good teamwork in which everyone knows his or her roles and responsibilities and the coach respects his or her capabilities of the moment. Don't base an offense on what you want but rather on what your players are capable of doing.

8

Playing Defense

Julie Backstrom and Mike Schall
Edited by Russ Rose

Photo by Scott Bjornlie

Of all of the skills and team concepts related to the sport of volleyball, nothing can quite compare to witnessing great defensive players—and ultimately, great defensive teams—battling to keep the ball off the floor.

In today's game, team defense is paramount.

Today's volleyball players—both male and female—are taller, stronger, and faster than ever before. As a result, offensive play—attacking, in particular—has exploded into a fast-paced, power-driven, hard-hitting element of the game. At the international level, players are spiking the ball over the net in excess of 90 miles per hour.

And someone needs to be on the receiving end of that spike.

A team with players who can dig that ball to transition to a successful attack and ultimately a point of their own is a team that will win matches, tournaments, and championships.

In addition, the advent of the libero player (a defensive specialist who plays only in the back row) has shifted the focus somewhat from offense to defense. Sure, fans are still looking for that exciting, powerful attack at the net; but now, the crowds also expect the players on the receiving end to respond with a sensational dig to their own setter to keep the ball in play.

Coaches in nearly every sport exclaim, "Defense wins championships!" Although some might argue that defense is not the only way to win a championship, teaching players and teams to play relentless defense should be an enjoyable part of the coaching job. At the very least, great defense helps a team move in the direction of a championship. For offensive players, there's nothing more gut-wrenching than taking a great swing at the ball, only to have it dug out and returned by a determined opponent on the other side of the net.

In essence, team defense takes the concepts of individual defense and develops them into successful ball control for all players on a team. Only a group of six players working in complete synchronization can transition a hard-driven spike from the opponent into an effective dig to the setter who, in turn, sets the hitter to unleash a similar attack for the players on the other side of the net to respond to.

Mastering team defensive skills begins with a proper attitude. Once the attitude is in place, a suitable game plan versus the opponent must be developed. Although the actual rally will vary each time, teams must be prepared for twists and turns. Penultimately, the sequence of events is established as play unravels. Finally, a team must decide which type of defense to play against an opponent. Depending on the skill level of both teams, that defensive scheme will change during the course of the match.

DEVELOPING DEFENSIVE ATTITUDE

Volleyball players hear all too frequently of the mentality they must possess to develop into a better defensive team, especially if a solid defensive tradition has been established by those who came before them. In fact, it's safe to say that they hear coaches speak of the proper defensive "mindset" as much as they hear lectures on the proper defensive position or technique. Different physical techniques have proven effective over the years, so it would be erroneous to suggest that one particular style of teaching defensive technique is superior to another (provided the basic principles are sound). Regardless of the technique that is taught, great defensive teams will be hindered in their development if the "never say die" attitude does not permeate the fiber of the team.

A volleyball program can operate smoothly without a long list of rules and regulations. However, one rule that players do pass on from class to class is the "go for every ball" decree. It's quickly understood that if a ball is traveling toward the floor, a player must go after it. The moment a player feels that he or she can't get to the ball and so doesn't make an effort is when he or she starts watching from the sideline. Once this concept is established, players begin to police each other; the older players assist the younger ones in understanding the value of playing every ball with maximum effort. This rule should be enforced during every drill; it's one of the building blocks of a solid volleyball program. Once all players on the team have embraced the "go for every ball" mentality, you can begin teaching them specific techniques and instructing them on strategic and tactical points.

PHYSICAL POSITIONING OF THE DEFENSIVE PLAYER

Much of the strength training and early-season conditioning should center on solidifying a strong base of support, from the feet to the legs to the lower back. Most players have the ability to make an occasional great defensive play, but outstanding defensive players make great plays consistently. Such players typically have the physical strength, muscular endurance, and mental toughness to maintain a solid defensive position for extended periods of time.

The basic posture of a defensive player might change several times during the course of a rally, depending on what's happening on the other side of the net. A team should begin each rally in a "medium position" (figure 8.1), in which front- and back-row players are relaxed and ready to move, with eyes watching the opponents and feet slightly wider than shoulder width. Front-row players have their hands high in preparation for blocking and remain in this position unless they retreat from the net to assume a defensive position for an attacked ball that they're not involved in blocking.

Figure 8.1 Medium position.

Back-row players assume a defensive position each time the opponent has a chance to put the ball on the floor. Back-row players might drop if a setter can dump the ball, then drop again for a quick attack, then drop again if the ball is set high to an outside hitter. The only time a back-row player is back in the medium position is when adjusting his or her position on the floor.

The basic defensive position remains the same across the board, regardless of age level or experience. The major difference between the beginner and advanced player's ability to demonstrate and maintain the basic position is physical strength and stamina. Following are the mechanics of the basic position:

- The feet are balanced, spread slightly wider than shoulder width.
- Body weight is slightly forward, on the balls of the feet.
- The knees are bent, extending beyond the toes.
- The waist is bent so that the back is as flat as possible.
- The chest is down, and shoulders are in front of the knees.
- The head is up, with eyes focused forward.
- The arms are loose and relaxed, ready to form the platform to dig or to release the hands for an overhead dig.

From this defensive position, players should be able to move laterally, forward, backward, or even into the air (figure 8.2).

At the highest levels of play, the goal is to maintain the lowest and most stable defensive position continuously. The harder the ball is hit, the more available reaction time will decrease, which means the player must be low and ready sooner to have a better chance to play the ball successfully.

Figure 8.2 Basic defensive position.

DEFENSIVE PREPARATION

At the beginning levels of play, coaches and players are justifiably more concerned with learning the proper skills and getting comfortable with the nuances of the game. As skill level increases, however, game tactics and strategies become more relevant.

Many defensive decisions depend on the strengths and weaknesses of your team and your opponent's team. Through hours of watching video and analyzing statistics, coaches and players can formulate a defensive game plan to give their team both the opportunity and ability to score points.

Begin looking at team defense at the origination point (with your team's own serve) and move on to the proper base positions, the responsibilities at the net and in the backcourt, and the subsequent actions affected by each contact of the ball.

To be solid defensively, players must know a number of things before each rally begins. First, they must acknowledge and make a mental note of how many hitters are in the opponent's front row, who the hitters are, and where the setter is located (front row or back row). Work every day in practice on identifying various offensive patterns by opponents so that proper defensive adjustments at the net and in the back row can be made. Doing this will familiarize your players with several defensive situations so that they're prepared for what's to come. For example, does the opposing setter set the player who has just made a mistake or will the setter avoid that player and give someone else a chance to score? Is the opposing setter an "equal opportunity" setter—one who gives each of the hitters the same number of swings?

Understanding general offensive systems and strategy becomes more critical to a team's defensive success as the players progress to more competitive levels of play. At the highest levels, detailed scouting reports are compiled that outline specific tendencies of the opponent's offensive system and individual players. The more information players can digest, the more advanced the coach's teaching approach to blocking and defense can be. For example, you can spend significant time working at particular blocking assignments at the net and consequently the back-row base position in two-hitter versus three-hitter rotations of the opponents. You can also work diligently on defending specific tendencies of the individual players your team will face.

An effective way to teach team defense, especially at the lower levels, is to break the game down into six minigames (one minigame for each rotation). The first minigame, for convenience, will be with the opposing setter in the right-back position. If this is the first minigame in a series of six, the coach must ask, "How will our team defend the opponent in this rotation?" One way to answer this question is to serve the "opponent" 10 balls and see what they like to do in this particular rotation. Once your players understand the options available to the opponent in rotation 1, rotate so the opposing setter is in the middle back (rotation 2). Repeat the same process for all six rotations or minigames. At all levels, the serve is critical in helping to dictate what options the opponent has.

The first priority regarding team defense is to look at how your team's serve also affects the outcome of the rally. Don't attempt to be a team that traditionally goes to the endline and bombs the serve in search of aces. This can result in a serve that is out and, when rally scoring is used, a point for the other team. Rather, look at serving as the first step in limiting the number of options for the opponent. This makes the team defense more efficient and more effective. Some serving strategies you might try are (1) serving the opponent's weakest passer, (2) serving one of the opponent's front-row players, or (3) serving short to test the rhythm and pattern of the opponent's middle hitter. If a serve can successfully limit the options of the opponent, there's a significantly greater chance to form a solid block on the available attacker(s). Thus, your team can cover the floor defensively to dig more balls.

SEQUENCE OF EVENTS ON DEFENSE

Once the ball is served and a team goes on defense, the rally can take any number of twists and turns. It's the coach's job to prepare the players for the many variables that will occur throughout the course of a rally. It's imperative that players remain focused on the correct actions and that they're agile enough for this to translate into the proper position and movement to keep the ball alive.

Before the Serve

On the defensive side of the ball, when the ball is served, players should assume a base position with the left-back and right-back players at about 12 feet (3.6 meters) from the net and 3 to 4 feet (91 to 122 centimeters) from their respective sidelines. The middle-back player will play deeper, about 5 feet (1.5 meters) from the endline. Coaches should reserve the right to change the base alignment, depending on the opponent's strengths and weaknesses. At the net, start the blockers in spread formation (figure 8.3), pinched formation (figure 8.4), or a combination, again based on the tendencies of the opponent in that particular rotation.

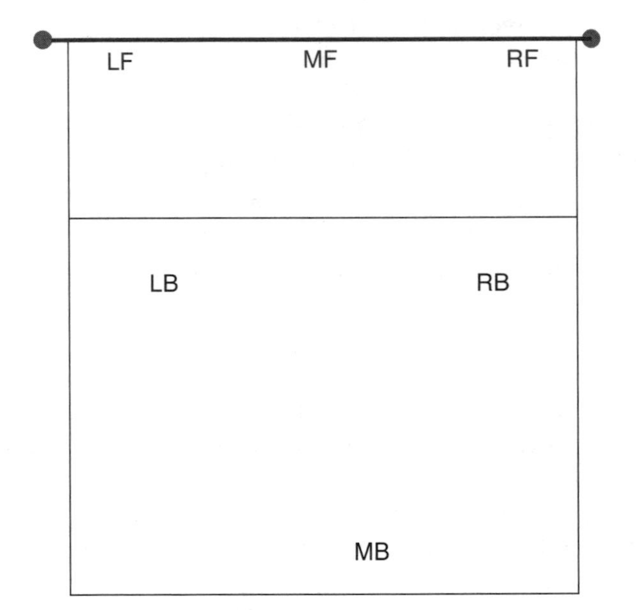

Figure 8.3 Base defensive position with spread block.

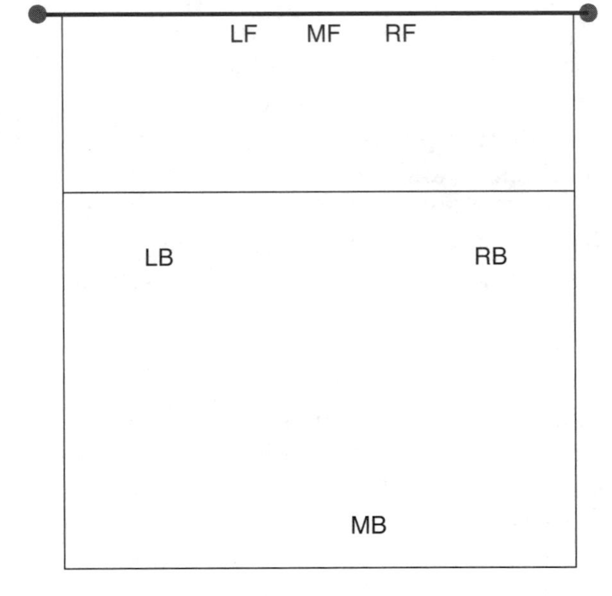

Figure 8.4 Base defensive position with pinch block.

Ball Served Over the Net

Option 1: Defending the overpass. Generally speaking, players should begin the rally in the base position to prepare for the varied ways in which the ball could come over the net. The first way a ball could come over the net to the defensive side is an overpass, which occurs when the receiving team attempts to pass the ball to its own setter, but inadvertently hits the ball long, sending it over the net into the opponent's court. Front-row players need to be ready to hit, tip, or block the ball down on an overpass. Back-row players need to be ready for a ball that is overpassed on the first contact by the opponent but is too deep in the court for a front-row player to attack.

Ball Passed to Setter

Option 2: Defending the tip. If the ball has been successfully passed to the setter on the opponent's side of the net, players should stay in their base positions to defend a possible setter tip. Offensive-minded setters can attack the ball in several ways. If the setter is in the front row, he or she can jump to attack, which would mean that the defenders should be in a low position, ready to pop the ball up. If the opposing setter is in the back row, he or she could stand and set the second ball over the net—a play that seems to score all too frequently. To prepare for this play, the right- and left-back players should be alert and ready to pursue the ball. Depending on the angle of approach of the quick hitter, explore the possibility of designating one wing player to take the setter's tip.

Setter Does Not Tip

Option 3: Defending the quick attack. If the setter doesn't tip the ball, it's a good idea to keep the players in their base positions to defend the quick attack by the opposing team (figure 8.5). This ensures that right-back players see the middle attacker on the opposing team and are in position to dig the cut back or power shot. Depending on the strength of the opponent's quick attacker, use one, two, or even three blockers at the net who are trying to block the ball. Regardless, the left-back and right-back diggers should be in a position from which they can see the attacker outside the block. In this defense, the middle-back player will read the hitter based on his or her angle of approach and will have an idea of what the middle blocker is going to take away at the net and position him or herself accordingly. Never allow a digger to play directly behind a solo blocker.

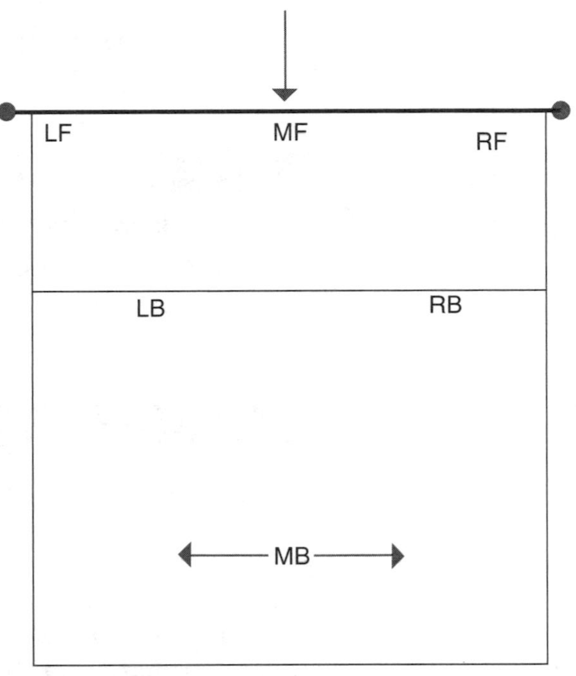

Figure 8.5 Defending the quick middle attack.

No Quick Attack

Option 4: Defending the set to left, right, or middle. If the opponent chooses not to set the quick attacker, players should now look to establish a new defensive position based on the location of the set (left side, right side, or combination play in the middle of the net) and the type of defense the team is playing. This new defensive position will vary based on the type of defense that the coach feels will best fit his or her personnel and the level of play at which the team is competing. Before discussing the specific defensive systems, first ask the following questions:

- Who are my best defensive players? Usually, it's a good idea to play the best defensive player in the left back and operate with a "green light theory." In other words, he or she has the green light to dig and pursue any ball possible.
- How can I get my best defensive players in position to dig the most balls? In practice, as a team, work quite a bit at coordinating the block and the defense so that if the ball is not blocked, it's channeled to the best defenders, who are ready and waiting to do their jobs.
- How can I best use substitutions to maximize the strengths of taller players at the net and the best defenders in the back row? With the introduction of the libero

position within the past several years, coaches will always have their best defenders on the floor, but there are still opportunities to use the other defensive subs to impact the game. It's possible that the libero will need to be comfortable in all three back-court positions. Following the set to the right or left side, players must work diligently to assume the proper position to defend the court. Three basic defenses will be diagrammed and the strengths and weaknesses of each will be noted. If your opponent sets the ball to a back-row attacker on a consistent basis, the defenders should stay deep in the backcourt, along the sidelines and the endline; meanwhile, the blockers should delay their block at the net.

Coaching Points to Prepare for Any Possible Sequence of Events

- Acknowledge who the hitters are and their court positions (front or back row).
- Acknowledge the setter and his or her court location (front or back row).
- Identify various offensive patterns used by the opponent.
- Use your team's serve to influence the rally defensively.

DEFENSIVE SYSTEMS OF PLAY

Hopefully it is clear that the main concerns on defense are attitude and effort. However, it must be understood that certain types of defenses have proven effective over the years. In the following pages, various defensive systems of play will be outlined and diagrammed. Coaches should be encouraged to have a rationale for choosing a particular defense and be willing to adjust if the situation dictates, based primarily on the skill level of the players. To begin making the decision on which defense to use, a coach should determine where the opponent attacks most of the balls—do they like to tip, for example? Do they hit cross court or down the line? Who is their best attacker and from where does he or she attack? Each of the defenses described below will address defending these types of attacks.

Perimeter Defense

The perimeter defense is probably the most common defense played, and its benefit lies in the positioning of the defenders to dig hard-hit balls. The floor is balanced, but there's a large open area in the middle of the floor. It's a good idea to use the left-front player to pick up tips in the middle of the floor against a left-side attack (figure 8.6) and the right-front player to pick up tips in the middle of the floor against a right-side attack (figure 8.7). In both situations, have the middle-back player stay deep so he or she can read the play. The middle back is responsible for balls hit high off the block or balls hit deep into either corner of the court. The left-back player is the primary digger for balls hit cross court from the opponent's left side, whereas the right back is the primary line digger. The roles are reversed for an attack from the opponent's right side.

Because this is a defense that can be used quite often, a team can spend considerable time on a drill called Four Person. In addition to allowing the players to

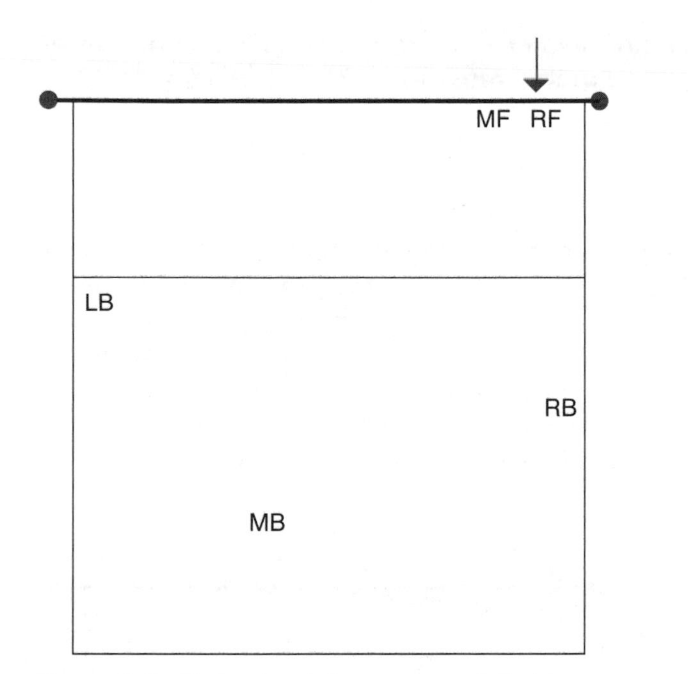

Figure 8.6 Perimeter defense versus left-side attack.

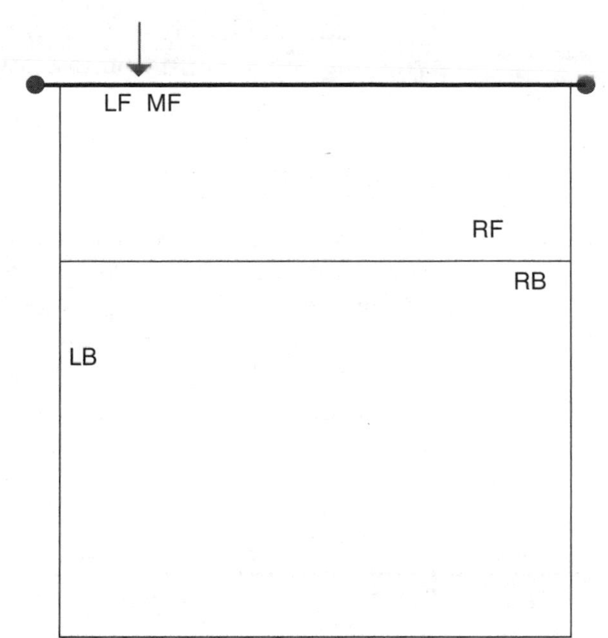

Figure 8.7 Perimeter defense versus right-side attack.

get comfortable in their defensive positions and accustomed to playing alongside their teammates, this drill allows the coaches to observe which players possess the necessary traits of great defenders. This drill also allows the setter to gain valuable setting repetitions in many situations (see drills at the end of the chapter).

Middle-Up Defense

The middle-up defense has proven quite effective when used in the right situations. If competition is against a team that tips quite frequently or uses a variety of off-speed shots, this is a great defense. In figures 8.8 and 8.9, it's indicated that

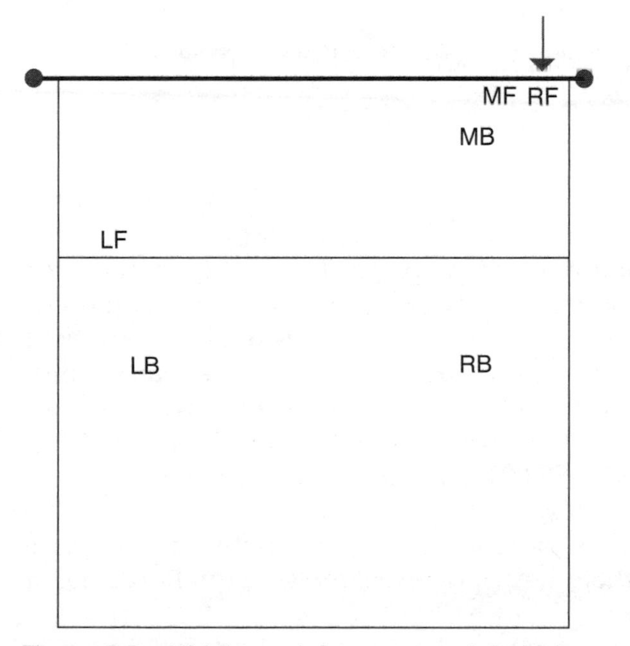

Figure 8.8 Middle-up defense versus left-side attack.

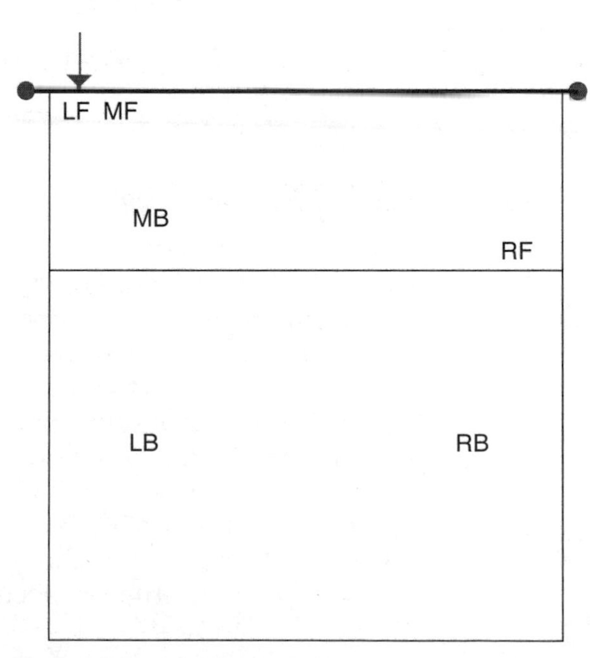

Figure 8.9 Middle-up defense versus right-side attack.

the middle-back player pulls in behind the block to dig (it could also be the setter who releases for the tips to allow for a quick transition). Internationally, this has been very popular.

Rotation Defense

The rotation defense can also be effective under the right circumstances. The proper execution of this defense depends on a disciplined block that allows the hitter to attack the line. The block should take away the seam and cross-court shot and allow the middle-back digger, who has rotated to the line, to dig the ball. Against a left-side attack, the right-back digger will release and pick up off-speed shots, while the left-back digger will release for tips against a right-side attack (figures 8.10 and 8.11). An excellent drill for the rotation defense is called Acceleration.

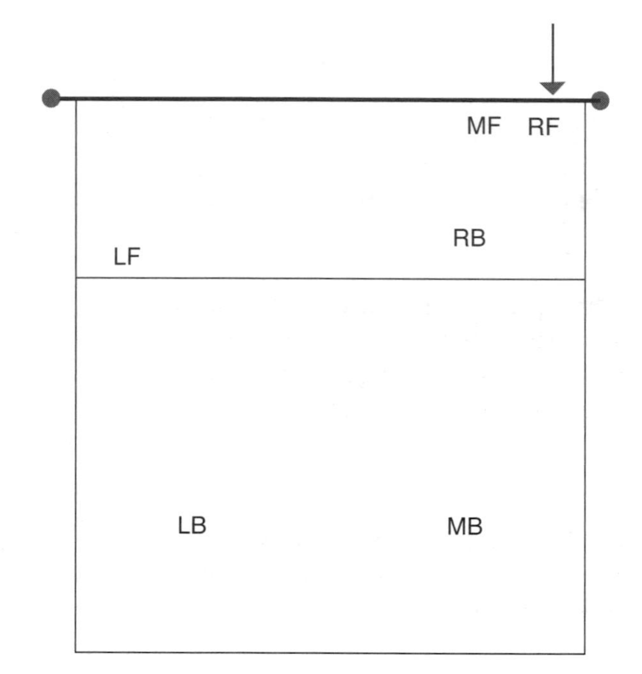

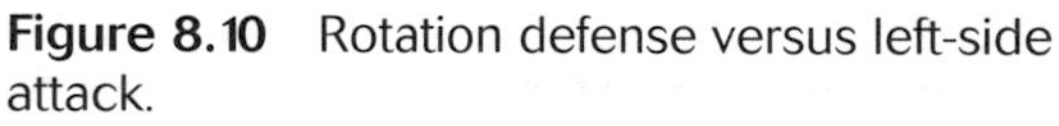

Figure 8.10 Rotation defense versus left-side attack.

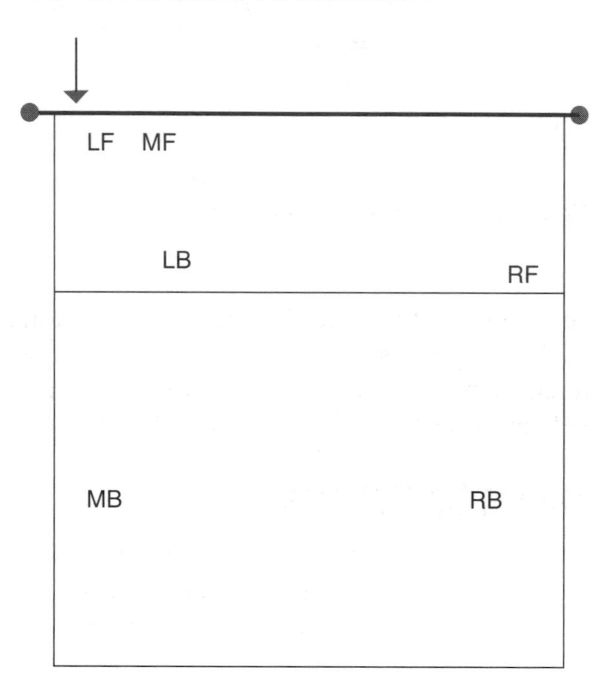

Figure 8.11 Rotation defense versus right-side attack.

Out-of-System Plays

There might be rallies in which the ball is not passed directly to the setter that could result in one of two different types of out-of-system plays. The first type, the "free ball," occurs when the opponent is forced, usually because of a poor first pass or a miscommunication, to pass the ball over the net easily. In this free-ball situation, encourage all players to communicate by yelling "free!" so each player can get into proper position to pass the ball. The setter, if he or she is in the back row, releases to the net to establish position and await the pass from a teammate (figure 8.12). The front-row players simultaneously pull off the net and are available to pass the ball, while the other back-row players balance the court.

The other type of out-of-system situation teams might encounter is the "down ball." A down-ball situation occurs when the opponent can't get a quality swing at

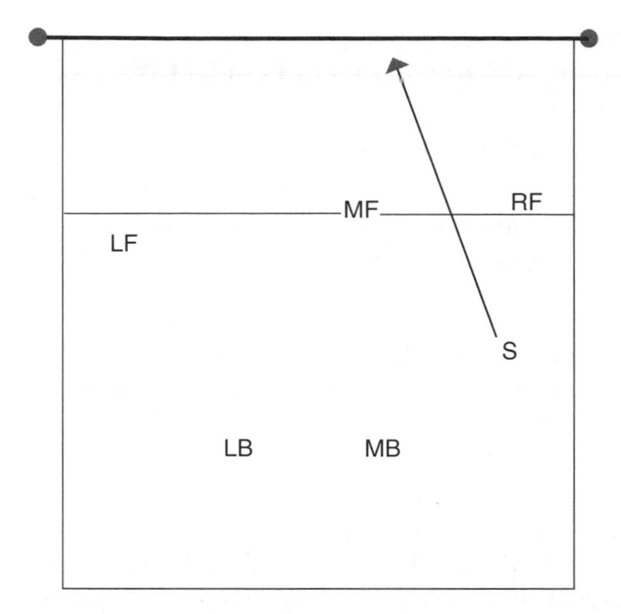

Figure 8.12 Free ball alignment.

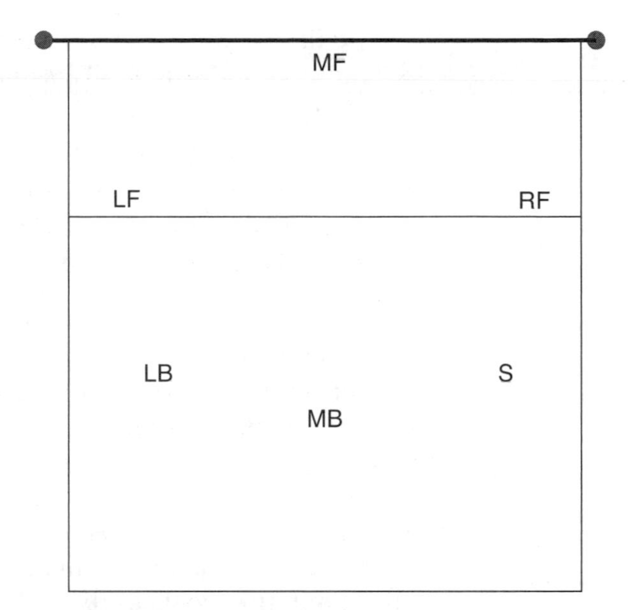

Figure 8.13 Down ball alignment.

the ball, but he or she can stand on the ground and swing. The worst thing to do in this situation is give the hitter an easy target at which to hit. In this situation, the middle blocker should stay at the net in case it's a ball that he or she can block; don't encourage the middle blocker to jump before the ball is attacked. Right-front and left-front players are expected to pull off the net but still be alert and available to pass the ball. The setter will remain in the right-back position until he or she sees that the ball is hit elsewhere. Left-back and middle-back players will also hold their positions (figure 8.13). An excellent drill to deal effectively with the down ball in practice is called Scramble.

USING THE LIBERO FOR MAXIMUM PERFORMANCE

In 1998, the Fédération Internationale de Volleyball (FIVB), the International Governing Body for the sport of volleyball, instituted a new position, the libero, for international volleyball matches. The libero (or replacement player) is, in its most basic form, a passing and defensive specialist. Men's collegiate volleyball in the United States began using the libero during the 2000 playing season, and USA Volleyball (USAV), the National Governing Body for the sport in the United States, adopted the rule in 2001. By 2002, women's collegiate volleyball had also adopted the rule. Since 1999–2000, the FIVB rulebook has incorporated the information specific to the libero into the text of each individual rule. In addition, the entirety of chapter 6 of the FIVB rulebook has been dedicated to the libero. The libero is defined in the 1999-2000 FIVB rulebook, rule 8.5.2, as follows:

- The libero must wear a different color uniform, shirt, or jacket in contrast to the other members of the team.
- The libero is allowed to replace any player in a back-row position.

- The libero is restricted to perform as a back-row player and is not allowed to complete an attack hit from anywhere if at the moment of contact the ball is entirely higher than the top of the net.
- The libero may not serve, block, or attempt to block.
- A player may not complete an attack hit from higher than the top of the net, if the ball is coming from an overhand finger pass by a libero in the front zone. The ball may be freely attacked if the libero makes the same action from behind the end zone.

It should also be noted that the replacements involving the libero are not counted as regular substitutions. They are unlimited, but there must be a rally between two libero replacements. The player whom he or she replaced can only replace the libero.

The standard method of using the libero is to replace the two middle blockers with the libero following the loss of the serve by the back-court middle blocker. There are several advantages to this method of replacement. First, middle blockers are traditionally the weakest defensive players on the floor, and by using this replacement pattern, they're only on the floor to play defense while they are serving. Also, the libero is available to serve receive in all six rotations. Finally, depending on its structure, a team's serve-reception pattern might allow for the front-row outside hitter to avoid significant serve-receive responsibilities and focus on scoring.

Of course, the previous paragraph outlines the standard method of replacement with the libero, but coaches know the strengths and weaknesses of their teams; thus, a coach should study and experiment with the possibilities of using this position to the benefit of the team. One collegiate team began each game using the libero to replace the middle blockers, but once they got into their routine substitution pattern, the libero replaced the outside hitters. This allowed the team to "save subs" so the strongest defenders were in the game at the end. In essence, the libero replaced four different players during a typical game.

Regardless of how coaches choose to structure their defensive pattern, it's critical to maximize the libero position. Many of the top collegiate teams in the United States play the libero in the left-back position. Some play the libero in the middle-back position. Basing judgment on the type of defense a team plays and the tendencies of each opponent, a coach might choose to use the libero where he or she is going to have the opportunity to pass and dig the most balls. It could happen that the libero changes defensive zones based on the location of the opponent's set.

DEFENSIVE DRILLS

Four-Person

Purpose: This is a team pepper drill that allows players to get comfortable in their defensive positions while becoming accustomed to playing alongside their teammates. Coaches can observe which players possess the necessary traits of great defenders.

Setup: Four defensive players take the floor, plus a setter. Two coaches hit at the defenders (figure 8.14).

Execution: The ball is put in play by C1 or C2. The defenders' goal is to keep the ball off the floor, preferably digging it to the setter. If C1 hits, LF goes to the net, and S pulls off the net as the right-front digger. The ball is kept alive as long as possible. Players can substitute after a certain amount of time or certain number of digs. Be sure to have a new ball in play immediately after a ball hits the floor.

Coaching Points: Look for players who are comfortable in the proper defensive positions.

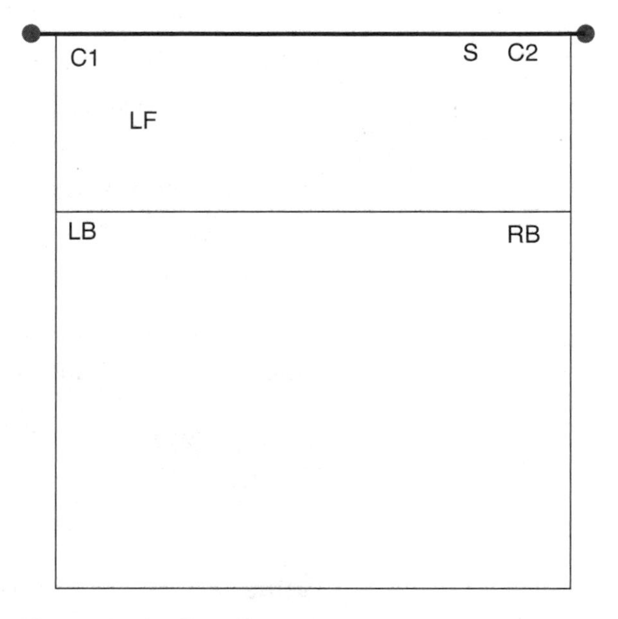

Figure 8.14 Four-Person.

Acceleration

Purpose: This drill allows defenders multiple opportunities to accelerate and pursue the ball while running forward.

Setup: A coach stands on a box on the opposite side of the net. The LB, MB, and RB line up along the endline.

Execution: The coach tips or tosses a ball so that the RB player, who begins on the endline, must accelerate and pursue the ball while running forward. The RB player then runs back to the endline to get ready for the next opportunity. Meanwhile, the MB pursues the next ball and is then followed by the LB (figure 8.15). Continue the drill for 15, 20, or 25 good digs to target. The coach can adjust the position from which the ball is tipped over the net (i.e., left side, middle, right side).

Coaching Points: You can dictate the area of coverage required and increase the tempo of the drill to include conditioning.

Variation: You can do this for any of the defensive schemes you're employing by placing the ball into the exposed areas of coverage.

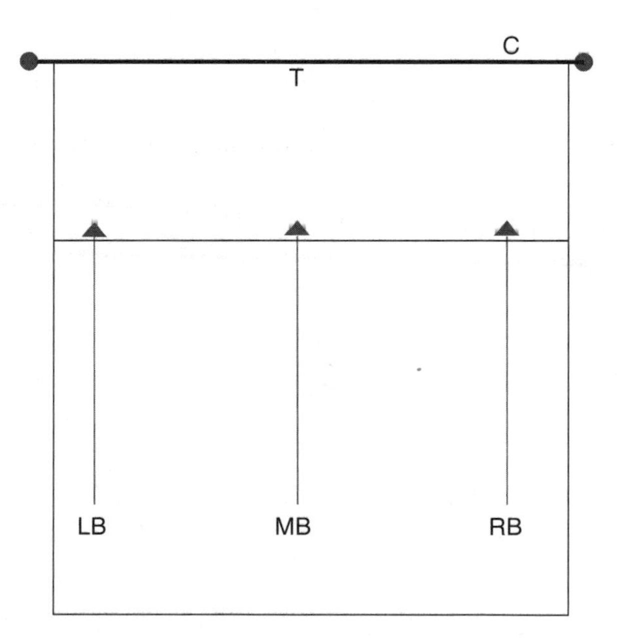

Figure 8.15 Acceleration.

Scramble

Purpose: This drill gives players a variety of gamelike situations in which they must scramble to get into position and play the ball out while keeping in-system.

Setup: Players play six versus six.

Execution: The coach can initiate play in several ways:

- Put the ball directly into play to side B.
- Give the first ball to side A, and they pass, set, and attack.
- Give the first ball to side A, and they must give a free or down ball to side B.
- In each of the situations, the two sides play the rally out.
- Play each of the six rotations. Side B must win five out of 10 rallies to rotate.

Coaching Points: Always provide gamelike situations while drilling players (especially on defense) to ensure the proper reaction to all balls played.

Weave

Purpose: This drill makes players move their feet to get to the ball at all costs.

Setup: A coach stands on the floor on the same side as the diggers. The diggers line up in the middle back area of the court.

Execution: The coach puts the ball into play with an underhand, controlled toss to the right-back or left-back area of the court. The next toss goes to the opposite area, and so on (figure 8.16). The toss should force the player to move his or her feet to get to the ball. After the player plays the ball, he or she retreats to the back of the line. It's best to use small groups of three to five players so standing around is minimized. The coach can toss for a set time or for a specified number of tosses.

Coaching Points: Adjust the degree of difficulty based on the skill level of the players.

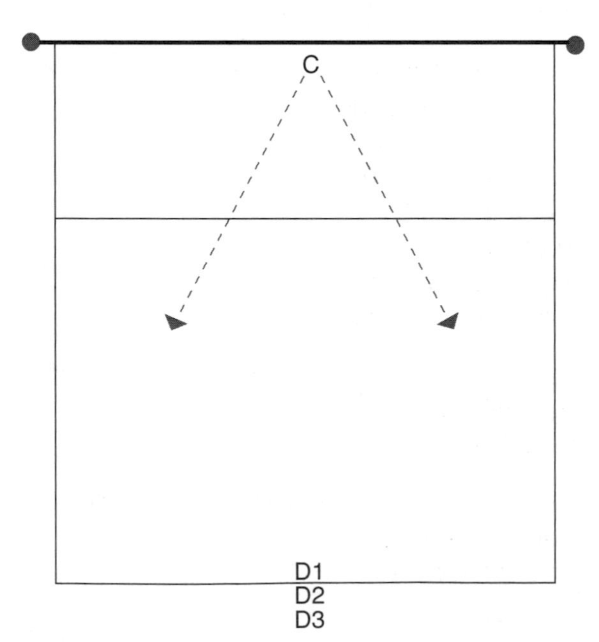

Figure 8.16 Weave.

Crossfire

Purpose: This drill allows players to practice digging cross court and down the line in rapid-fire succession.

Setup: Two coaches are on boxes on one side of the net. LB and RB set up just behind the three-meter line on the other side.

Execution: Coach 2 hits the first ball down the line at the RB player. Coach 1 then hits a ball cross court at the RB player. Coach 2 hits the next ball cross court at the LB player, followed by coach 1 hitting the next ball down the line at the LB player. Essentially, each player will dig two balls in a row (one cross court and one down the line). Change the order in which the players dig the ball. The pace of the ball depends on the skill level of the players in the drill.

Coaching Points: Use gamelike introduction of the ball so players can practice digging one after another.

Variations: This drill can be continued for a number of successful digs or for a set time. You can also put a player in the middle back position.

Dig 10

Purpose: This drill provides an opportunity for defensive players to become accustomed to reading the setter and gives them a chance to work on various defensive alignments.

Setup: Three coaches are on boxes on one side of the net. A group of six players set up on the other side (figure 8.17).

Execution: The group of six on the floor attempts to dig 10 balls. The ball is put in play from a setter on the opposite side of the net so the defense becomes accustomed to reading the setter. The setter sets in the general direction of one of the coaches. That coach then tosses a ball to attack or tip against the defense. Repeat the sequence 10 times before switching players on defense. Work on various defensive alignments. Compete to see which group gets the most digs out of 10.

Coaching Points: The ability to read the setter is paramount for a successful defense. When introducing live hitters, the drill becomes even more gamelike.

Variations: The drill can be done with three live hitters at each position instead of coaches.

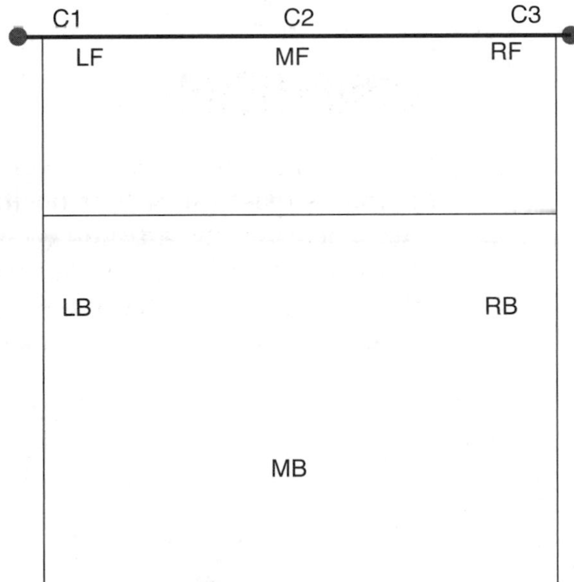

Figure 8.17 Dig 10.

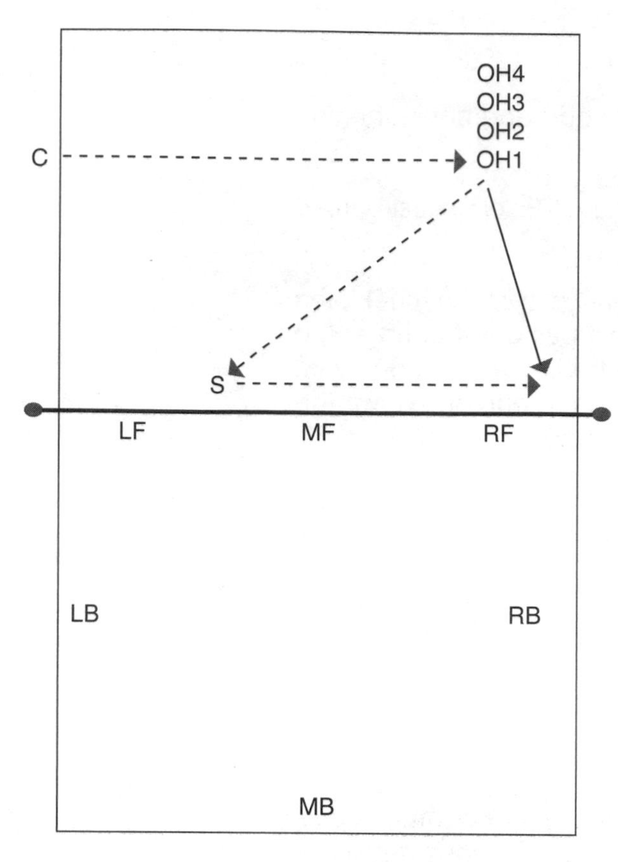

Figure 8.18 Hitters Versus Team Defense.

Hitters Versus Team Defense

Purpose: The drill allows the team defense to practice stopping the opponent's attack, either by block or dig. Simultaneously, the hitters are able to practice attacking in a gamelike situation.

Setup: A group of three to four hitters begins on one side of the net beginning with OH1 and a setter.

Execution: The ball is put into play to OH1 from a coach. OH1 passes the ball to the setter and then attacks versus the team defense, trying to score. After OH1 attempts to score, OH2 then tries to score. While the team defense is pursuing the goal of getting five stops, either by a block or a dig into a transition swing, the hitters are competing with each other to see which player can get the most kills. This drill is then repeated for middle hitters and right-side hitters (figure 8.18).

Coaching Points: Providing gamelike opportunities for all hitters and defenders to hone their skills is the key to successful defense of your court.

CONCLUSION

Players must possess a "never say die" attitude. Although many possibilities and opinions exist for proper positioning and techniques related to playing effective team defense, the attitude each member of the team possesses in pursuit of each ball in every rally is the greatest predictor of success. Playing effective team defense doesn't guarantee that your team will be successful, but it does give you a solid chance for victory in every match.

9

Transitioning

Stephanie Schleuder

Transition is best described as the movement of players from one phase of the game to another. In basketball, transition is the movement from one end of the court to another, but in volleyball, transition is much more subtle. Every time the ball passes over the net, transition occurs on each side. Generally, when coaches think of transition, they think of the movement of the players between actual defensive and offensive execution. But transitions also occur at other times during a game, such as when preparing for defense, switching positions before the serve or after receiving the serve, covering hitters, and preparing to receive a "free" or "down" ball. Watching teams execute transition effectively is like watching a well-choreographed ballet with synchronized movement on each side of the court.

Top coaches might debate over which skill in volleyball is the single one most important to a team's success. However, virtually all highly successful coaches agree that efficient and effective transition ranks among the top three. This is particularly true for higher levels of competition, where all teams have highly skilled players. Teams with higher levels of skill have faster and more efficient transition. In essence, the speed at which the game is played increases with skill, and the speed and efficiency of the game is directly proportionate to the speed of the transition within the game. Coaches can greatly enhance the competitiveness of their teams—without significantly improving skills—by improving the speed and efficiency of the transition game.

TRANSITION CONCEPTS

Transition skills can be broken down into individual skills and team-related skills. Factors affecting good, efficient transition for both the individual and the team are ball control, reading (or anticipation), and familiarity with specific formations. All of these skills are interrelated and interdependent and play key roles in the ultimate success of a team. The old saying about the team being only as strong as its weakest link definitely applies to the transition game.

Ball control is the ability of the individual or team to pass, dig, or overhead set the ball effectively coming from the opponent to the target area so that the setter can run the offense. A team that can get the ball to the setter in the target area near the net immediately increases the likelihood of successfully attacking and scoring. Scoring with this kind of ball control is the goal for all transition offense.

Reading and anticipation are critical aspects of being in the right place at the right time—definitely a huge advantage in playing the ball successfully. Reading is a visual skill that allows players to respond to the setter's release of the ball, effectively moving into position while quickly ticking through a mental checklist of the options available to the hitter in each circumstance. Anticipation enables a player to get a jump and get to the most advantageous position to make a play on the ball effectively. Focus of the eyes in a specific sequence is an important part of developing reading and anticipation skills and will be discussed later.

Knowing the formations and getting to position quickly are essential for performing good transition. These concepts are equally important. It does little good to be in the right spot on the court if you have arrived there too late to play the ball. Coaches must be specific about where each player should be in each situation and give them movement patterns for transition to the right spot in a quick, efficient way. Teaching players when to be in a specific formation and how to get there are big keys in training for good transition.

Base position (or starting position) is the term used to describe the place on the court from which all movement or transition begins. The base position is the position to which players return each time their team sends the ball over the net. A team's base position for a match depends on the defense and the alignments desired by the coach. Frequently, individual base positions will change over the course of a match based on the strengths and weaknesses of the opponent and the defenses being employed. Base position can also depend on whether the opposing setter is a front- or back-row player. One front-row player should be assigned to communicate this information to the team before every serve. It's critical for players to know their base positions and, more important, to "hit" the position every time the ball is returned to the opponents. During long rallies it's common for players to get out of position and never get back into position. Such a lack of discipline usually results in the loss of a point. The proper execution of this particular concept—getting back to base—can markedly improve the success of teams at any level.

Figure 9.1 shows players in a typical base position as the opponent's setter prepares to set the ball. Here, the opposing setter is a back-row player. The left-front blocker must take a position that allows her to help the middle blocker and also to transition to the left when there's a back set to execute a block on the opposing right-side hitter. Putting up a double block on the opposing middle, as well as a double block on the left- and right-side hitters, is frequently seen today. It's also common in the men's game—and even in the women's game—for teams to attempt a triple block against outstanding hitters. Obviously, this requires quick, agile blockers. In the back row, players' base positions can vary depending on the defensive system and the strengths of each hitter. Generally, the left- and right-back players are positioned slightly behind the three-meter line and about 5 feet (1.5 meters) in from the sidelines. They should turn toward the opposing setter and be ready to play any setter dump. The middle back player is usually positioned about 6 feet (1.8 meters) inside the endline and equidistant from either sideline. Note the body postures of the players. The blockers have a high posture with arms up and ready to block; the back-row players are in a medium posture with their arms relaxed and extended at about waist level, ready to move and play a ball.

Figure 9.1 Base position for defense when the ball is with the server.

Figure 9.2 shows another example of a team in base position. The ball is on the opponent's side of the net in the setter's hands, with three opposing hitters ready to approach and attack. In this figure, the back row is positioned for rotation defense, and the left-front (LF) player is positioned to help the middle block the opposing middle hitter. If the opposing middle is not much of a threat, you might adjust the left front's base position further to the left, as shown in figure 9.3. When the opposing right-front/opposite (RF/OPP) player is a very strong hitter and receives a high percentage of the sets, you might move your left front's base position out near the left sideline to focus on the opposing hitter, as shown in figure 9.4.

If the opposing setter is a front-row player (in a 5–1 or 4–2 offense), one of the front-row players might be assigned to block the setter in an attempt to stop an attack or dump on the second ball. One of the common reactions by a setter in this

Figure 9.2 Base position for defense when ball is with setter.

Figure 9.3 Base position with left front more left.

Figure 9.4 Base position with left front on left sideline.

situation is to dump the ball backward to area 4 (left front). Figure 9.5 shows this situation with the wing (left back) moved up to cover a dump to the left-front area. This strategy is especially effective if the setter has a pattern of dumping to one specific area. Figure 9.6 shows a situation in which the setter is a front-row player and the opposing middle attacker is very strong. Here, you might opt to use the left front as a blocker, freeing him or her from responsibility for the setter's dump or attack, and assign the wings (left back and right back) responsibility for digging the second-ball attack by the setter. Figure 9.7 shows the team in base position for perimeter defense with the opposing setter in the back row. When the setter is in the back row, the defense needs to be less concerned about a second-ball attack from the setter and, usually, play deeper in base position. Defensive players should be aware that some back-row setters will still use a two-handed set to dump. If this happens, the wing players are responsible for digging these dumps.

Figure 9.5 Left wing moves back to cover dump into left-front area.

Figure 9.6 Left wing moves to blocker positions, using the left back and right back for digging the second ball attack.

Figure 9.7 Team in perimeter defense with opposing setter in the back row.

The adjustments in base position shown here and used by many coaches are very subtle. But even such small adjustments can be extremely important in giving players an edge, helping them to be in the right place at the right time. Base positions can vary significantly with each coach's defensive philosophy. Many examples have been given here, but coaches should be creative in finding the best options for their teams. Clearly, the important point is to establish, teach, and require proper execution of base positions.

Checklist for Transition to Base Position

- Each time the ball is sent over the net, players return to base position.
- Base positions can vary depending on defensive strengths and the opponent's tendencies.
- Front-row players should verbalize whether the opposing setter is front- or back-row.
- Back-row wings (left back and right back) often have responsibility for dumps.
- Train efficient and quick movement routes so players "hit" their base in all situations.

USING VISUAL KEYS FOR EFFECTIVE TRANSITIONING

Eye sequencing and visual keys provide players with valuable information for effective transition movement. From their base position, players should use this sequence of eye checks to enhance transition.

1. *Watch the pass and quickly evaluate it.* Judge whether the pass will allow the setter to exercise all setting options (quick middle attack and both left and right). If the pass is good, the blockers and the defense should hold to watch the setter release the ball. If the pass is poor or the setter is unable to set the ball, the defense has an advantage in making early adjustments for the block and defense.

2. *Find the hitters.* After the ball is passed, blockers and defense should check the routes and positions of the opposing hitters. Hitters might be running static patterns (no movement), crossing patterns, or varied routes, which would require adjusting the blockers and defensive players.

3. *Watch the setter release the ball.* Some setters give clues to the intended location of their sets by their body position or the way they hold their hands. Once the setter releases the ball, the defense should make a strong, quick transition.

4. *Watch the flight of the set to its peak and evaluate it.* The location of the set along the net gives the blockers and defense important information for their transition. Additionally, the further the set is off the net, the less likely the hitter will be able to hit straight down. This allows the defense to play deeper on the court. On the other hand, a tight set (close to the net) gives the hitter a chance to bury the ball at or in front of the three-meter line. If the block is not positioned to take away the shot straight down, the defense should move up and hope they can dig it!

5. *Find the attacking hitter and note the angle of his or her approach.* Most hitters attack the ball along the same angle as their approach. Highly skilled hitters can change the attack angle after seeing the block form, but this is an advanced skill.

6. *Watch the hitter's jump and the initial forward swing of the hitting arm.* The general rule is for the blocker to jump a split-second after the hitter jumps. The defense traditionally sets up around the block, unless there's a hole in the block or a one-on-one situation in which the hitter has more options. When there's a mistake

by the block resulting in a single block or no block at all, the defense must resort to emergency protocol and scramble like crazy. In every case, the coach should discuss each possibility, and players should know where and how they transition for each situation.

7. *Keep eyes open.* This sounds pretty basic, but some players' eyes can wander or even close. All players should see the ball being contacted.

MOVEMENT PATTERNS AND TIMING

Movement patterns and timing should be specific for each situation and formation. Equally important to eye sequencing and where players direct their attention is how they move from one spot to another. There are three functions that coaches should train related to movement and timing: footwork, posture, and movement routes.

- *Footwork*—Practicing footwork skills is critical to ensure a high level of efficiency and quickness. Many transitions require footwork training, including blocking transition, back-row defensive transition, offensive transition, setter penetration, switching (position changes), and hitter coverage. Coaches have different opinions on the type of footwork best used for each situation. Some prefer to use a cross-over step; others prefer teaching a side step for most sideways and diagonal movement. The important thing is to train footwork that players can effectively execute and replicate without thinking—it must be a trained response. Once they have mastered the techniques, players need to practice footwork at normal game speed.
- *Posture*—Coaches often forget to teach players the types of postures they should hold in different transitions. The photos in figure 9.8 show the three postures used in volleyball. The first player is holding a fairly upright (high) posture, common to blockers in base position. They are upright with knees slightly bent and weight distributed evenly on the balls of the feet. Arms and hands are held high (above the head) but are slightly relaxed; the palms are open and the fingers spread (figure 9.8a). Depending on the type of blocking taught, the hand and arm position of the blockers during movement is important. Some coaches prefer to have blockers move with their hands and arms high and parallel to the net, whereas others allow players to drop their arms to perform a swing-blocking motion. The second player in the figure shows a medium posture. When transitioning off the net, blockers will be moving from a high posture to a lower (medium) posture in preparation for digging or offensive transition. In medium posture, the legs are bent and the feet spread about shoulder width; weight is slightly forward and evenly distributed on the balls of the feet; hands and arms are slightly extended from the waist, ready to play the ball. This posture is used for serve reception and movement in the back row for defense (figure 9.8b). Finally, the third player in the figure shows a low posture, with feet spread wider, weight forward, back relatively straight, and arms forward and slightly extended, ready to play the ball. A low posture is used for digging or emergency skills and should be employed in the final preparation stages for defense (figure 9.8c).
- *Movement Routes*—A player's movement routes are obviously important in coordinating transition for the team. Coaches should first teach the cues for timing the movement. Eye sequencing is an important part of the training, but coaches

Figure 9.8a High posture.

Figure 9.8b Medium posture.

Figure 9.8c Low posture.

will also have other cues to use. For example, as soon as the ball crosses the net to the other side, players should return to their base positions. Another example of a cue is when the opposing setter releases the ball to the outside hitter. In this case, the offense immediately transitions to defense, with the middle blocker moving to the right to form a double block with the right front (opposite blocker), while the off-blocker (LF) transitions off the net to defensive position. Simultaneously, the back-row players transition to their respective defensive positions. The second issue with training routes is to teach players where they go in relation to the other players. The first rule is that the setter always has the right of way, and the team stays out of his or her way. The setter always takes the most direct route to the target area and back to base position. Players should clear a path for the setter so he or she doesn't have to run around teammates. More specific routes for other players will be discussed in the section on rotational transition.

Figure 9.9 shows the set leaving the setter's hands. This action triggers the defense to begin transition from base position to defense—in this case, rotation defense. Note that the middle blocker steps along the net toward the right-side blocker as the left-side blocker (off blocker) uses a drop step to move off the net and transition for playing defense. The middle-back player moves toward the right sideline, and the left-back player transitions deeper toward the back corner. The right-back player moves slightly into the court and behind the forming block at about the three-meter line. During transition, players should keep their eyes on the action, never turning their back to the play.

Figure 9.10 shows the final transition position of the defensive players in rotation defense before the hitter contacts the ball. The left front (off blocker) is positioned at about the three-meter line and is lined up in such a way as to see the ball outside

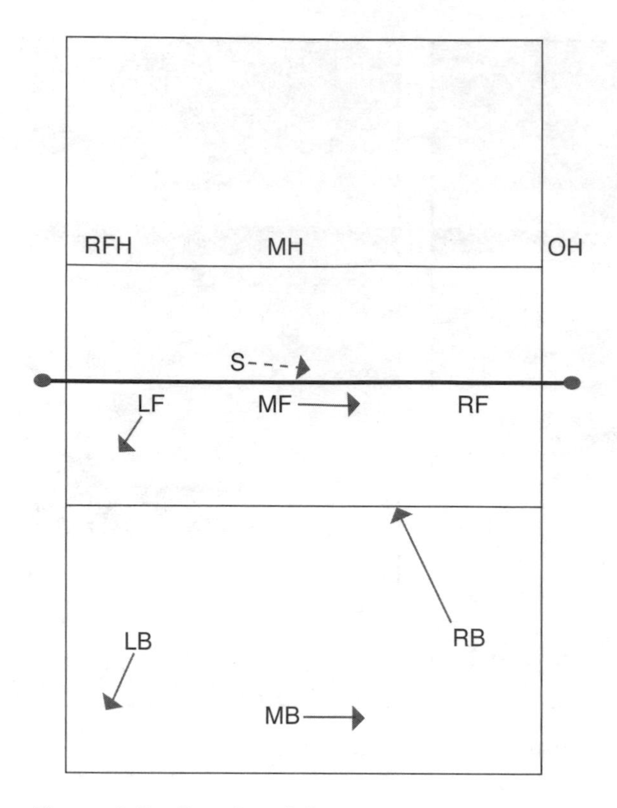

Figure 9.9 Rotation defense.

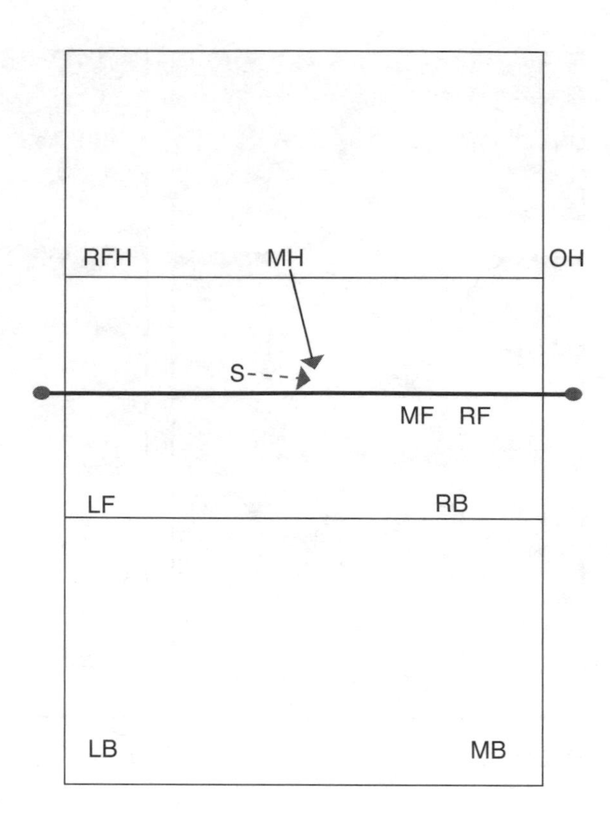

Figure 9.10 Rotation defense before the hitter contacts the ball.

the left shoulder and arms of the middle blocker. The middle- and right-side blockers have formed a double block, with the right-side blocker setting the position of the block relative to the hitter. The left back has transitioned toward the left back corner, and the middle back has moved to the right sideline about six feet in from the endline. The right back plays at about the three-meter line and lines up between the two blockers. It's critical for the defensive players to arrive at their defensive positions before the hitter contacts the ball.

Checklist for Movement Patterns and Timing

- Footwork training should be specific for each position and transition.
- Teach the type of posture (high, medium, low) desired for each transition.
- Use drills that focus on timing and movement routes for each individual transition.
- The setter always has the right of way and the most direct route.

TRANSITION TACTICS

Rotational transition (or “switching”) is the term used to describe the movement of players immediately after the ball is contacted on the serve. Most coaches elect to use specialization in which players are assigned to a specific front-row position and a specific back-row position (assuming they play both front and back row). At some levels of beginning play, some coaches decide to have players play the position they rotate into rather than specialize. This concept is called generalization. When generalization is used, there’s no need to discuss rotational transition, in which players move to their assigned front- or back-row position on the contact of the serve. With generalization, players simply stay where they are—a different position in every rotation.

Any offensive system that uses players specialized as hitters and setters needs to cover the concept of rotational transition. Common offensive systems using specialization are the 4–2, 5–1, and 6–2 offenses. Generally, players in these systems are assigned one front-row position and one back-row position. For example, a player might be assigned to be an outside hitter (left front) and then play left back when in the back row. A player opposite him or her in the rotation order would be assigned to play the same positions, so at any given time one would always be in the front row and the other in the back row. Figure 9.11a shows the numbers commonly used to name the areas of the court, and figure 9.11b shows the rotation order using specialization. The wheel shows a 5–1 offense with the setter (circled) as #9 starting in right back (rotation 1). Typically, the middle hitters would be opposite each other in the lineup, as are #13 and #5; the outside hitters would be opposite each other, as are #4 and #10; and the right-side or opposite player (#14) would be opposite the setter. Using specialization requires that players switch into their assigned positions after every serve. There are two specific aspects of rotational transition.

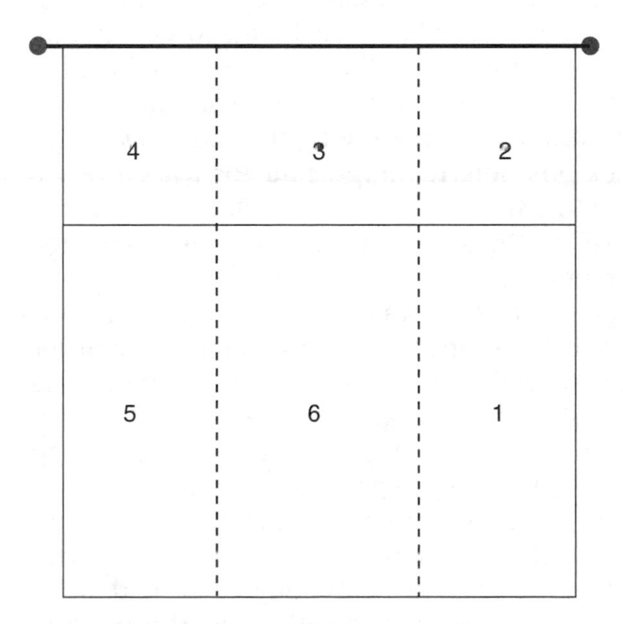

Figure 9.11a Areas of the court.

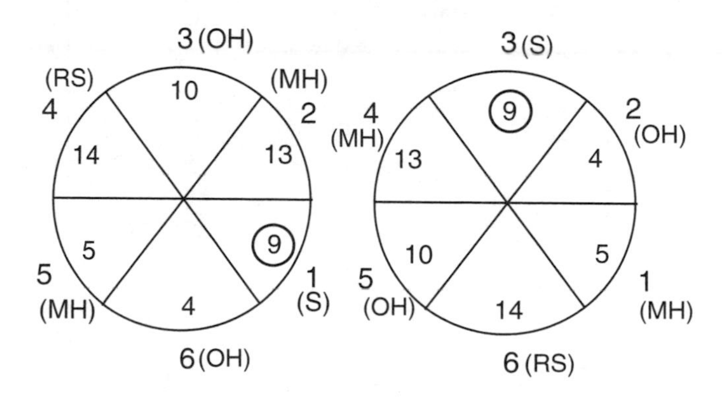

Figure 9.11b Setter in rotation #1.

The first and most straightforward part of rotational transition is employed when the players' own team is serving. Here the transition to assigned positions is relatively easy. As soon as the server contacts the ball, players immediately transition to their assigned front- or back-row positions. Train players to switch positions when they hear the server contact the ball. It's important for the team to focus on the opponents, not the server. The server's location is unimportant to the pending action, but the opponents' positioning is critical.

In the front row, the middle hitter transitions closest to the net, while the end hitters/blockers take paths around the middle by running behind them as directly as possible to their positions. The outside hitter takes the widest route around the middle and the right side/opposite takes the route immediately behind the middle blocker. Transition of back-row players is usually simpler, with players going backward, forward, or sideways with few traffic problems. Before the rule change allowing players to serve from anywhere along the endline, the longest rotational transition was often the left-back player serving from right back and then having to run to the left-back wing position near the three-meter line. Now players usually take a serving position more adjacent to their assigned back-row position. Crafty, opposing front-row setters often check the server and dump to their respective back-row base position if they notice the serving player is slow in getting into base position. If for some reason a player is serving and making a long transition to the base position, it might be advisable to have another player cover for him or her until he or she gets to base—this can discourage the opposing setter from dumping. The switch could then be made when the server reaches base or later, after the first completed play. This type of "cover" is usually made with the middle back and left back or sometimes left back for the right back. If this technique is used, one player should be assigned to coordinate the switch verbally. The exception to this plan is for the back-row setter, who should always transition immediately to the assigned right-back position. It's important for the setter to play to either right back or right front, making the transition to set the ball from the target area uncomplicated.

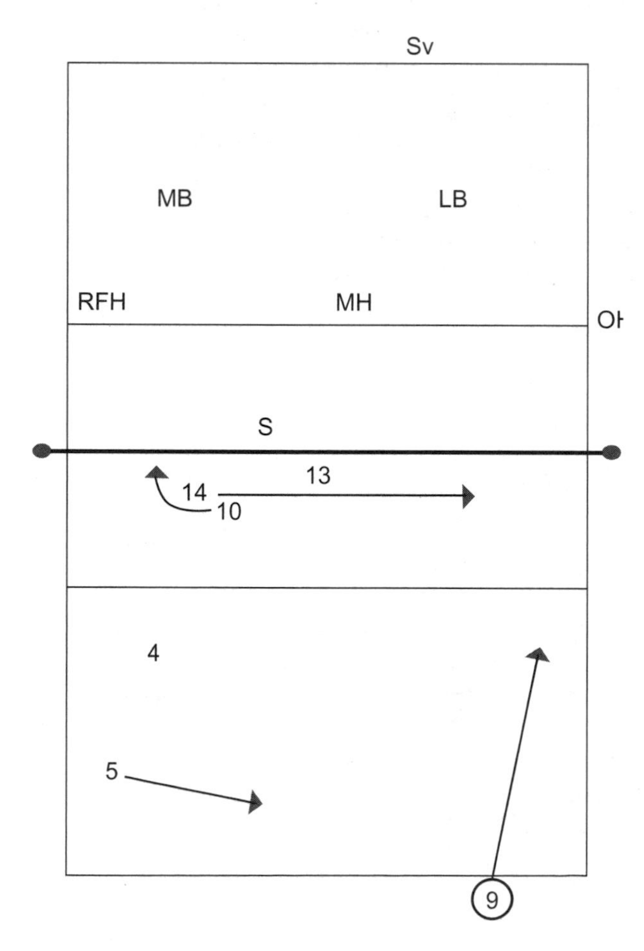

Figure 9.12 Transition order with opposing setter in the back row.

Figure 9.12 shows a typical rotational transition for a serving team using the rotation order shown on the wheel in figure 9.11b. When the opposing setter is back row, there's less concern about a dump, so players can move closer to their eventual base positions before the serve. In the front row, note that the middle blocker should always have the movement route closest to the net. The right-side players should move directly behind the middle, and the outside hitter takes the longest route around both other front-row players. When serving, players can also bunch up a bit to reduce the distance for the transition movement. However, be careful not to form a screen which blocks the opponent's view of your server or to overlap positions; either can cause a violation and the loss of a point.

Figure 9.13 shows a situation in which the left back "covers" for the setter (right back) until he or she serves and runs to base position. As mentioned, this tactic can discourage the opposing setter from dumping.

The more complicated rotational transition occurs when the team is receiving the serve and must switch to assigned positions. For coaches, the first consideration should always be to position the players to get the best possible passers in serve-reception formation, regardless of where they'll eventually be transitioning. In addition, take care to design a serve-reception formation that allows the setter to have a fairly easy transition to the target area. Having the setter transition from the middle-back and left-back is difficult. In these situations, you might consider moving the setter to the net with the adjacent front-row player. Figure 9.14 shows an example of this formation, in which the setter is in the middle-back position (rotation 6), and the setter and player #14 move to the net, allowing an easy transition to the target area. Once you have positioned the best possible players in their best possible places to receive the serve, you can think about designing offensive plays to help ease the eventual transition.

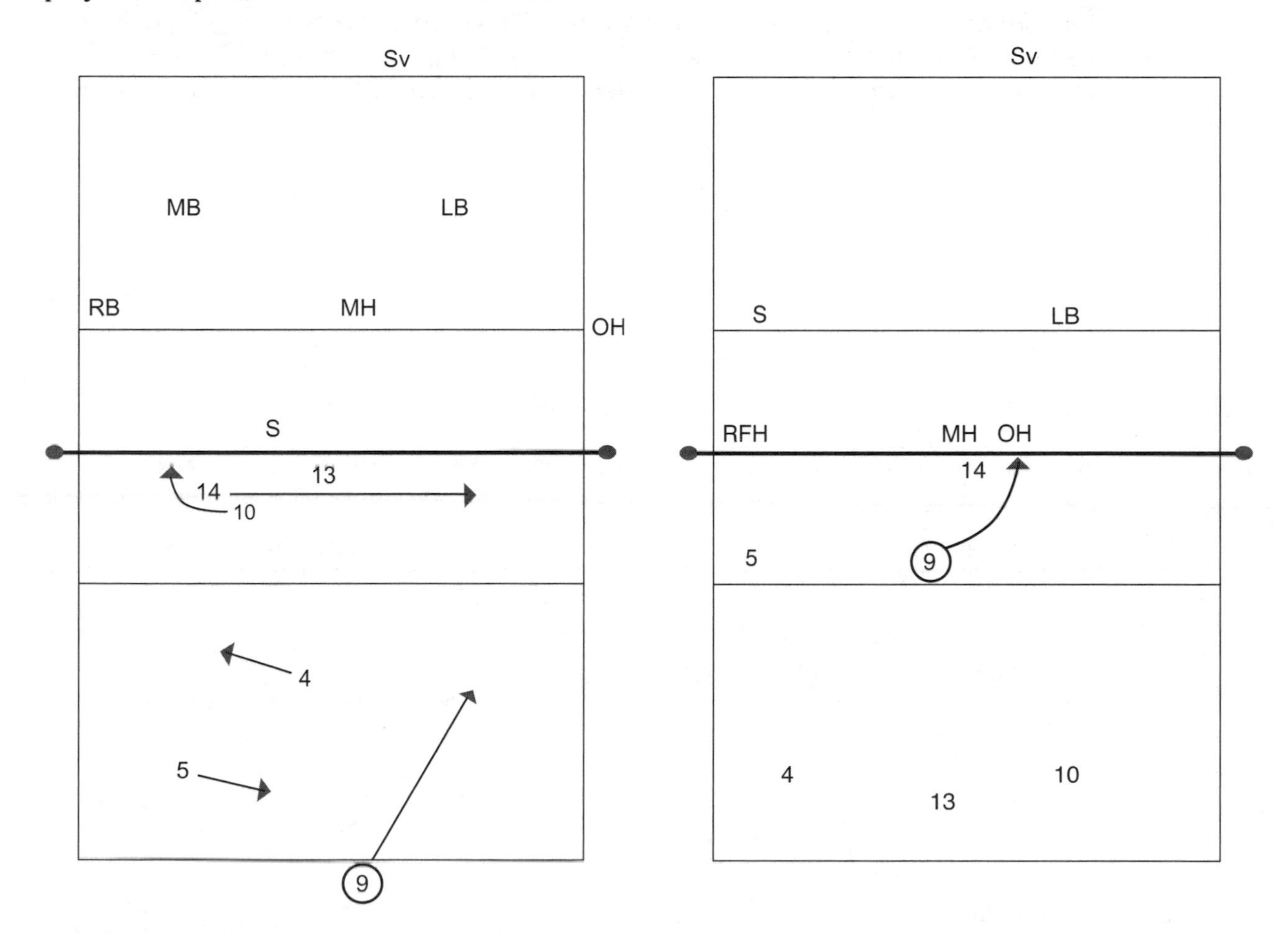

Figure 9.13 Left back covers for the setter.

Figure 9.14 Setter moves to net for easy transition.

Figure 9.15 shows a play ("Right Cross") that helps facilitate transition. The outside hitter (10) runs a right cross toward his or her eventual assigned position in left front, and the opposite (14) transitions immediately to his or her normal position and runs a pattern to hit from right front. In figure 9.16, note that 14 has moved to the right, making a small adjustment in his or her starting position. This eases transition. In both cases, the middle hitter has remained constant, running a pattern directly to his or her middle position.

The final aspect to address regarding rotational transition during serve reception is hitter coverage. After the ball is passed to the setter and the setter delivers the ball to a hitter, the remaining players must cover the hitter. Covering is a formation designed to prevent the ball from hitting the floor if the opponents block it. Because players often haven't switched positions—especially the back-row players—the team must be trained to cover the hitter from each of the six serve reception formations. If the ball isn't blocked, players can transition to their assigned front-row or back-row positions. On a blocked attack, the team must try to play the ball up and attack without switching. Once the ball goes over the net and the players see that it will be a normal pass-set-hit situation, they can safely switch positions quickly. If this process isn't practiced, the result is usually chaos on the court.

Figure 9.17 demonstrates typical hitter coverage transition from the offensive play run in figure 9.16. The setter has delivered the set to #10, and the rest of the team immediately transitions to cover the hitter. This particular coverage formation is called 3–2 cover. There are three players covering in the cup immediately around the hitter and two players covering deeper in the gaps. Players should be in a low

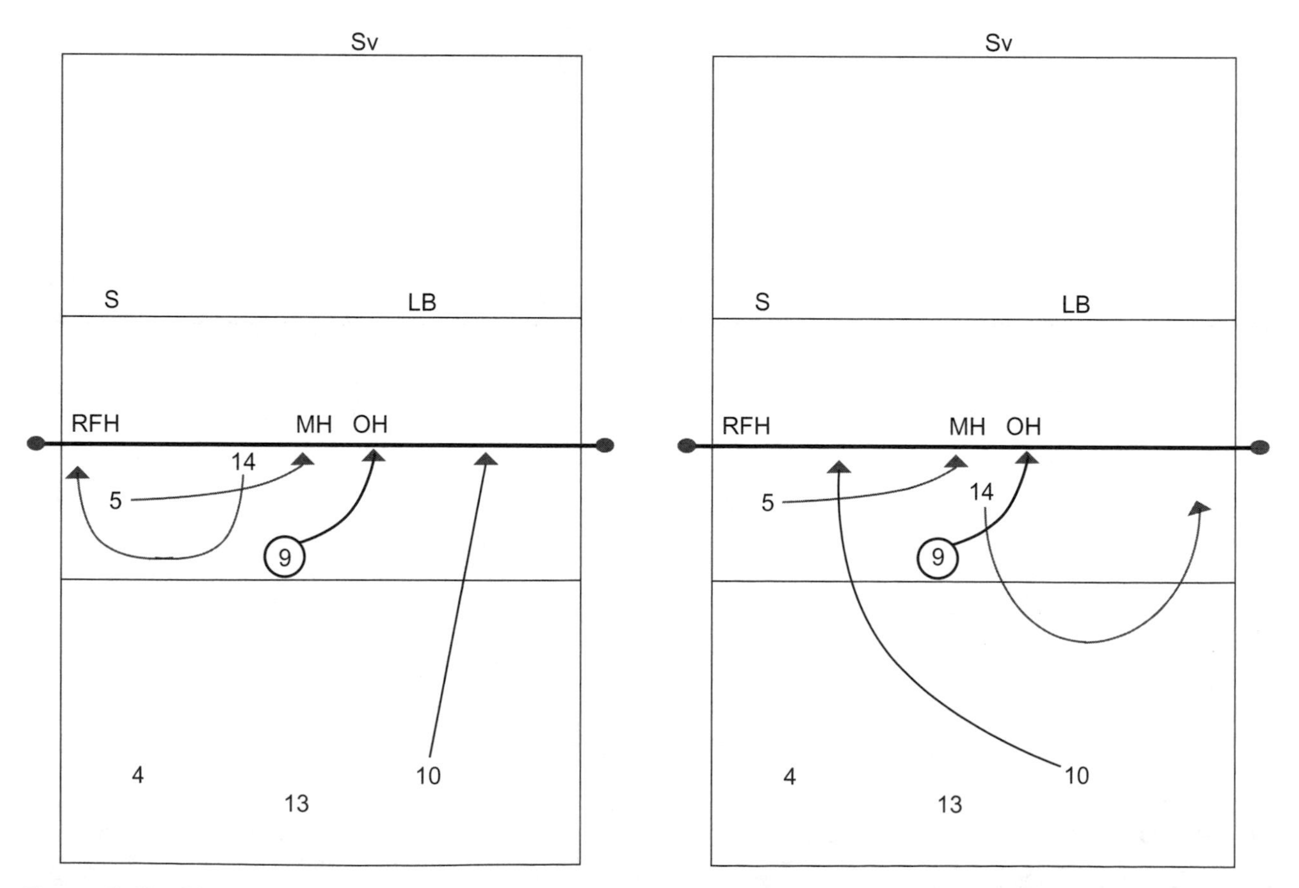

Figure 9.15 Right Cross.

Figure 9.16 Middle hitter runs a pattern directly to the middle position.

posture before their attacker contacts the ball. Normally, the setter is trained to follow his or her set and cover the hitter in the cup immediately surrounding the hitter. There are other formations for covering the hitter, but they are all characterized by the nonhitting players collapsing around the hitter while transitioning into a low posture, ready to dig up any blocked attack. If the attack crosses the net without being blocked, players immediately transition to their base positions, as shown in figure 9.18. Simultaneously, on the other side of the net, the opponents have played defense and are transitioning from defense to offense and preparing to attack.

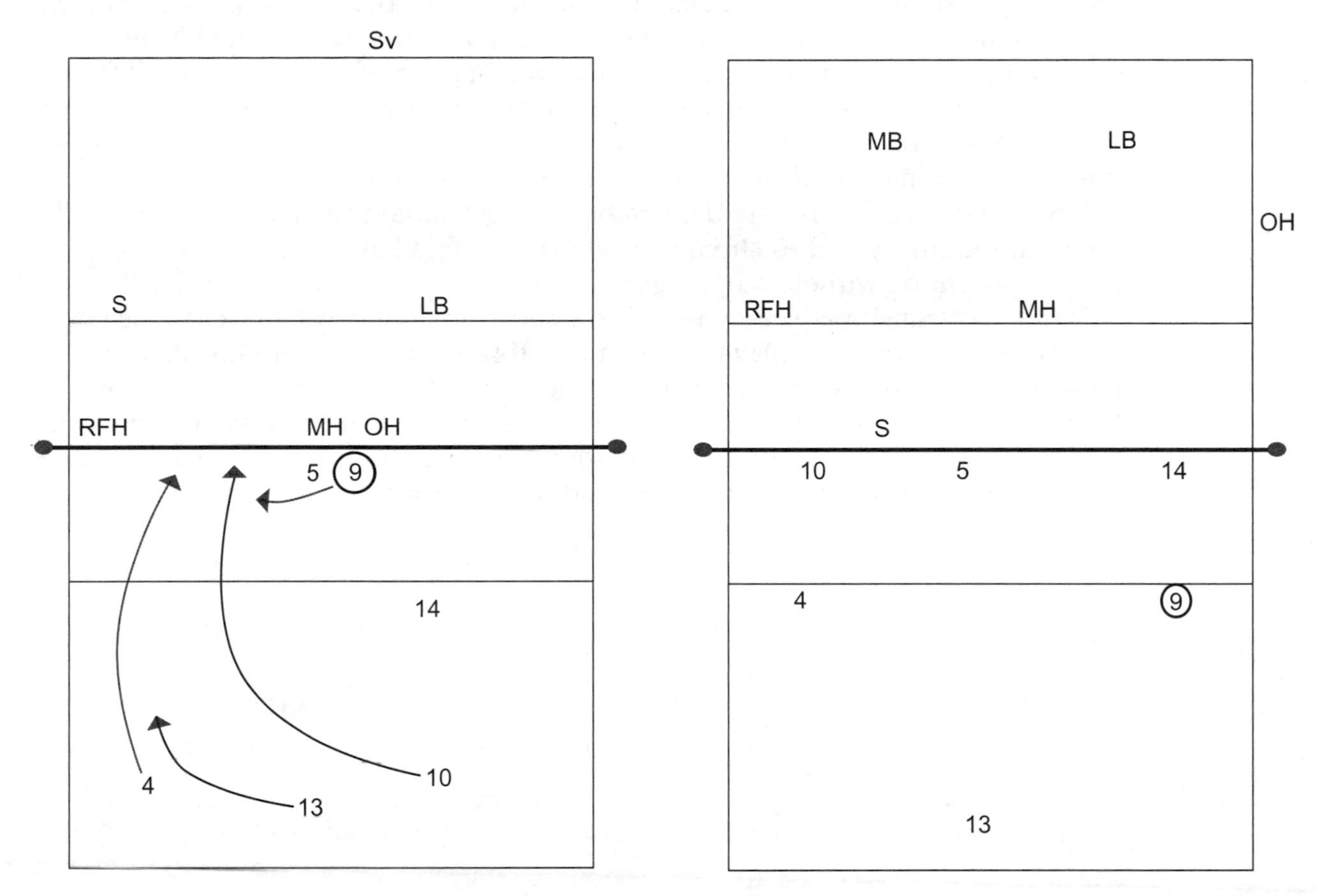

Figure 9.17 3-2 cover.

Figure 9.18 Players immediately transition to bases if attack crosses the net.

Checklist for System Transition

Areas to be covered for each rotation

- Base position
- Transition to defense
- Transition to offense
- Hitter coverage
- Free-ball transition
- Down-ball transition

System transition encompasses all other types of transition on the court. The flow of the game moves from base position to defense, from defense to offense, from offense to attack-offense, from attack-offense to hitter coverage, and finally, from hitter coverage back to base position.

Figure 9.19 illustrates the general transition phases used in the normal flow of a game. However, within these generalized transitions are more intricate formations, such as free-ball transition and down-ball transition. All phases of transition should be trained. Initially, teaching can be at a slower pace, and phases of transition can be broken down so that only one phase is practiced at a time. Once players know their responsibilities, get the team into gamelike drills that encompass all aspects of the game. This is best accomplished in drills designed to be gamelike in which the ball continues in play rather than just training in one specific phase of transition. Run these drills at a fast pace; don't discuss errors at length; keep the drill moving. Focus on giving players mass repetitions at game speed or faster. One of the best coaching tips of all time has been attributed to Russ Rose, head women's volleyball coach at Penn State University, who said about practice: "Run your drills, not your mouth." Coaches should use short, succinct key words or cues to direct players' attention without stopping play.

In free-ball transition (see chapter 8), the setter immediately releases to the target area while the front-row players transition off the net to prepare for offense. The middle and left back can split the court and easily get into position for a free ball. Back-row players should normally play free balls so the front-row players are available to run the offensive routes. Coaches differ on the philosophy of free-ball offense. Some prefer to run a relatively simple attack pattern to increase the chances of

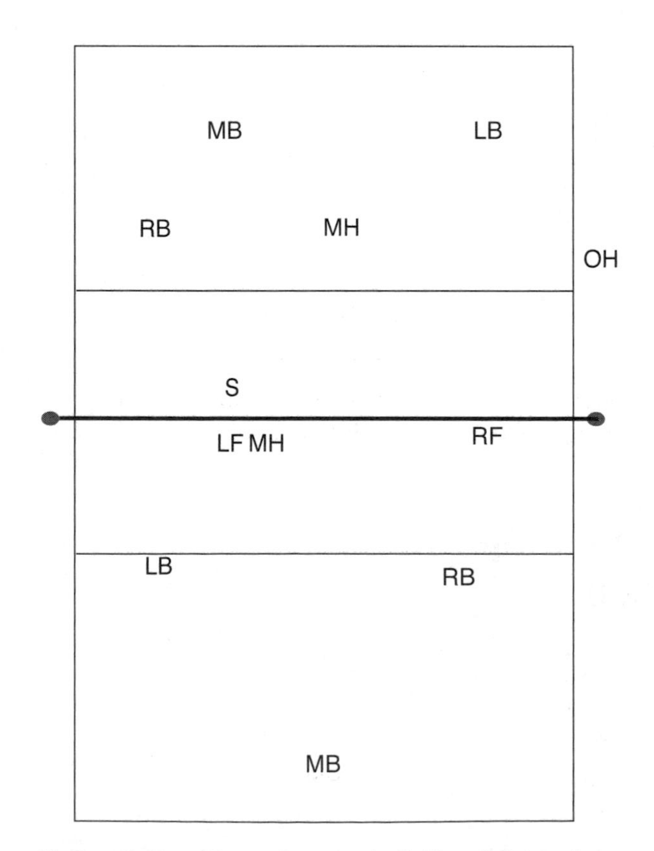

Figure 9.19a Setter has the ball. The defense is in base position.

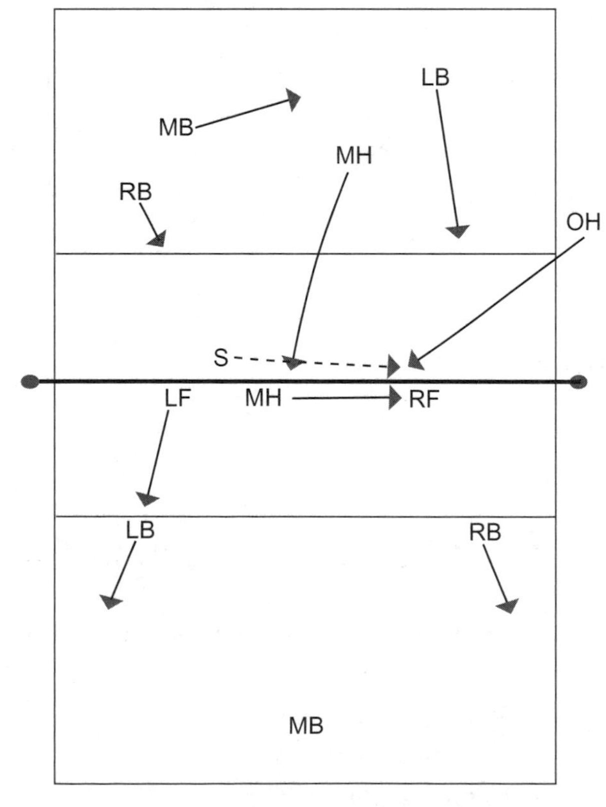

Figure 9.19b The setter sets to the OH. The offense transitions to cover the OH. The defense transitions to a perimeter defensive.

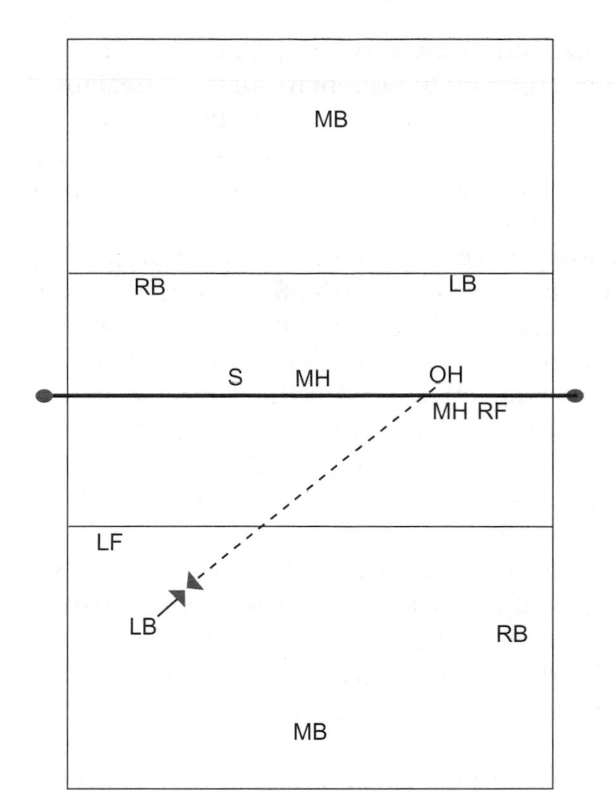

Figure 9.19c Attack is hit to the LB. The offense covers their hitter while the defense plays the perimeter.

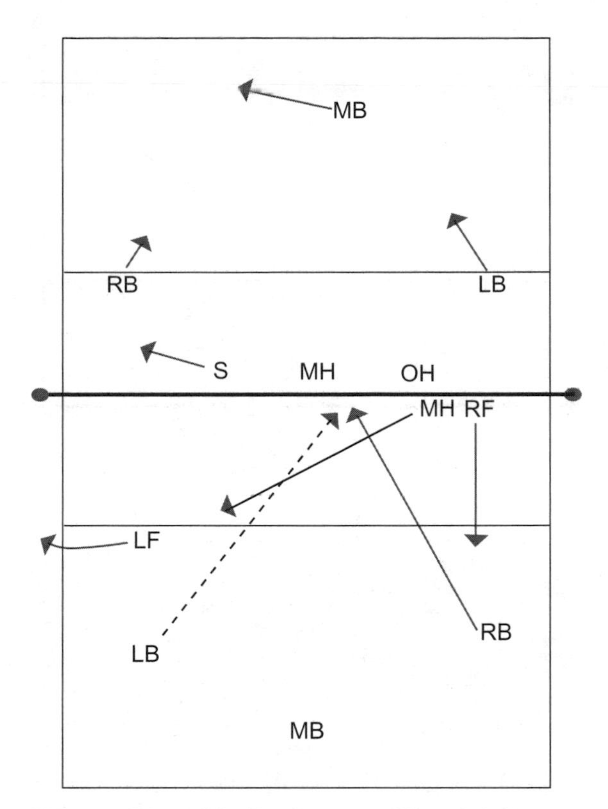

Figure 9.19d LB digs to target. The defense transitions to offense. The other team transitions to the base position.

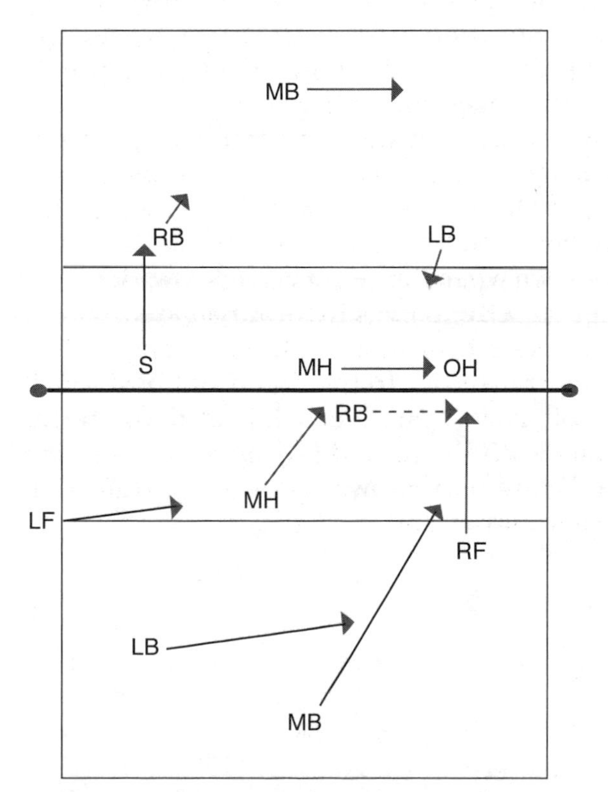

Figure 9.19e Ball is set to the RF. The offense transitions to cover their hitter. The other team transitions to a rotation defense.

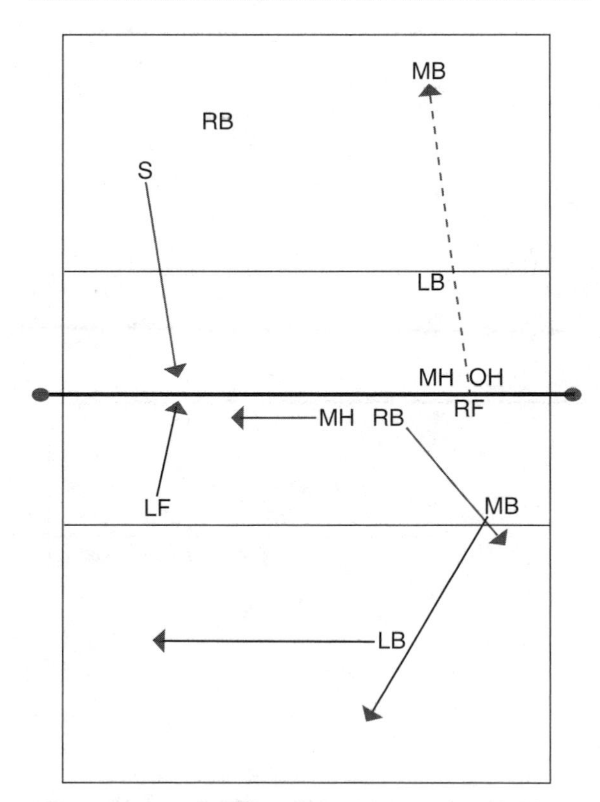

Figure 9.19f Setter releases to target as the MB digs. The defense returns to base position.

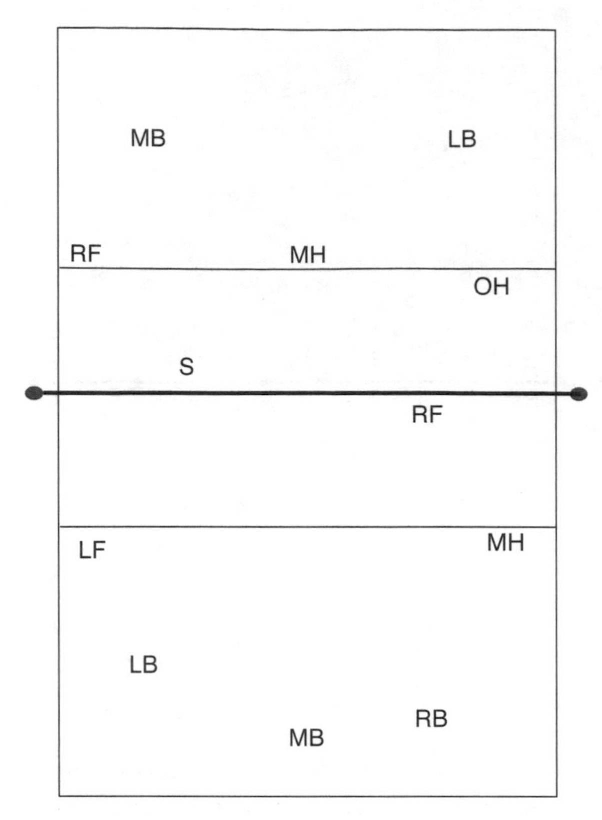

Figure 9.20 Down-ball transition. Back-row setter stays to dig. RF stays and may set.

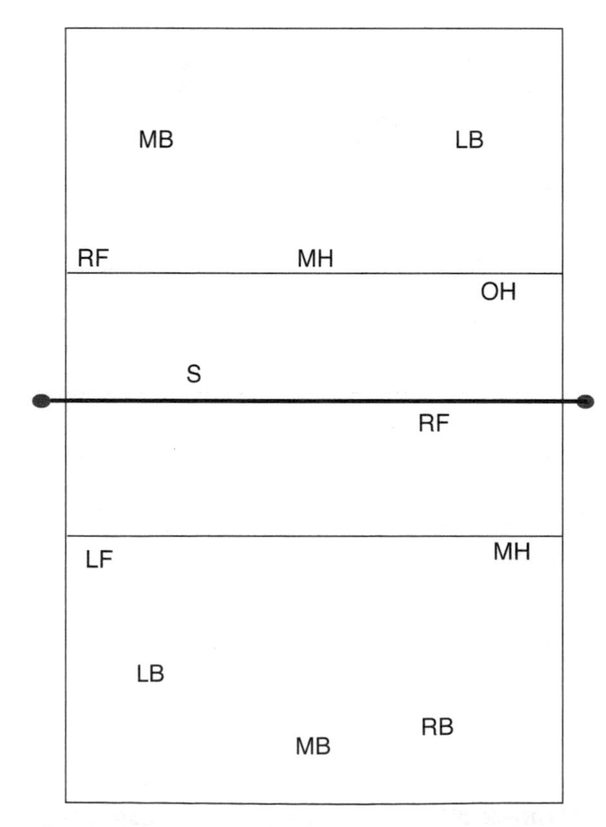

Figure 9.21 Down-ball transition. Front-row setter moves to target. MH transitions to right front.

good execution and scoring. Others prefer to run a more complicated offensive pattern designed to challenge the block and defense. Whatever the choice, the free ball is a great opportunity to get a good swing on the ball and shouldn't be squandered.

A down ball can be called in several situations (see chapter 8). In this transition, the back-row setter doesn't release—he or she stays to play defense and releases only if the ball doesn't come to his or her area. Even if the back-row setter doesn't have to dig the ball, it's a long transition, especially on a less-than-perfect pass. One of the blockers should remain at the net to play a dribbler (a ball that hits the top of the net and comes over). The front-row player at the net should also be designated as the setter if the back-row setter has to dig the ball. Some coaches prefer to have the middle blocker stay at the net, and others like to use the right-side blocker, who's more accustomed to setting. If the right-side player stays at the net, the middle blocker should transition to the right side of the court, not the middle front. All other players transition off the net to a position behind the three-meter line and slightly inside the court. The back-row players should transition deep on the court around the perimeter. Figure 9.20 shows a down ball transition with a back-row setter.

On a down ball with the setter in the front row, some coaches like to use the same formation used for a free-ball transition. However, it's more common to use a formation similar to the one shown when the setter is back row. Here, the front-row setter moves to the target area, and all the blockers transition off the net. The middle blocker transitions to the right-front position. If a 4–2 offensive system is being used, the setter will already be in the middle front near the target area. Figure 9.21 shows a down-ball transition with a front-row setter.

Checklist for Coaching Transition

- Posture: Cue for high, medium, or low, depending on transition.
- Eyes: Cue for eye sequencing.
- Hands: High for blockers; ready position for defense or cover.
- Quick: Cue for movement.
- Talk: Cue for blockers and hitters or to cover player describing the forming block.
- Base: Cue for returning to assigned base position.
- Teaching can be done one phase at a time at a slower speed.
- Once players know the formations, all drills should be gamelike with continuous, fast-paced action.
- Run your drills, not your mouth.

TRANSITION DRILLS

The drills presented here cover many of the topics in the order they're discussed in the chapter. Most drills can be adapted to focus on additional aspects of the game. Once again, it's important for coaches to remember that slower-paced teaching drills should be used only when introducing concepts. Gamelike drills at a fast pace should be used once players are familiar with their assignments and specific formations. Using a scoring system is a major component in running successful team drills.

Scoring for Team Drills

Fast score (rally score): The team winning the rally each time the ball is served scores a point.

Handicaps: One team starts with a greater number of points. For instance, team A starts the drill with 20 points, and team B starts with 25 points—the first team to 30 wins.

Consecutive points burden: A team must score two or more points in a row to get credit for one point. For instance, team A must score twice (or more) in a row to get one point, and team B has normal scoring.

Wash drills: Big points and little points are used. To score a "big" point, the receiving team must convert a serve reception for a "little" point and a free ball for a second little point.

Triangle

Purpose: To train base position, posture, movement, and defensive systems when players are first learning to transition

Setup: Two teams play six versus six on one court; one side plays defense.

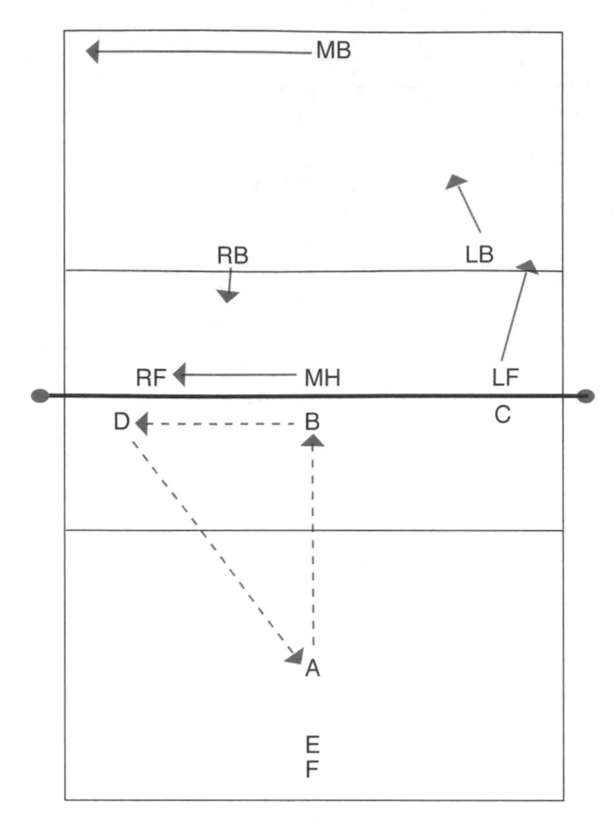

Figure 9.22 Triangle.

Execution: The ball starts with A, who sets to B. B sets either to C or D, and D (or C) then sets the ball back to A, who immediately sets it again to B. As this happens, the other side is in base position, and when B releases the ball, the defense transitions. The defense must get back to base by the time A goes to set again (figure 9.22).

Coaching Points: Use cue words such as "base" or "posture" to coach the defensive side while the ball is in play—don't stop play to talk. Focus on players getting back to base. Make the defensive side get 5 to 10 perfect transitions and then wave through. Players B, C, D move to the front row on defense, the defensive front row moves to back row, and the back row moves to the other side. Put a player in A position who can set if there are problems keeping the ball going. Count perfect transitions out loud and yell out errors: "base fault!" (and so on). The count goes back to zero with a fault.

Variations

- Add a "setter" between B and C so the defense must be aware of a middle hitter and play defense when the middle gets set.
- Change defenses between transitions—assign one court player to call the defense as B sets the ball.

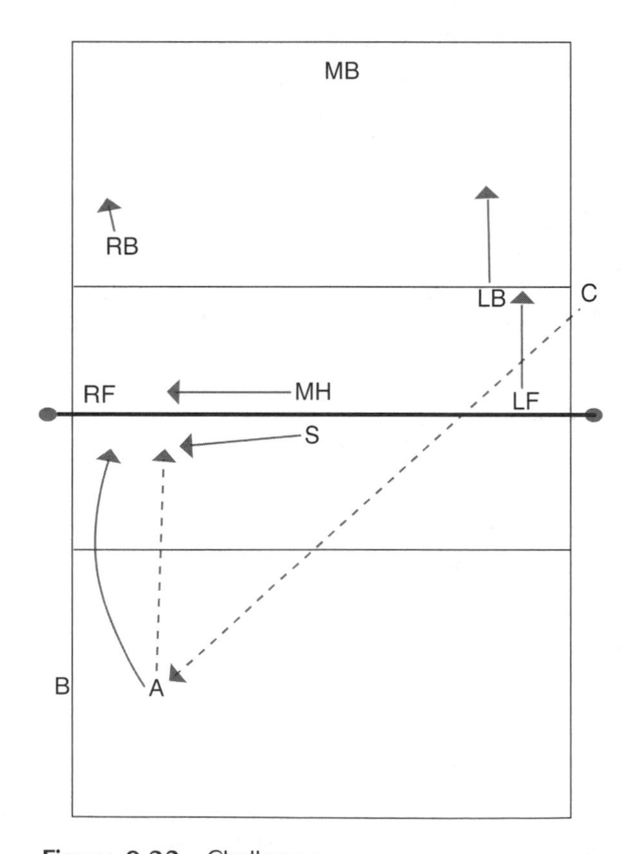

Figure 9.23 Challenge.

Challenge

Purpose: To work on eye sequencing and visual keys, posture, movement, timing, and transition

Setup: The defense sets up on one side of the court, with two players and a setter on the other side. A coach has a basket of balls.

Execution: The coach enters the ball to player A. Player A passes the ball to the setter in the target area; the defense starts in base position, watching the pass and going through eye sequencing while player A approaches and hits (figure 9.23). The defense plays the ball out. The coach then enters another ball to player B, and the same process occurs. If the defense gets the ball back with a good transition (everyone transitions where they should be with good posture) and an attack, they score a point. If they transition and get an attack but there's a breakdown in transition, it's a wash. If the offensive players get a kill, unreturned ball, or a free ball back, they score a point. Play to a set score or give a total of 20 balls to each offensive team (A and B).

Coaching Points: One coach should focus on the defense and judge their posture, transition, and movement. If there's a problem, use cue words to help correct, but don't stop play. Yell "base foul!" or "position foul!" and so on to let players know something is wrong.

Variation: This drill can be done with outside hitters, middles, or opposites; players can call the type of sets they want to hit: the setter can be designated a front-row player and "live" (he or she can dump). The competition could be player A versus player B, or one complete team could compete against the other, switching defenses with each hitter or every other attack.

Middle Hitter/Right-Side Transition

Purpose: To work on right side and middle transition at the net

Setup: A passer, two setters, right-side players, and middles set up on a court. A coach has a basket of balls.

Execution: The coach enters the ball to the passer (P), and the right-side player (RS) transitions off the net. P passes to setter 1 (S1), and S1 back sets to RS, who hits, and new RS steps in. Blockers on the other side are all middles (M), and they transition to block RS. If they don't block RS, the middle player transitions off the net as the coach tosses a pass to setter 2 (S2), and S2 sets to M. Play is continuous, middle players rotate, and the coach enters another ball to P (figure 9.24).

Coaching Points: Encourage considerable talking by players; keep the speed of the drill gamelike; make sure players are using good transition footwork.

Variations

1. The right-side attacker can hit slides or crosses.
2. Middles can hit slides or quick sets (or others).
3. Middles have to hit two or three in a row with an abbreviated transition back and forth off the net.
4. Add a middle hitter on the other side to block and hit different sets.
5. Substitute some outside hitters to double block in their position with the middles versus the right-side attack.

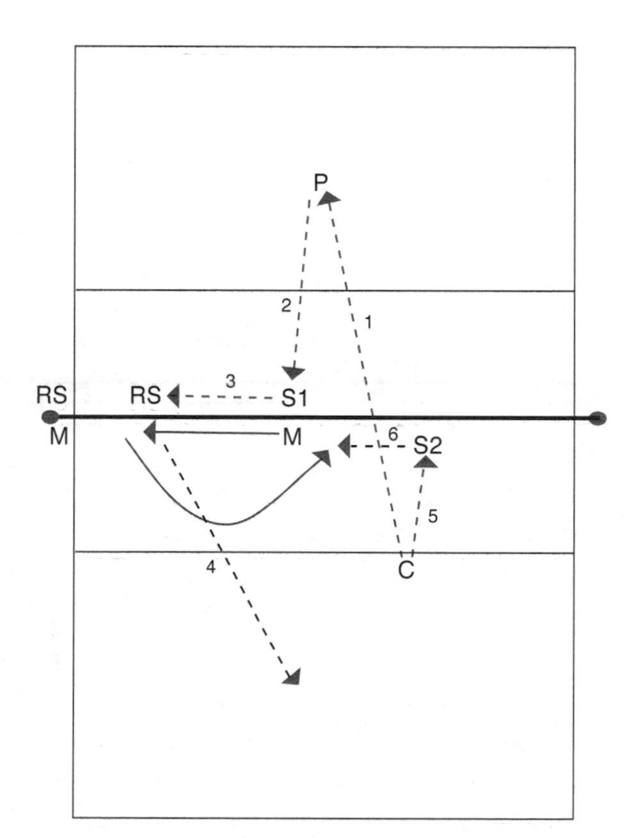

Figure 9.24 Middle Hitter/Right-Side Transition.

Wash Drill

A wash drill is an activity that employs all aspects of team play, usually with two full teams competing against each other. It's a team drill rather than an individual skill drill. Coaches often choose to emphasize a specific aspect of team play by setting rules on how teams score points within the wash drill. For example, a coach might have one team focus on offensive transition and the opposing team focus on defensive transition. Wash drills are fast-paced and gamelike. The following wash drill emphasizes offense and defensive team transition.

Purpose: To practice gamelike team transition

Setup: Two full teams set up on a court.

Execution: Player A serves to team A (figure 9.25). Team A plays the ball out while team B defends. If team A scores, it gets a little point, and C1 enters a free ball. If team B successfully defends, it gets a little point and receives a free ball from C2. If either team scores off the free ball, they win a big point and rotate. If the opposing team wins the free ball, it's a wash, and team B serves again. The first team to score six big points wins. Penalties can be given for missed serves.

Coaching Points: Keep the pace of the play fast. If players are less skilled, have a coach serve. When playing the varsity team against the junior varsity, let the varsity receive serve most of the time, and give the junior varsity a point if it scores on the serve; try to keep the competition even by giving the better team a higher burden to score.

Variation: Make the higher skilled team score on two consecutive points to get a big point; keep the ball in play continuously until one team wins two free balls in a row. Other variations on the Wash drill are detailed more thoroughly in the next two drills.

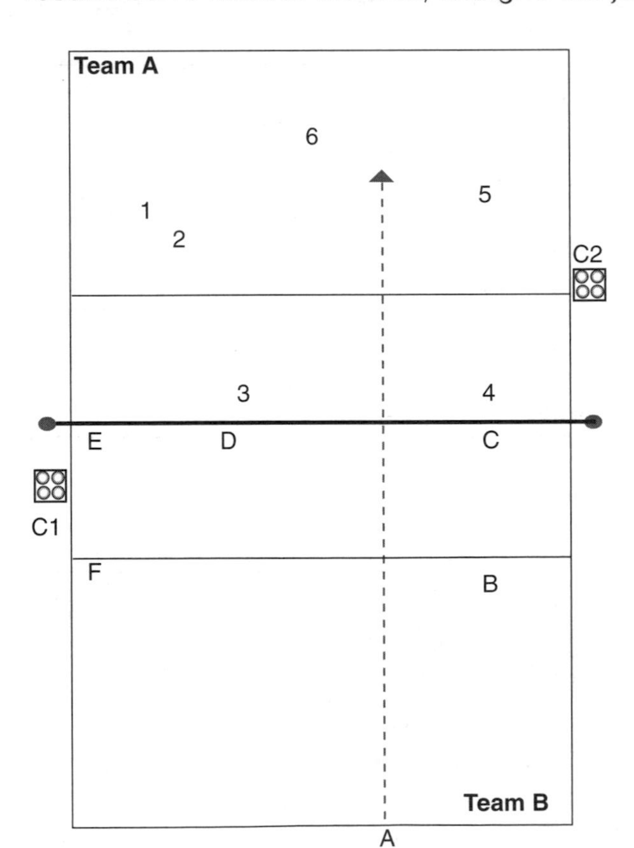

Figure 9.25 Wash Drill.

Wash Drill: Middle Attack

Purpose: To practice serve reception and transition

Setup: Two full teams play on a court.

Execution: Team A serves to team B, allowing team B to work on serve reception. Team B receives and must set the middle hitter to score. If team A scores off serve reception, a coach (C1) enters a free ball, and team A must set the middle again to score a big point. If team B wins the point, a coach (C2) enters a free ball, and team B has a chance to score a big point. If team B wins a little and a big point, they rotate and serve again. The middles can call for any type of set, or setters can be "live."

Wash Drill: Further Variations

Purpose: To customize gamelike play to work on problem areas

Setup: Two full teams play on a court.

Execution: Play the entire drill (first team to six points) in one rotation.

Variations

1. **Defense/transition offense.** A coach enters free balls to team B; team A must get two sideouts in a row.
2. **Serve reception/transition offense/defense.** Team A receives serve. Whichever team wins the rally gets down balls until they win two points in a row.
3. **Handicap the first team.** Team A must win three rallies in a row to get a big point.
4. **Use rally scoring.** Don't use big points and little points, but handicap one team by starting the score at 20 or 25; the first team to 30 points wins.
5. **Coach control.** The coach enters the serve to the first team (the coach can serve to problem areas).
6. **Focus on one or two hitters.** Only the middle hitters can side out on free balls.

CONCLUSION

Fast and efficient transition is the hallmark of teams with highly skilled players. However, transition is not only the movement from defensive to offensive play; transitions occur at more subtle times during the game, culminating in what many liken to a synchronized and well-choreographed ballet. Indeed, as the speed of the game increases, so does the speed of the transition. As a result, teaching and mastering effective transition should be a major component of the game of volleyball at all levels.

10

Practicing

Paul Arrington

Courtesy of the University of Florida

Many factors must come together for a volleyball team to be successful. One of those factors is coaching, which is largely teaching. Undeniably, the vast majority of this teaching occurs during practice. A team can't enjoy success without quality practices. In this chapter, three components of quality practices—preparation, execution, and evaluation—are discussed in detail. Coaches can use or modify the ideas presented in this chapter in setting up their practices.

PREPARATION

If you don't know where you're going, then any road will get you there. However, if you hope to have a successful season, you must set goals. Effective planning can't occur without goals in place. Primary objectives such as winning the league are important, but weekly, seasonal, and annual goals are essential to the ongoing development of your program. Your team's goals should be process oriented (e.g., use several ball-control drills to achieve a serve-receive average of 2.3 by tournament time) rather than outcome oriented (e.g., win the game).

Along with emphasizing process over outcome, goals need to be specific, challenging but realistic, achievable during the time frame established, and measurable. You can't use the same goals for all teams; they need to be team specific. Clearly, you can't expect a 12-and-under team to pass a 2.3 average on serve reception, so this is not a realistic goal for this team. Once weekly, seasonal, and annual goals are established, a team's road to success becomes much clearer.

You must plan your practices carefully. No matter how good a coach you are, poorly designed practices won't help you reach your goals. Well-designed practices are the result of considerable forethought and planning. The old saying "failing to prepare is preparing to fail" certainly holds true for practices.

Experienced coaches often come to practice and run effective workouts apparently off the top of their heads. Nothing could be further from the truth. After 20 years of coaching, I still come to every practice with a written plan. My players might not know it, but my notes are in my pocket should my memory fail.

Some novice coaches don't realize how much time and effort needs to be put into preparing for practice. As a rule, at least two hours of preparation are required for each hour of practice. And beginning coaches might need more; they might require three or four hours of preparation per hour of practice to develop a good practice plan.

Planning practices for the entire season before it begins can be done in only a limited way. For example, you might want to follow an outline similar to the one in table 10.1, adjusting the numbers to fit the experience level of your athletes.

After setting general guidelines for the season, you can begin your weekly planning. A sample of a weekly plan during the preseason is shown in table 10.2.

Once you have your weekly plans in place, you can start developing your daily plans, which will most likely involve several different drills. There are many considerations in choosing a drill.

- When possible, drills should be gamelike, with the ball crossing the net.
- Random drills in which players perform several skills are superior to block drills, in which players repeat one skill many times.
- Use "whole skill" drills instead of those focusing on parts of a skill, with later reconstruction of the entire skill.

Table 10.1
Seasonal Practice Plan

	Preseason	Midseason	Late season
Individual skills	60%	30%	10%
Group skills	30%	40%	40%
Control scrimmage	10%	30%	50%

Table 10.2
Weekly Practice Outline

Individual skills: 75 minutes (total) per practice (Goal: to instill proper form and movement)	
Forearm pass	5 days per week
Face pass	2 days per week
Attack	3 days per week
Individual defense	3 days per week
Floor play	2 days per week
Service	5 days per week
Group drills: 40 minutes (total) per practice (Goal: to begin to work together as a team)	
Team serve receive	3 days per week
Ball control	1 day per week
Transition	1 day per week
Intensity	1 day per week
Court movement	1 day per week
Team defense	3 days per week
Controlled scrimmage: 15 minutes (total) per practice (Goal: to begin to develop a competitive mindset)	
Queen of the Mountain	As many days per week as necessary
Wash drills	As many days per week as necessary

- Use drills that involve many contacts and minimal time waiting in line. If an athlete is waiting, his or her focus is wandering.

Some coaches find a drill they love and use it over and over again until players are thoroughly bored with it. Try to use a variety of drills to accomplish your team's goals.

In formulating practice plans, begin by identifying the goals for the practice. Start with the length of time available per workout. Practices should be two hours or less and may be as short as one hour for very young athletes. Change drills frequently; most drills should last 10 to 15 minutes or less.

In writing your daily practice plans, begin by identifying the goals identified for that period of the season and work backward to determine the types of drills needed to achieve those goals. For example, if your players are inexperienced, and your goal is for them to be able to pass to the setter consistently, gear drills toward footwork and basic passing form (although eventually they'll need to work on fine adjustment of their platform).

An example of a fairly detailed plan for a single practice is shown in table 10.3. This plan is not intended to serve for any particular team but to illustrate the thinking that needs to go into developing a practice plan.

Table 10.3
Detailed Plan for a Single Practice

Time	Drill name or description	Goals of drill	Performance goal	Consequence	
				Type	Result
10 min	Butterflies with tip, block, and dig	Warm-up; multiple touches; random	10 consecutive	+Re	QOM
3 min	Queen of the Mountain (QOM)	Reward; competition	Call every pass	+Re	1 min QOM
5 min	Group stretch	Stretch; leader experience			
15 min	Three-player serve receive with setter	Control pass	Each player completes five 3-passes	–Re	Avoid rolls
	Quick hitters and servers	Service control			
	2 rolls for non-3-passes	Setter and hitter connection			
1-minute water break					
15 min	Coach-on-3 defense	Read hitter; dig hard hits; floor play; focus; persistence	2 minutes (no ball hitting the floor unless the player is on floor, too)	+Re	Out of drill
15 min	Hitting overloads (two at a time)	Getting in position to attack while a pass is being made; focusing on attack when tired	10 each	+Re	Out of drill
12 min	Service using targets	Control serves to multiple areas of the court	3 consecutive areas 1-6	+Re	Water
2-minute water break					
10 min	Team QOM (3s)	Team play; competition	First team to 10 points	+Re	Stickers
18 min	Error correction; control scrimmage	Skills; focus; perseverance	Make the play	–Re	Repeat effort
10 min	Dynamic stretches	Cool down; increase flexibility			

When putting together your practice plans, you also need to decide whether to positively or negatively reinforce your drills (discussed in detail in the next section) and what actions to take to trigger the consequences you want to see.

EXECUTION

With a good practice plan in hand, you can turn attention to its actual execution. Although a practice plan is necessary for a quality practice, a good plan alone doesn't ensure a quality practice. How the practice plan is executed is also extremely important.

After developing a good plan, the most important action is to follow it. Unless you have an excellent sense of time, you'll need a watch (perhaps even a stopwatch) to ensure you're sticking to the time allotted for each drill or activity. If it becomes apparent that although the plan looked great on paper, it's bombing on the court, have a plan B ready to go.

In the previous section on practice planning, we mentioned avoiding down time when running drills. During a practice session, it's imperative to move from one drill to the next as quickly and seamlessly as possible. The biggest mistake a coach can make is to take the time between drills to "talk." Keep verbal instruction at this time to a minimum. Briefly describe the goals of the drill and how long it will run (duration or set number of successes) and quickly demonstrate or discuss how the drill should be done—and then get the drill underway. If a drill is going to be used more than once during the season, name the drill so that you don't have to describe it every time. This way you can say simply, "Now we're going to do drill X to focus on control of our passes on serve receive. Each of you needs 10 successes to get out of the drill."

In-Practice Feedback

The coach's feedback is one of the most important contributors to the proper execution of a practice session. The quality of your feedback has a major impact on the amount of learning that takes place; your feedback also influences how willing your players are to take risks, exert increasing levels of effort, and persevere in all attempts. Keep two very important things in mind regarding feedback: It must always be on the attempt, not the outcome, and it must always be on the performance, not the athlete.

When giving feedback, the coach's teaching role comes to the forefront. The most effective feedback is "positive specific" feedback. Feedback in this form follows a pattern of first telling the athlete specifically what aspect of the skill he or she is performing well and then what aspect of the skill can be improved and how. For example, you might say, "You're using a very good quick approach on your spike, and when you use your armswing (like this), you'll increase your jump even more."

When giving positive specific feedback, coaches frequently make the mistake of giving the positive aspects of the attempt and then saying "but." The word "but" is a mental eraser. Players won't remember what has just been said because once they hear the word "but," they're thinking, "Uh-oh, here comes the hammer." Instead, connect the positive phrase with "and when," as in the example given in the previous paragraph. This is more encouraging to players and keeps them from getting defensive about the instruction you're trying to impart.

Because most coaches are programmed to look for mistakes and then tell players what *not* to do, it requires effort to phrase feedback in positive terms. A typical piece of feedback might be, "Don't drop your elbow when you serve." This is ineffective feedback in several ways. First, the mind often doesn't register the negative *don't*. The mind hears, "Drop your elbow when you serve." If someone says to you, "Don't think of elephants," how effective is that instruction in preventing you from thinking of elephants? Not very. Another problem with this kind of feedback is that it doesn't tell the player what he or she *has* done well, if anything.

Along with "but" and "don't," "try" is a third word to avoid. In the words of Jedi Master Yoda in *The Empire Strikes Back,* "Do or do not, there is no *try.*" "Try" gives the athlete an excuse. So when you say, "Try to keep your elbow up," your player might say, "But coach, I *am* trying."

A positive but generally ineffective form of feedback is to shout out to a player something like "Great hit!" Such a remark leaves the player wondering what exactly was great about the hit. Was it the jump? The armswing? Was it avoiding the block? Or was it simply that the ball landed in the opponent's court? Although this feedback is positive, no information is given to help the athlete repeat the action in the future.

A coach's nonverbal feedback is also critical. Too many coaches act like a radar station during practice—they stand on the sidelines, arms folded across the chest, eyes scanning for errors to correct. This certainly doesn't send a message to players that they can relax and perform at their best. A good way for coaches to detect any negative nonverbal feedback they're communicating is to watch video of themselves during a practice session. Once you *see* what you're doing, it's far easier to adjust and improve upon your actions.

Initiatives and Consequences

Regardless of the drills selected, the coach must use a combination of initiatives and consequences to get the most out of a practice session. If you don't use initiatives and consequences effectively, you're leaving your players' progress up to chance. An initiative is something that gets a player to try something at least once. Threats, directives, requests, goal striving, and yes, even begging are all examples of initiatives. Whether players persist in an activity depends on the consequences, or result, of the action. Frequently, too much emphasis is placed on initiatives and not enough on the consequences of behavior. Initiatives and consequences must be paired for maximal impact. It's better to introduce initiatives and consequences in practice rather than during a competition, when doing so can be disruptive, not to mention too late.

There are two general types of behavioral consequences. First, there are those that increase the chances for repeating a behavior, including both positive and negative reinforcement. Second, there are consequences that decrease the chances of repeating a behavior; these include punishment and extinction.

To understand behavioral consequences a little better, examine some descriptions Aubrey Daniels uses in his book *Bringing Out the Best in People* (1994). Daniels describes positive reinforcement as "getting something you want," including praise, rewards, or anything else the recipient values. Negative reinforcement can be thought of as, "avoiding something you don't want," such as criticism. Each of these consequences encourages a player to repeat a behavior. In contrast, a consequence that reduces the chance of repeated behavior is punishment—that is, "getting something you don't want," such as laps or push-ups. Another consequence that reduces the chance of repeated behavior is extinction, which is "not getting what you want." An example of extinction is making repeated phone calls to someone and finding the line is always busy. After a few attempts, you decide maybe you didn't really want to talk to that person anyway.

Consequences that are immediate and certain are much more powerful in changing behaviors than future and uncertain consequences. The consequences in practice should occur as quickly as possible after the action, not at the end of practice—or even worse, at the end of the season.

Negative reinforcement is the other form of consequence that leads to repeated behaviors and is the most efficient method of getting athletes to perform at a minimally acceptable level. Yet, there are no consequences for progressing beyond this level. Although the use of positive reinforcement is not the fastest way to steer behaviors to a minimally acceptable level, it's the only type that allows and encourages athletes to continue to progress beyond the minimally acceptable.

Punishment and extinction are the forms of consequences used to decrease repeated behaviors. Extinction, as a consequence, is the weakest method of achieving behavioral changes; really, its only use is in ignoring intentionally bad behavior directed at getting attention. Unfortunately, punishment seems to be the most commonly used type of consequence. Punishment is intended to incite pain or fear into the recipient; fear is an extremely potent motivating factor. However, punishment has some serious drawbacks: it's effective only over a very brief period of time, it causes the receiver to be angry at the punisher, it doesn't result in the receiver wanting to strive for excellence, and it loses its motivational features over time.

On the surface, negative reinforcement and punishment might seem the same, but in fact they are extremely different. Confusion between the two is common because the consequences appear to be the same. The real difference is that with negative reinforcement, players know in advance what they need to do to avoid an unpleasant event. With punishment, players don't know how to avoid the unpleasant event. For example, in a negatively reinforced serving drill, each athlete will serve 10 balls and then do 5 push-ups; however, if all 10 serves are in the court, he or she doesn't have to do the push-ups. In a punishment-based drill, each athlete again serves 10 balls. But in this case, if the server doesn't get all 10 serves into the court, he or she is told to do 5 push-ups (without having known this from the drill's onset). In the punishment-based drill, the athletes are angry with the coach, whereas in the negatively reinforced drill they are angry with themselves and must take personal responsibility for a lack of success.

The types of initiatives and consequences we choose will be determined in part by the mindset, experience, and maturity of our athletes. Regardless of the choice of reinforcement we make, punishment should be used only when there's an infraction of team rules. Use extinction only to stop inappropriate behaviors. For best success in instruction, we need to apply our understanding of initiatives and consequences and develop an approach that allows our athletes to take ownership of their own improvement, continue to improve throughout their careers, and be uplifted by the experience.

A major decision for coaches is in determining what combination of positively reinforced and negatively reinforced drills to use. Keep in mind that although negative reinforcement generally gets athletes to a minimally acceptable level faster than positive reinforcement does, it won't encourage them to progress beyond that level.

If your athletes are young, new to the program, or slow to buy into your system, a significant number of drills should be negatively reinforced early in the season. As they mature, the emphasis should be changed, predominately or exclusively, to positively reinforced drills. If your players are all mature returning players who are self-motivated, you need not use any negatively reinforced drills.

Praise is universally perceived as positive reinforcement. However, the method in which praise is given can have a negative impact. Generally speaking, male athletes like public praise, whereas female athletes feel uncomfortable with it. Female athletes like praise, but many of them prefer that it be given privately. In this case, stickers and other tokens of praise can be quite effective, but they should be given immediately—not at the end of a practice session. With female athletes, this must be done without ceremony or fanfare. In practice sessions, even the high school varsity girls go quietly to the sticker container after reaching a goal, get the sticker, and discretely place it in their goal books. By the way they respond, you might think a particular achievement is unimportant to them—but they never fail to go get their sticker.

The difference between positive reinforcement and other types of consequences is in the eye of the receiver, not the giver. The same is true for negative reinforcement and punishment. Because there seems to be confusion about the real impact of various consequences, how can you tell what your players consider to be positive reinforcement? One way is to ask them. However, this sets up expectations on their part that we might be unwilling to fulfill. In such cases, we might have been better off not to have asked.

One approach is known as "Grandma's Rule." That is, "If you eat your broccoli, you can have ice cream." Pick a drill that your players would consistently select from a list of options to use as positive reinforcement for less popular drills. With our team, "Queen of the Hill" is a drill we can use almost any time as positive reinforcement.

If positive reinforcement is so great, why does punishment sometimes seem to be more effective? To answer this, we need to understand a statistical phenomenon called "regression to the mean." When there is any behavior well above or well below the average behaviors, the next attempt will be back closer to the average. During practice, often the only time a coach praises a player occurs when the attempt is much better than average. Statistically speaking, the subsequent attempt will be worse (back toward average). However, when we chastise or otherwise punish, we do so because an attempt was below average. After the punishment, the next attempt will be better (back closer to the average). In other words, the feedback was inconsequential. However, many coaches assume the improved attempt was a result of the punishment, which promotes the misconception that punishment is more effective than positive reinforcement.

MAKING PRACTICE FUN

Keeping practice fun is extremely important. Coaches often erroneously feel that learning sport skills is incompatible with fun, and thus problems arise. We simply need to rethink our definition of "fun." Focus and fun are not at all incompatible; in fact, focus is necessary for fun to occur. This can be clearly understood if we define fun as "being deeply involved and uplifted by an experience." We can be deeply involved because of fear, but we probably won't find the experience uplifting. However, it doesn't mean that at all times during an activity the athlete is doing something pleasurable.

This definition of fun arises from Mihaly Csikszentmihalyi's work on the psychological state called "flow." In explaining the concept of flow, Csikszentmihalyi takes various activities that people might call fun and divides them into two different concepts. The first of these he calls "pleasure," which is the conscious state we're in when we have satisfied a biologic or socially conditioned need. Examples include the taste of food when we're hungry and relief of boredom by the diversion of our attention. He refers to the other concept as "fun." By this definition, fun has many components, including the following:

- The activity matches challenges with ability.
- Focus on the task is required.
- Focus is possible because there are clear-cut goals and immediate feedback.
- The worries and frustrations of life do not intrude.
- There is a sense of control over actions.
- Self-consciousness is absent.
- The sense of self is stronger after the activity.
- The sense of time is altered.

If players are having this kind of fun, they might not only meet prior expectations but perhaps exceed them and have an experience that was unexpected. In fact, after having these experiences, the player might be permanently changed; he or she might feel the change and feel unique because of it. Paradoxically, while feeling unique, he or she might feel a closer union with people and with ideas beyond themselves.

After a particularly grueling outdoor activity, an Outward Bound participant was asked by his instructor, "How was your experience?" The participant responded, "It was fantastic, except at the time," implying that although the activity was not at every moment totally pleasurable, the overall experience was uplifting. Athletes frequently experience pain, extreme fatigue, nagging injuries, or severe disappointment as a result of their activities, yet they come back to them because they find them rewarding overall.

Clear goals are very important for fun to occur. If the goals are not clear at the beginning of the activity, reflection on their results sometimes allows the participant to view the activity as fun. However, immediately after completing it, the response may have been, "I never want to do that again." For most activities, process goals work far better than outcome goals. If players have only outcome goals (e.g., winning), at least half of them (those who lose) aren't going to have fun.

There are many goals in athletic competition other than simply to outscore the opponent. These include demonstrating competence, creatively expressing oneself, improving one's self-image, feeling the joy of skilled movement, testing one's ability, and, perhaps most important, experiencing fun. Fun is a major motivational factor for continued persistence in any activity.

Some people are better able to experience fun than others. This occurs when—as a result of genetics or training—they have better control of their mental energies and are better able to focus their attention on the tasks to be done; they are able to set process goals instead of only outcome goals; they have a higher level of self-confidence and learned optimism; and they are less distracted by physical discomfort.

As a coach, what can you do to ensure that players have fun in your practices? If you think of the practice court as an "idea stage" on which to experience fun, the major goal for coaches is not to interfere with the process. Very few players view lectures as "fun." Too many coaches give their athletes long lectures. Despite our desire to impart our athletic wisdom to our athletes as directly as possible, we need to keep verbal instructions to a minimum. One of my favorite quotes in this regard is from Herman Hesse's book, *Siddhartha.* Siddhartha (Buddha as a boy) tells his friend, who is desiring his secrets of wisdom, "Wisdom is noncommunicable." We can't verbally communicate to our athletes everything they need to learn. What we can do is run our practices so that our players have ample opportunities to learn lessons for themselves.

Let's consider coaching activities with respect to some of the components of fun.

- *Match challenges with players' abilities.* In unsupervised athletics, kids will always match challenges with abilities, if necessary by handicapping much stronger competitors in some way. When coaches are involved, sometimes the challenges are too great for inexperienced athletes or, conversely, the challenges are not great enough. In either case, fun does not occur. Coaches must be sure that the challenges they present to their players are commensurate with their abilities.

- *Help them focus on the task.* In this area, coaches can have, perhaps, the greatest impact. Practice sessions should be planned to allow for minimal time between contacts with the ball. When athletes are standing in long lines in coach-directed drills, boredom sets in quickly, and players will seek pleasure by directing attention to things other than the task at hand. Decreasing "down time" increases the athlete's ability to maintain focus.

  It's well known that fatigue has a negative impact on focus and, as a result, on having fun. If practices are too long or the players are not conditioned, no one will have fun. After 90 minutes, their ability to focus begins to diminish. After 120 minutes, they might be too tired to focus at all.

  Teaching players how to focus their attention can be helpful. On the other hand, if it comes while they're trying to focus, feedback is not going to help them. Think how distracting it would be if in the middle of a ballet, the ballerina's teacher yells at her from offstage, "For God's sake, point your toes!" Yet coaches do this kind of thing to their athletes all the time, and their activities require no less focus than those of the ballerina. Allow your players to develop focus without your distractions.

- *Have clear-cut goals with immediate feedback.* Make certain that the goals of a drill are clear prior to starting the drill. For the most part, feedback is inherent in the activity itself. If any question exists in a player's mind about his or her performance of a particular skill, positive verbal feedback can clarify the situation. But players seldom need to be told when they make a mistake—they're usually painfully aware of it.

- *Help players leave their worries and distractions outside the gym.* The practice court should be a sanctuary from outside distractions, a place where players can come and have positive experiences. As long as practices allow them to focus on individual performance, this is not a problem. However, when players aren't having success, are getting bored because of long-winded tirades and nonchallenging drills, or are being disrupted by negative comments, their attention is going to wander and come to rest on the worries they wanted to leave outside the gym door.

• *Give players a sense of control.* Focus your drills on the players, not on the coaches. If drills are set up so that it's difficult for players to succeed, players will begin to feel they lack control over outcomes. Frequent success leads to a sense of control. It works best to also give players some say in the goals they are trying to achieve.

• *Try to minimize players' self-consciousness.* Self-consciousness in athletics is largely fear of what others think of our performance. If a coach is nonjudgmental in his or her approach and helps players overcome their fears of failure, players can leave their "self" out of their performance. Correcting fear of failure isn't easy, but when players can clearly focus on a task, it's less likely they will feel self-conscious.

• *Help the players' sense of self grow stronger after an activity.* Help players reflect on the positive things that occurred during a game, drill, or other activity. Many times, players don't consciously note positive things as the activity is taking place. Discussing the positives can help players, on reflection, experience a greater sense of fun.

EVALUATION

Evaluation is the final step in the practice session and must not be omitted. Soon after each practice session ends, the coaching staff should discuss the session. Were the plans effective? Was the execution good? Here are some questions that should be addressed as part of your discussion:

- What parts of practice went well and why? Did players seem more motivated during portions of the session? Which drills fully met the established goals? Were there any drills that players wanted to continue longer than they did?
- What parts of practice did not go well and why? Were the drills appropriate to the skill level of the players? Did players seem to lack motivation? Were the drills boring? Did coaches make effective use of initiatives and consequences?
- Were the goals for the session accomplished? Were the goals too easy, too hard, or about right? Did the chosen drills lead to established goals for the session? Were players able to complete the drills in the time allotted? If goals were not met, what changes are needed to make the drills more effective in reaching established goals?
- Was feedback given appropriately? Were all coaches attentive, actively involved, and giving positive verbal and body language feedback? Are there areas of feedback that need to be focused on more closely?
- Were players focused and intense during practice? If not, why not? Were they bored? Were the drills too hard? Were players focused early but lost focus as the session progressed? Were they tired?
- What needs to be worked on at the next practice? Can we proceed toward our next established set of goals, or do we need to spend more time on the goals for this last practice?

Coaches should take all of these considerations into account as they begin to make plans for the next day's practice.

PRACTICE DRILLS

Butterflies

Purpose: To engage athletes in a series of warm-up drills that can be used with players at all levels

Setup: The court is divided longitudinally between two groups with a line of servers, passers, and setters for each group.

Execution: Phase 1 can be used for beginners who are just learning the forearm pass. In this phase, the servers (Sv) can put the ball into play to the passer (P) with either a serve or an overhand throw in preparation for developing an overhand serve. After the server has put the ball in play, he or she joins the line of passers. The passer then passes to the setter (S) and joins that line. In this phase, the setter is only a target. He or she then takes the ball and joins the server line (figure 10.1a).

Phase 2 incorporates a second pass by the setter to a target stationed in the attack zone. The player movements are the same as in phase 1, except the setter now becomes the next target, and the target takes the ball and joins the server line (figure 10.1b).

In phase 3, a third contact is added in the form of an approach, with a tip or off-speed shot by the attacker (H). If enough players are available, a blocker (B) can be added to this phase. Additionally, after the server has served, he or she needs to play up the tipped ball on defense before going to the passer's line. Depending on the goals for the practice, everyone can rotate through the setter's position, or a designated setter can be used and that position bypassed in the rotation (figure 10.1c).

In phase 4, use a designated setter. In this phase, the passer must pass and then transition to the outside to be ready to attack the set with either a tip, off-speed shot, or line attack. The server plays defense after the serve and digs up the ball to the outside blocker, who has opened up to the court after the block attempt. The inside blocker moves to the outside and the passer becomes the inside blocker. In this phase, with both groups working efficiently, 60 to 80 touches occur per minute (figure 10.1d).

Coaching Points: There is considerable movement, little waiting time, and a lot of touches for everyone in this drill. The drill can also be used as a ball-control drill by setting performance goals of consecutive successes.

Variations: If a blocker is used, the attacker becomes the next blocker, and the blocker goes to the service line. The servers can also make the passers move one step up, back, left, or right. Passers can be moved a step closer to the net and forced to receive the serve with an overhead pass instead of a forearm pass.

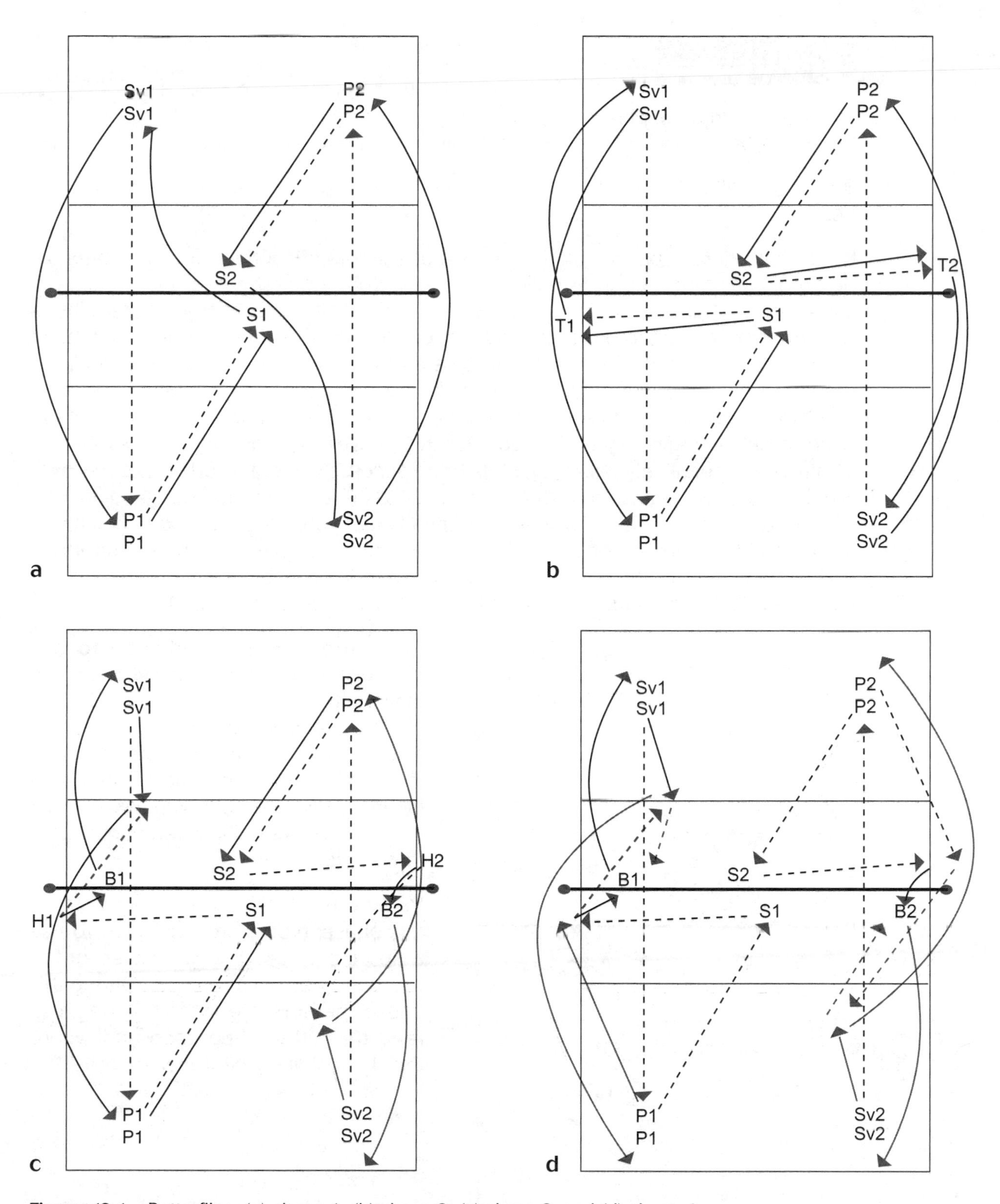

Figure 10.1 Butterflies. *(a)* phase 1, *(b)* phase 2, *(c)* phase 3, and *(d)* phase 4.

Frustration

Purpose: To improve players' ball control by practicing a drill that should be very easy, but which proves to be annoyingly difficult to complete—hence the name

Setup: It is difficult to run this drill with fewer than 10 players; 12 to 14 players works best.

Execution: Players position in lines of two as passers (P), setters (S), and hitters (H) on both sides of the court. A ball being tossed from the first passer on one side to the setter on that side starts play. After tossing the ball, the passer joins the setter's line. The setter sets the ball to the hitter and moves to that line. The hitter two-hand passes the ball over the net to the passers on the other side of the court and goes around the net to join that line. The passer forearm passes the ball to the setter on his or her side and continues in that fashion until an error is made, at which point the entire process begins again. The goal for this phase is for the ball to cross the net 10 times consecutively. When that has been accomplished, the drill is started over with both passers simultaneously tossing a ball to the setter on that side, and the drill continues as before. Now, however, with two balls in play, focusing becomes much more difficult. Movements need to be faster, and communication becomes important. Again, the goal is for the ball to cross the net 10 times consecutively. If enough players are available, introduce a third ball as the drill progresses (figure 10.2)

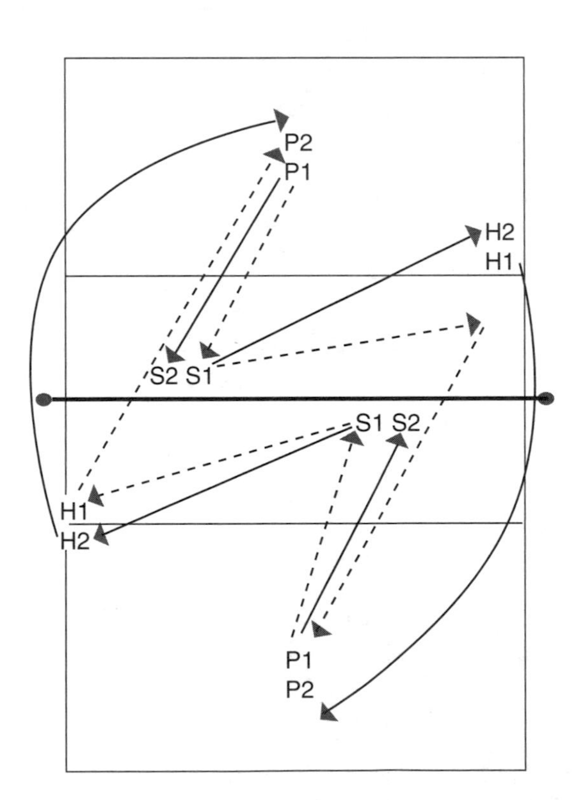

Figure 10.2 Frustration.

Coaching Points: In addition to ball control, this drill is very useful in helping players focus on their responsibilities at all times and not just the ball. This drill also helps with reading on defense and in fostering communication. This would be an excellent warm-up drill except that it often takes a significant amount of time to complete.

Variations: When players have mastered this phase, hitters are instructed to use a tip or controlled spike instead of the two-hand pass over the net. During this phase, passers are forced to begin to read the hitter's approach and where they'll most likely hit the ball.

Error-Correction

Purpose: To practice handling errors in a controlled scrimmage that fosters focus on perseverance

Setup: Place two teams on the court; a coach or two stand off the court with baskets of balls.

Execution: A coach tosses a ball to either side as a free ball to begin play (figure 10.3). Play continues until the ball hits the floor. At this point, the coach immediately directs another ball toward the player who made the error so he or she can make another attempt. This is repeated until the attempt is completed correctly. If the error was a hitting error, a ball is tossed to the setter to set the same hitter again and again until he or she is successful, and then play continues. If the error was a defensive one, the coach hits another ball to the defender in the same manner as the one in which the error occurred. This is repeated until the player is successful, and then play continues. Rotations can be done after a particularly good kill or after a set time.

Coaching Points: It's important for players not receiving the ball for the error correction to kick the errant ball off the court or to a coach so that a player is not injured on a loose ball. This is a very strenuous drill and becomes like a continuous rally, so give players a breather after 10 minutes.

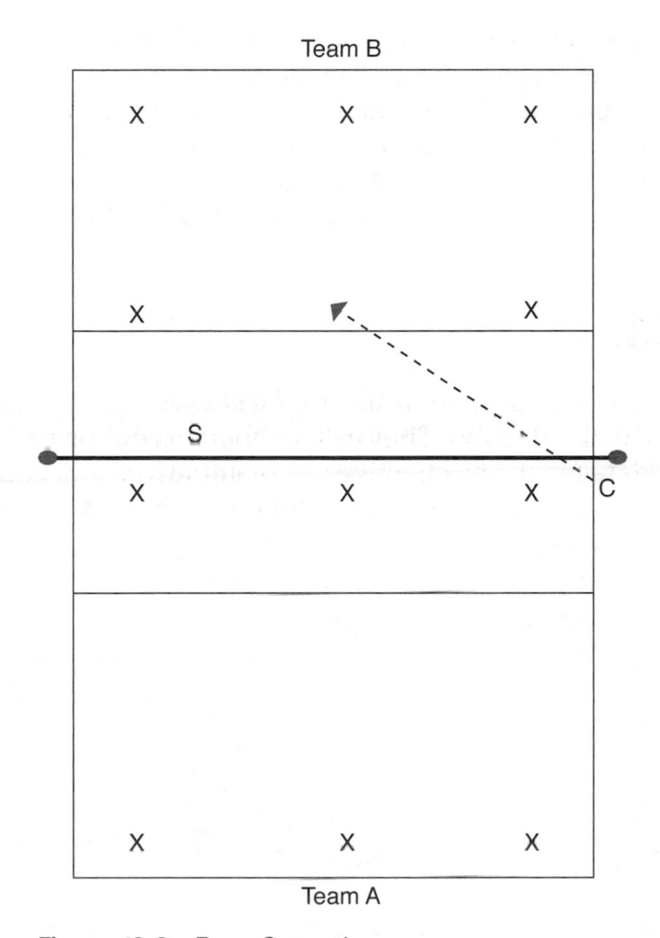

Figure 10.3 Error-Correction.

Serve Receive With Quick Attack

Purpose: To improve serve-reception accuracy and create three attacking options; it also provides serving, setting, and quick attacker repetitions

Setup: Four servers line up on one endline, with a blocker at the net, while three passers line up on the opposite court, ready to pass to a setter and a middle hitter. An extra passer waits behind the endline on the same side.

Execution: The drill can be run in several ways. As it is shown, it is set up as a negatively reinforced drill. Each passer must pass five perfectly passed serves and then do two barrel rolls. The pass's degree of perfection is determined by the setter's ability to set a quick middle attack as a result. If it's a perfect pass, the passer stays active in the drill without doing the rolls. While a passer is doing the rolls, the extra passer jumps into the position left by that passer. After serving, the server goes to the middle back, reads the middle attacker, and digs the attack, then shags the ball and gets back in line. After passers reach the assigned goal, others from the serving line replace them, as well as the middle hitters and blockers, until all have passed. The middle attacker and the blockers might need to be rotated frequently to prevent fatigue.

Coaching Points: Along with promoting passing accuracy, this drill forces the setter to attempt quick attack sets, even on less-than-ideal passes.

Variations: This drill can also be run as a positively reinforced drill. When every player has met the goal, the team plays "Queen of the Mountain" for five minutes. Or, it can be run so that each player gets a set number of opportunities (e.g., 10) and gets a "star" if the goal is met. The drill can also be run using a back quick attack alone or in conjunction with a front quick. A left-side attacker can also be added to run low trajectory sets or high-release sets on bad passes. More blockers can also be used.

CONCLUSION

Quality practices, prerequisites for a successful season, require much forethought in preparation and drill selection. They call for good execution of the practice plan, including appropriate feedback, effective use of initiatives and consequences, and thorough evaluation after each practice. Quite simply, quality practices require quality coaching.

About the American Volleyball Coaches Association

The mission of the **American Volleyball Coaches Association (AVCA)** is to advance the development of the sport of volleyball by providing coaches with educational programs, a forum for exchange of opinions, and opportunities for recognition.

Incorporated as a private nonprofit educational corporation in 1981, the AVCA currently has members in all 50 states and the District of Columbia as well as numerous international members. At the collegiate level, all major NCAA conferences are represented and membership among club coaches continues to rise.

About the Editor

Kinda S. Lenberg has edited 10 books about volleyball and has served as a writer and editor for two of the sport's major publications, *Coaching Volleyball* and *Volleyball USA*. She is the owner of Creative Liaisons, a consulting firm that works with the American Volleyball Coaches Association and USA Volleyball.

During the 1996 Olympic Games in Atlanta, Lenberg was the media subcenter manager for the inaugural beach volleyball Olympic tournament. Additionally, she was the AVCA's director of publications from 1992 to 1999.

In her leisure time, Lenberg is an avid reader who also enjoys playing volleyball and camping with her family. She, her husband, Eric, and their two children reside in Colorado Springs, Colorado.

About the Contributors

Paul Arrington, MD, has been a club volleyball coach for 23 years. During this time he has garnered numerous accolades, including the prestigious Bernice Reiff Epperson Award in 1996 for his contributions to juniors' volleyball. Arrington's club teams have finished first, second, and fourth at the Volleyball Festival, which is the largest girls' volleyball tournament in the United States. He began coaching the Waimea High School girls' varsity team in 1994, garnering seven league championships and six fifth-place finishes in the state tournament. Arrington has been named the league Kaua'i Interscholastic Federation (KIF) Coach of the Year six times. He is a USA Volleyball CAP level II certified coach and author of several coaching and scientific articles. Arrington has been a general surgeon in private practice in Waimea, Kaua'i, Hawaii, for 24 years. In the fall of 2005 he became a volunteer assistant coach at Dartmouth College in Hanover, New Hampshire.

Sean Byron serves as head coach for both the women's and men's volleyball programs at Rutgers-Newark in New Jersey. He led the Scarlet Raider women's team to a New Jersey Athletic Conference (NJAC) record of 20-3 and to the conference championship each year from 2002 to 2004. His women's team captured the school's first-ever NCAA Division III tournament berth, while his 2003 men's squad advanced to the Eastern Intercollegiate Volleyball Association (EIVA) semifinals, coming within a game of the Final Four. In 2002, Byron coached the USA youth men's national team to a bronze-medal finish in the World Championship qualifier. He also served as assistant coach for the USA junior national team, which posted records of 5-2 and 8-1 in international competition. Byron has been a clinician for the NCAA YES (Youth Education through Sports) program since 1995 and has received both NJAC and EIVA Coach of the Year honors.

Don Hardin has been the head women's coach at the University of Illinois since 1996 and has led his teams to five berths in the NCAA tournament, including two trips to the Sweet 16. He earned Big Ten Coach of the Year honors in 2001 and 2003. Before returning to his alma mater, Hardin guided the University of Louisville to six conference championships and five NCAA tournament appearances. While Hardin established elite programs at two different universities, his teams have averaged almost 21 wins per season, with an overall mark of 353-187. He earned Coach of the Year honors with the Cardinals in 1991 (Metro Conference) and in 1995 (Conference USA).

Taras Liskevych, PhD, was head coach of the U.S. women's national volleyball team from 1985 to 1996. He holds the record among U.S. women's volleyball coaches for most wins, longest tenure, and most international matches as a coach. Under his leadership, he U.S. squad captured the bronze medal at the 1992 Olympics, and their gold-medal finish at the 1995 World Grand Prix earned him Federation of International Volleyball (FIVB) Coach of the Year honors. Before his stint with the U.S. team, Liskevych headed the University of the Pacific women's team, raising the program from the intramural club level to a national contender. His teams won six NorCal Conference titles, landing him Conference Coach of the Year honors five times. In 1983 Liskevych was national Coach of the Year. He is currently the head women's volleyball coach at Oregon State University. Liskevych holds a PhD from Ohio State University.

Jim McLaughlin has served as head coach of the University of Washington women's volleyball team since 2001, helping to catapult the program from the bottom of the Pacific-10 Conference to a top-10 program and NCAA championship contender. After inheriting this program, which finished last in the Pac-10 standings in 2000, McLaughlin took the Huskies to the postseason in three of his first four seasons and led UW to a Final Four appearance in 2004. In 2002, he earned Pac-10 Coach of the Year honors after leading the Huskies to their best Pac-10 finish in five seasons and their seventh-ever NCAA appearance. A 14-year veteran head coach, McLaughlin has made 13 appearances in the NCAA postseason, including four consecutive seasons with Kansas State.

Marilyn Nolen retired at the end of the 2003 season after 32 years of coaching women's collegiate volleyball and 10 years at the helm of the Saint Louis University team. Nolen's overall record of 809-357-12 (.692) ranked third on the active NCAA Division I victory list when she retired, and she is just the third coach in Division I history to reach the 800-win milestone. She was named Conference USA Coach of the Year in 1998 and was inducted into the inaugural class of the AVCA Hall of Fame in 2003. Nolen's career began in 1969 at Sul Ross State University in Alpine, Texas, where she led teams to national championships in 1970 and 1971. She coached six seasons at Utah State University (where she won the AIAW national championship in 1978), led Kentucky to a 44-7 record in 1983, and helped restore the University of Florida as a national power during her seven-year tenure.

Coach Nolen would like to thank Kathy DeBoer, Doug Beal, Darlene Kluka, Stephanie Schleuder, and Sue Woodstra for sharing their knowledge and expertise through the years.

Penn State Assistant Coaches Julie Backstrom and Mike Schall, With Russ Rose

Julie Backstrom joined the Penn State women's volleyball staff in 2001 as an assistant coach, and after the 2004 season she became director of women's volleyball operations. As an assistant coach, Backstrom served as recruiting coordinator, and her specialties included working with the team's setters and defensive specialists. Since her return to her alma mater, the team has won 82% of their matches. During her playing career at Penn State, Backstrom earned both Atlantic 10 and Big Ten All-Academic honors.

Mike Schall has been an assistant coach to Russ Rose since 1991, making him the most veteran member of the staff other than Rose. Schall is involved in every aspect of the program, including match preparation and player development. The Nittany Lions have won more than 86% of their games during his tenure. Schall earned four letters as a defensive specialist on the Nittany Lion men's volleyball team, served as a two-year co-captain, and played in every Penn State match during his four-year career.

Russ Rose has been head women's volleyball coach at Penn State University since 1979, where his teams have never posted fewer than 22 wins in a season. Under Rose, the Nittany Lions have secured 30 or more wins in a season 18 times and 36 or more victories six times. In 2004 his squad captured its eighth Big Ten title in 14 seasons while Rose picked up his 800th career victory. His overall record of 828-151 (.846) ranks second nationally among active coaches. Rose was named AVCA Coach of the Year in 1990 and 1997, and he has been honored as Coach of the Year eight times at the regional level and 11 times at the conference level. In 2000, Rose was named the United States Olympic Committee Coach of the Year for his work with the U.S. men's team in preparation for the Sydney Olympics. He also led the U.S. men's team to a bronze medal at the 1985 Maccabiah Games and the U.S. women's team to a silver medal at the 1981 Maccabiah Games.

Tom Peterson entered his third year as head coach of the Brigham Young University men's volleyball program in 2005. In the 2004 season, he led the Cougars to a 29-4 record and a first-place finish at the NCAA tournament, marking the squad's fourth national championship game in six years. Peterson also coached four All-Americans in 2004. The BYU alum and 1994 NCAA Coach of the Year was also the first to guide a non-West Coast team to a men's title (Penn State in 1994). During his six years at PSU, Peterson led the Nittany Lions to a 127-49 (.722) overall record. He also served as head coach (1995) and assistant coach (1993) to the Olympic Sports Festival East men's team, which was the champion both years. In addition to coaching both men's and women's teams throughout his career, Peterson has served as the director of various community and university volleyball camps.

Joan Powell has coached the Coronado (Colorado) High School girls' volleyball team since 1976, leading the program to three state championships in 14 playoff appearances. Coronado also has won 3 regional titles, 10 conference championships, and 12 district titles. Powell's overall record is 449-208. Twenty-nine of her athletes have gone on to play volleyball in college, and 15 of them became coaches. She was named Women's Sports Foundation Active Female Coach of the Year in 1989. She also was the YWCA Sportswoman of Colorado Coach of the Year in 1983 and was inducted into its Hall of Fame in 2003. In 2004, Powell was inducted into the Colorado Springs Sports Hall of Fame. Powell has also been chosen to call the NCAA finals on six occasions, first in 1995 and most recently in 2004.

Joe Sagula entered his 16th year as the University of North Carolina's head women's volleyball coach in 2005. His 2003 squad finished 20-12, the sixth consecutive year it has collected at least 20 wins. The 2002 Tar Heels won 30 matches (32-4 overall) for the first time since 1985 en route to the program's first appearance in an NCAA tournament regional semifinal. They also took the Atlantic Coast Conference (ACC) regular-season championship with a 15-1 conference record. The most successful season in the history of the program concluded with Sagula garnering both Conference and Regional Coach of the Year honors. Carolina has won more conference titles—nine—than any other ACC volleyball program, and Sagula holds the most ACC wins (121) of any coach in history. He is currently serving a two-year term as president of the American Volleyball Coaches Association (2004 and 2005).

Stephanie Schleuder has served as head women's volleyball coach at Macalester College in St. Paul, Minnesota, since 1998 and has amassed more than 650 career wins at the Division I and Division III levels. Schleuder compiled 561 wins during her stints as head coach at the University of Minnesota (1982-1994), the University of Alabama (1974-1982), and Bemidji State University (1972). Her career record of 669-376 places her among the most successful volleyball coaches in NCAA history. In 2004, Schleuder completed a two-year term as president of the American Volleyball Coaches Association (AVCA), making her the only non-Division I coach to hold this post. She will continue to serve on the AVCA board of directors through 2006.